P9-DCP-771

first the DEad

TIM DOWNS

THOMAS NELSON
Since 1798

NASHVILLE DALLAS MEXICO CITY RIO DE JANEIRO BEIJING

Published in Nashville, Tennessee, by Thomas Nelson. Thomas Nelson is a trademark of Thomas Nelson, Inc.

Thomas Nelson books may be purchased in bulk for educational, business, fund-raising, or sales promotional use. For information, please e-mail SpecialMarkets@ThomasNelson.com.

Publisher's Note: This novel is a work of fiction. Names, characters, places, and incidents are either products of the author's imagination or used fictitiously. All characters are fictional, and any similarity to people living or dead is purely coincidental.

Page design by Mandi Cofer.

Library of Congress Cataloging-in-Publication Data

Downs, Tim.
First the dead / Tim Downs.
p. cm.
ISBN 978-1-59554-024-9 (HC)
ISBN 978-1-59554-486-5 (IE)
1. Polchek, Nick (Fictitious character)—Fiction. 2. Forensic entomology—Fiction. 3. Entomologists—Fiction. 4. Hurricane Katrina, 2005—Fiction. 5. Murder—Investigation—Fiction. 6. New Orleans (La.)—Fiction. I. Title.
PS3604.O954F57 2008
813'.6—dc22

2007045179

Printed in the United States of America
08 09 10 QW 6 5 4 3 2

For my beautiful Joy,
my first reader, best critic, lover, and friend

In memory of J.T. Walker,
who found his Father and spent his life helping others find theirs

And for the people of New Orleans:

"The God of heaven will give us success;
therefore we His servants will arise and build . . ."

Nehemiah 2:20

1

Saturday, August 27, 2005
The Louisiana Bayous

He wiped the hot sweat from his forehead with the back of his hand but forgot that his hand was sealed in a latex glove. The rubber squeaked across his skin like a squeegee on a windshield, pushing the sweat toward his right eyebrow until it ran down into his eye and burned. He pulled up his shirttail and rubbed at his eyes.

He looked down at the water around his knees that was undulating like oil against his waders. He twisted his legs and dug his feet in a little deeper; it wasn't easy keeping his balance standing in the soft peat that lined the banks. He turned and looked again at the abandoned tin shack, silhouetted like a gravestone against the starry sky. *This has to be the place,* he thought. *They must be around here somewhere.*

He shuffled forward in the water, probing with his toe until his boot finally struck something soft. He kicked at the object but it didn't move—whatever it was, it was large and heavy. He reached into the inky liquid with both arms until his chest almost touched the surface; the water seeped into his gloves around his wrists and ran down cool over his palms and fingertips. He pushed on the object; the lump felt spongy but firm. He felt along the surface until the lump abruptly narrowed at one end.

He felt the contours of a face—or what was left of one.

He pulled his arms from the water and looked at his gloves; he rubbed his fingertips together, making a mental note not to wipe his forehead again.

He looked across the water and saw the shadowy outline of the boat trolling slowly in the distance, its spotlight sweeping the water like a wandering eye. He took out his own flashlight and switched it on, then pointed it at the boat and waved it in a wide arc. A moment later, the boat's spotlight swung toward him and flooded his position with blinding white light. He covered his eyes with his forearm.

"Did you find 'em?" a man's voice called out.

"One of them!" he shouted back. "The other one must be nearby. Bring the boat alongside and get the tarp."

The moon was in its last quarter, allowing the stars to dominate the sky, and there were millions of them—more than he had ever seen before. You couldn't see them in the city, where the party never ended and the lights were never off. For stars like this you had to head deep into the southern bayous, which no one in his right mind ever did—at least not at this time of night.

It was a peaceful night, a beautiful night, a night a man could almost relax and enjoy—if he didn't know what was coming. The air was hot and heavy, allowing a thick gray mist to finger its way around the knees of the old bald cypresses and water tupelos that lined the banks of the water. Nothing in the bayou was moving—not the dangling strands of black moss, not the needle-sharp tips of the tall marsh grass, not even the mosquitoes—as if every living thing in the bayou was hunkered down and waiting. He thought about the stories he had heard, about the way animals and insects can sense a disaster before it occurs, and he wondered if it was true. Maybe it was; maybe the mosquitoes were smarter than the people in New Orleans. It wouldn't surprise him.

The boat's pilot brought the boat in close and killed the motor, then eased himself over the edge and into the black water. "Where is it?" he asked.

"You're almost standing on it. The head's up here; the feet are down there. Give me a hand."

Together the two men worked the plastic sheet under the body until it lay roughly in the center of the tarp. On the count of three, they slowly hoisted it to the surface and waited while the water drained from one end, revealing the badly decomposed body of a man in tattered clothing.

"He weighs a ton," the boat's pilot said. "How big was this guy?"

"His lungs and gut are full of water," the man said. "Let it drain for a minute."

The pilot made a gagging sound. "Ugh—the smell."

"What did you expect? He's been here two weeks. C'mon, let's get him into the boat."

A few minutes later, the two men stood panting, resting against the edge of the boat, staring down at the loosely wrapped figure lying in the bottom of the fiberglass hull.

"This is a lot harder at night," the pilot grumbled. "Did we have to do it now?"

"They didn't make the evacuation order mandatory until late this afternoon—some of the shrimpers and crabbers stayed behind to take their chances with the storm. If somebody spotted us, this would be a little hard to explain, don't you think? Besides, this is our last chance—you won't be able to get anywhere near this place tomorrow night."

The pilot looked up at the cloudless southeastern sky. The air was clear and still, without a trace of breeze. "Are you sure this Hurricane Katrina is coming?"

"She's coming," he said. "It's still a few hundred miles offshore, that's all—too far to see yet. They say it doubled in size today. The thing can't miss us—it's a couple hundred miles across. It's a category 4 now—it'll hit 5 by morning. The first feeder bands will reach us tomorrow."

"I talked to the state police," the pilot said. "They've implemented the contra-flow plan. Every road in New Orleans is one-way now—one-way out. A million people are trying to get out of town before it hits. All the highways are jammed; they say it takes ten hours just to reach Baton Rouge. They think this might be the Big One."

"It's big enough for what we need. The hurricane will push a storm surge ahead of it—some say it'll overtop the levees by ten feet. If that happens, the whole city will fill up like a toilet."

"You think the city's ready?"

"We're the ones who need to be ready. Let's find that other body."

The pilot let out a snort.

"Something funny?"

"I was just thinking: Everybody's trying to get out of the city."

"So?"

"We're the only ones bringing bodies in."

2

Same Time
Raleigh, North Carolina

From across the dinner table, Nick Polchak stared at the woman's mouth as it moved. It was a human mouth, just a simple pair of gloss-lined lips surrounding an oral cavity, but it was like no mouth Nick had ever witnessed before. It was the *way* it moved: rhythmically, mechanically, hypnotically. Her lower jaw swung in a constant, circular motion, like a cow grinding cud, only much faster. Nick adjusted his huge glasses and stared.

Like a cow on amphetamines, he thought.

Her chewing never stopped—not for conversation, not to shovel in another chunk of Black Angus beef, not even to take a drink of water. The woman even chewed water—or maybe the water only served as a lubricant, like the oil a machinist pours over a spinning drill bit to keep it from overheating.

From time to time her lips would part, and the tip of her tongue would dart across her teeth and plunge into the deep recesses of her gums, searching out tiny morsels that had somehow escaped the crushing molars. Whenever this happened a little lump would appear in her cheek like a mouse under a rug, dart left and right, then vanish again. Nick wondered how the tongue had survived so long—how it had avoided being shorn clean off, because the relentless teeth waited for nothing. He imagined what would happen if the tongue hesitated a nanosecond too long: He envisioned the severed tip dropping off and landing like a crouton on her Caesar salad.

Nick sat mesmerized. Another bite, another drink, another cobralike lash of the tongue, and all the time the words kept coming—though he had long ago stopped comprehending them.

"Unbelievable," Nick said unconsciously.

"You're sweet," she said. "I like you too. Pass the bread."

He slid the basket halfway across the table, using the misdirection as an opportunity to slide his cell phone from his pocket and check for messages. Unfortunately, there were none.

The woman smiled as she chewed. "You know, since we don't work in the same department, we probably never would have met. It was awfully nice of your friends to set this up."

"I owe them one," Nick said. *One Australian funnel-web spider in each of their shoes. Why can't they mind their own business?*

Every six months or so, Nick's married colleagues in the Entomology Department at North Carolina State University began to feel sorry for him, the only single professor in the department. Longing for Nick to share in their connubial bliss, his colleagues began to match him up with "compatible" women from the faculty and staff of other departments—the term "compatible" apparently being loosely defined, as in, "She's a carbon-based life-form too."

But what really infuriated Nick was that every six months or so he gave in, despite two tragic object lessons per year that should have kept his memory fresh. Like clockwork, every six months his colleagues began to feel sorry for him, and then for some inexplicable reason Nick began to feel sorry for *them*, feeling sorry for *him*. The inevitable result was a departmentwide pity party culminating in some comic tragedy just like this one—a blind date from hell.

The whole thing was nuts—but here he was again, right on schedule, and his luck was no better this time than it had been in the past. *Who chose this woman?* he wondered. Which one of his dewy-eyed colleagues actually thought that the two of them might be compatible, and what selection criteria had he employed? Was this actually someone's idea of a life partner? The woman wasn't unattractive; she was just—dangerous. If they crashed together in the Andes, she would probably eat him before he was even dead.

And to make matters worse, he had invited her to *dinner*—and not at just any restaurant, but at the Angus Barn, one of Raleigh's pricier establishments. Why did he have to commit himself to an entire meal? Why not a mocha grande at Starbucks—to go? Why didn't he ever *learn*? But no; every six months his optimism took over his common sense, and every six months Nick got stuck with the check—in more ways than one.

He glanced down at the bread basket; it was empty. She had done serious damage to the relish tray, grinding down the carrot sticks like a pencil sharpener and popping the olives like breath mints. She had single-handedly emptied two cheese crocks—both the sharp smoked cheddar and the tangy blue cheese; then came the three-cheese ravioli appetizer; then her ten-ounce filet, medium rare—

"What's the matter?" the woman asked unexpectedly. For the first time in forty-five minutes, she stopped chewing and looked at him.

Nick felt a twinge of panic, like one of his students caught sleeping in class. "What do you mean?"

"You're not eating."

Nick looked down at his plate. She was right—he had barely touched his own food; he had barely spoken, for that matter. For the last forty-five minutes, he had felt like a man pinned down by enemy fire.

"I've been—preoccupied," he said.

"You've been looking me over," she said with a grin. "A woman notices that."

Nick measured the distance to the fire exit.

"What is it you do again? I know you teach entomology."

"I teach entomology."

"So teach me something about entomology."

"What do you want to know?"

"I don't care. Anything."

Nick watched her knife and fork moving with the speed and precision of a hibachi chef. "Okay," he said. "The locust is a member of the genus *Schistocerca*. It has the unusual ability to change its habits and appearance according to its population density. By nature, the locust is a solitary creature that migrates individually. But as their numbers enlarge, the competition for food increases and they become more and more aggressive—that's when they begin to swarm. In the 1870s there was a swarm of locusts eighteen hundred miles long and a hundred miles wide over the Great Plains. Three and a half trillion locusts formed a dark cloud half a mile high. They ate everything in sight: grain, fabric, small animals—even one another."

"What happened to them?" she asked.

"They suddenly died off."

"All of them?"

Except for their queen. "Yes, all of them."

"So that's what you do—you teach about locusts?"

"No. I'm a forensic entomologist, actually. I only teach to pay the bills."

"A *forensic* entomologist. What is that, exactly?"

"I study necrophilous insects."

"What kind of insects?"

"*Necrophilous.* It means 'dead-loving.'"

"They love to be dead?"

"No, they love to *eat* the dead. I study the insects that eat people after they die."

Her mouth dropped open, which was not a pretty sight. "There are bugs that eat people?"

"Of course. What did you think happened to bodies after they die?"

"I never thought about it."

"Americans die at a rate of six thousand per day. That's a lot of corpses piling up. Where do you think they all go?"

"To funeral homes, I suppose."

"To funeral homes—where they drain your blood and powder your nose to make you look nice for your family and friends. They're not fooling nature; they're just buying time."

"What does that mean?"

"The instant you die—the very *instant*—your body begins to decompose. Every cell in your body needs oxygen to survive, but when the heart stops and the lungs cease to function, there is no more oxygen.

Without oxygen, the mitochondria fail; the cells begin to starve. In desperation they begin to cannibalize themselves, consuming their own enzymes and membranes until the dying cells rip apart at the seams, scattering cellular debris everywhere—which is exactly what the bacteria have been waiting for."

"The bacteria?"

"Bacteria are everywhere in the bloodstream, ordinarily held in check by the body's immune system—but after death there is no immune system, so the bacteria engorge themselves on the cellular remains. They multiply exponentially, producing heat and gas as they grow. The body bloats, the gas escapes through the body's natural orifices, producing packets of scent molecules that drift away in the breeze—where the insects are waiting."

"What insects?"

"The dead-lovers. Iridescent blue-and-green blowflies; gray, blunt-bodied flesh flies; insects that have adapted to feed solely on the decomposing tissues of the dead. The pregnant females circle in the air, tracking those scent molecules back to the body. They land, looking for a place where the tissues are soft and moist—the eyes, the ears, the oral and nasal cavities."

The woman's face began to slowly contort into a disgusted sneer. Nick didn't notice. He was a bug man and he was talking about bugs now; this was his subject area, his one true passion in life. Besides, he hadn't spoken in forty-five minutes, and he was on a roll.

"The flies lay their clutch of eggs," he said. "Three, maybe four hundred each—and then they take off again. The eggs hatch and maggots emerge; the maggots stuff themselves on the decomposing tissues—thousands upon thousands of them, consuming the body at an astonishing rate. As the famous taxonomist Carolus Linnaeus once said, 'The progeny of three flies can consume a dead horse more quickly than can a lion.'"

She closed her eyes and held up one hand. "Nick."

"Since insects pass through distinct developmental stages, by studying the insects on a corpse we can determine almost exactly how long they've been there—and thus, the time of death. All you have to do is collect maggot samples from the various orifices. Take your filet, for example: It's basically a thick slab of muscle tissue, much like—oh, let's say a cross section of the human thigh—"

"Nick!"

Nick stopped. The woman had a strange look on her face—the sort of look a person gets when they first learn that calamari is really squid.

"Can we talk about something else?"

"You asked me what I do."

"I know, but I didn't know you did . . . *that*. Do you really have to work with dead people?"

"It helps."

"How can you stand it?"

"As coworkers go, I recommend them."

She shuddered. "Well, let's talk about something else."

"Like what?"

"Something besides work—*your* work, anyway."

Nick shrugged. "Okay. What do you do?"

She glared at him. "I've been telling you that for the last forty-five minutes."

Nick blinked. "Would you excuse me a moment?" He pulled out his cell phone and checked for messages again.

"You keep looking at your cell phone," she grumbled. "A woman notices that too."

"Sorry. I'm sort of on call."

"In case somebody dies?"

"In a way, yes. I volunteer with an organization called DMORT—the Disaster Mortuary Operational Response Team. DMORT is a part of the National Disaster Medical System, under FEMA. Whenever there's a disaster involving mass casualties—like the World Trade Center or United Flight 93 in Pennsylvania—then DMORT is called in. Whenever the number of casualties is too big for the local coroner's office to handle, we show up. Our job is to help collect and identify human remains."

"You *volunteer* to do that?"

"Sometimes I can't believe the things I volunteer for."

"Has there been a disaster somewhere?"

"There's a hurricane called Katrina moving northwest across the Gulf of Mexico right now. It was a category 1 when it hit Florida the night before last; then it was downgraded to a tropical storm. But now it's out over the Gulf again, and it's sucking up energy from the hot sea; it's up to a category 4 now, and some say it might become a 5. The National Hurricane Center says it's heading for New Orleans; if it keeps going, my DMORT unit will be activated—just in case."

At that moment, Nick's cell phone mercifully rang. He scrambled to open it.

"Nick Polchak."

"Nick. It's Denny with DMORT."

"It's about time."

"I called your office first. You're usually there on a Saturday night."

"I should be there now."

"Some grad student answered your phone. He said you were on a *blind date*—in a *restaurant*—with a *woman*."

Nick didn't reply; he just kept nodding and staring straight ahead.

"Nick, is it true?"

"Denny. Please."

"Just tell me: How's it going?"

"A disaster of unprecedented proportions," he said. "It makes you wonder if there's a God."

"That bad, huh?"

"All the needless suffering—all the wasted resources—it could have been prevented. Why don't we ever learn?"

"Well, then, I've got good news for you. We just got word from the Emergency Operations Center: NDMS has activated us—Katrina's predicted to make landfall early Monday morning. How far are you from the airport?"

"Twenty minutes. My go-bag is in the car."

"Whoa, slow down. NDMS has to call you back with travel arrangements first. You should have four hours at least. Relax, have a cup of coffee. Enjoy your date."

"*Ten* minutes? Okay, but I'll have to leave right now."

"Do what you want. I'll see you in Baton Rouge."

Nick folded the phone and looked apologetically at his date.

"You have to go, don't you?" she said.

"Sorry."

"It sounds terrible."

"Relief is on the way. Have you seen our waiter? I'll grab him on the way out."

After repeating his condolences and offering a fictional promise to reschedule at a more opportune time, Nick hurried toward the exit.

The maître d' met him in the doorway. "Leaving so soon, sir?"

"Gotta run. I was at that table over there—see it? The lady with the long red hair." Nick pointed and the woman waved back.

"Yes sir, I see it."

Nick handed him a ten-dollar bill. "She needs more bread."

3

Sunday, August 28
St. Gabriel, Louisiana

"Folks, I need to ask you to pack in a little tighter so you can hear. Please move all the way into the warehouse. The wind is starting to pick up a bit, and we'd like to get you all out of the weather." Denny Behringer, the DMORT incident commander, motioned with both hands as if he were parking a 737, and the group began to move forward slowly.

Nick caught Denny's eye, and the two men nodded a silent greeting.

Nick looked at the group bunched tightly around him. He counted about seventy-five people, thirty of whom he knew. They were all members of his regional DMORT team—DMORT Region IV, consisting of forensic professionals from eight different states across the southeastern U.S. There were pathologists to conduct autopsies; anthropologists to examine fragments of bone; odontologists to match dental records; fingerprint specialists to establish lost identities; and a dozen other forensic subspecialties, including his own. The rest of the group consisted of computer experts, security personnel, and the myriad support staff necessary to run a morgue the size of a football field.

Less than twenty-four hours ago, each of them had been sitting comfortably in his or her home in Atlanta or Memphis or Nashville or Miami. Now, they huddled together in the darkness in the tiny town of St. Gabriel, Louisiana, seventy miles west of the city of New Orleans and just outside Baton Rouge. St. Gabriel had been selected from a short list of candidates as the location for DMORT's temporary morgue, the place where victims of the coming disaster could be collected and processed away from prying eyes.

St. Gabriel seemed the perfect choice: it was close to Baton Rouge, the location of FEMA's regional headquarters; it was situated just off Interstate 10, the major artery into and out of New Orleans; and it had no way to say no. The little hamlet of fifty-five hundred people, home to two prisons and a half dozen chemical plants, had been politely but bluntly informed that they would soon have the privilege of contributing to rescue-and-recovery efforts on behalf of their big sister to the east. Before long, a cadre of refrigerated tractor trailers would begin to deliver decomposing bodies right to their own back door. Not everyone in St. Gabriel appreciated the honor; but after repeated reassurances about safety and security, the little town resigned itself to its inevitable role.

FEMA, anticipating the closing of Louis Armstrong New Orleans International, and not wishing to add to the chaos at the airport in Baton Rouge, had decided to assemble the DMORT members at DFW in Dallas—not exactly a stone's throw away. From there, Nick's DMORT team had caravanned 370 miles by car and van, arriving just before midnight central time. The roads were desolate when they first headed east out of Dallas, but once they passed Shreveport and turned south on I-49, they found a steady and ominous increase in traffic coming from the direction of the Gulf Coast. By the time they reached Baton Rouge six hours later, the outbound lanes were aglow with headlights rising out of the south like sparks pouring from the mouth of a furnace.

In obedience to their commander's instructions, Nick's group dutifully shuffled forward through the entrance of the 150,000-square-foot warehouse. They were more than happy to move inside; the August heat and humidity were stifling and a light rain was beginning to fall, a presage of what was headed their way. As he approached the doorway, Nick looked up into the sky; in the brilliant light of the mercury-vapor lamps, raindrops magically appeared from the infinite darkness and streaked toward him like silver needles. Above the doorway was a sign in Latin: *Mortui Vivis Praecipiant*—"Let the Dead Teach the Living."

Nick felt a tap on his shoulder. A voice behind him said, "A woman walks into a funeral home."

Nick turned and found himself looking into the face of a very large man. The man looked directly into Nick's eyes, rivaling his six-foot-three stature, but the man outweighed Nick by at least forty pounds.

"C'mon," the man said. "A woman walks into a funeral home."

Nick rolled his eyes. "Go ahead."

"A woman walks into a funeral home. She tells the funeral director, 'I want my husband buried in a blue suit.' 'What's wrong with the black one he's wearing?' he asks. 'No, it has to be blue,' she says, and she hands him a blank check. "Whatever it costs," she tells him. So, at the viewing, the husband is wearing a beautiful blue suit. 'It's perfect,' the woman says. 'How much did it cost?' 'Not a thing,' the funeral director tells her. 'After you left, a body came in wearing a blue suit. The man was exactly the same size and build as your husband, so—I switched heads.'"

Nick just stared.

"C'mon, Nick, that's my newest joke."

"I believe you, Jerry."

The two men shook hands.

Jerry Kibbee was a member of Region V, the Great Lakes Region of DMORT. Jerry was a funeral director from Fort Wayne, Indiana, a town that Nick had visited once and vowed never to do so again. Kibbee's Funeral Home served the good people of Ft. Wayne in all the conventional ways: selling caskets, ordering headstones, providing memorable floral arrangements, and coordinating with police over solemn funeral processions to local cemeteries. For his part, Jerry was a simple mortician with a two-year associate's degree in mortuary science from a local community college. Beyond that, Jerry had no forensic expertise, a fact those new to DMORT might find surprising—but DMORT was founded by people just like Jerry. In the early 1980s, the National Funeral Directors Association assembled the components of the nation's first portable morgue, and many funeral directors are still counted among its members. The simple reality is that people like Jerry will always be needed at DMORT; there's always a place for those who are comfortable handling the dead.

Jerry's weight was all in his torso. He wasn't fat; he just had a barrel-shaped trunk that overshadowed the rest of his body. His arms, by contrast, were slender, and his legs even more so—like a marshmallow on toothpicks, Nick always said. His face was wide and friendly, and his cheeks were always rosy regardless of temperature or season, giving him a look of constant energy and health—*and making him look*, Nick thought, *like a poster boy for the embalmer's art.*

"Didn't know if I'd see you for this one," Nick said.

"You kidding? Wouldn't miss it for the world. They've activated all ten regions this time, did you hear that? They say it's the first time; they only activated seven after 9/11. Everybody's here, or over in Gulfport. That's where they set up the other DPMU."

"What is this for us, Jerry? Five? Six?"

"Beats me. Are you counting the Houston flood in 2004?"

In fact, it was the seventh time the two men had been deployed together, beginning with the Oklahoma City bombing in April of '95—DMORT's first major duty. Like Nick, Jerry often volunteered to deploy with other regional teams to shorten the downtime between assignments. In the past, half of DMORT's deployments had been in response to major transportation accidents, like the Flight 801 tragedy in Guam or the crash of Flight 587 in the New York borough of Queens. Each assignment posed its own challenges, but everyone knew that New Orleans would be unique—and everyone wanted to be there.

Nick and Jerry had become close friends over the years, perhaps bound together by each man's own "uniqueness"—Jerry because he was a simple mortician among forensic specialists, and Nick because he was a forensic entomologist: a scientific discipline that even some in DMORT found bizarre. Nick never saw Jerry apart from these deployments, but that's how DMORT worked. They were like a family, gathering only for special occasions but picking up right where they'd left off when they did.

In the doorway the two men anticipated a rush of cooler air, but they were both disappointed; the portable air-conditioning units had not yet been installed. The sounds of frenzied construction were everywhere, even at midnight.

"Heard any more about the storm?" Jerry asked.

"I listened to the radio on the way down," Nick said. "Not much new. Katrina keeps picking up steam; they declared it a category 5 this morning."

"Wow. She's a big girl now."

"No kidding. Sustained winds of 175 miles per hour and gusts up to 215."

"That's hard to imagine."

"That's the problem—nobody knows what to expect."

"Is she still headed for New Orleans?"

"The National Hurricane Center's sticking to its original prediction: landfall at 6:00 a.m. this morning near some town called Buras-Triumph—about sixty-five miles southeast of the city."

The two men continued to exchange the miscellaneous bits of information that each had been able to collect in transit. The Louisiana governor, Kathleen Blanco, had declared a state of emergency on Friday afternoon; in response, President Bush had declared a federal state of emergency the following day, triggering the activation of DMORT. Jerry said that the mayor of New Orleans, Ray Nagin, had refused to order a mandatory evacuation of the city until just the day before; he had planned instead to stick to his city's preexisting emergency evacuation plan. Nick replied that no preexisting emergency plan had ever anticipated a storm of this size or magnitude, and no one knew what would happen when it actually hit. Only residents of the parishes closest to the Gulf had actually been ordered to evacuate, and even then there was no one to enforce the order, so many had stayed behind. In the city itself untold thousands more remained, reluctant to leave their houses or pets or possessions, unwilling to believe that this storm would be any different from the last—or unable to comprehend the potential destructive power of the fourth-largest hurricane in recorded history.

On the radio, political pundits and talk-show hosts had delighted in unearthing the latest dark secrets about the city and its vulnerabilities: New Orleans, they said, is one of the poorest and most violent cities in

America; 28 percent of the city's residents live below the poverty line, more than twice the national average; most of the poor are black, living in the most crowded and lowest-lying neighborhoods; more than half of the elderly have disabilities, making it difficult—if not impossible—for them to flee the city.

And most ominous of all: The city of New Orleans, situated on a narrow bridge of alluvial silt between a river and a massive lake, is the lowest point in the United States besides Death Valley.

The two men finally reached the warehouse and stepped out of the misty rain. The building itself was an abandoned rubber-storage warehouse, but it was rapidly being converted to house DMORT's Disaster Portable Morgue Unit—the DPMU, as it was commonly known. The DPMU was a marvel of portable medical engineering, a complete and transportable morgue-in-a-box. FEMA maintains two of these units in constant readiness at its logistics centers in Rockville, Maryland, and San Jose, California. Each DPMU contains more than ten thousand individual items, from scalpels and forceps to autopsy tables and full-body X-ray machines. It also includes computers, fax machines, and state-of-the-art communications equipment, everything necessary to carry out the business of dealing with the dead—in very large numbers.

The concrete floor was covered with a heavy-gauge black polyethylene sheet to help insulate against the dampness and to facilitate the process of repeated decontamination. Nick stepped onto the plastic and felt his wet soles slide just a little and then catch, the way they would on snow-covered ice.

With everyone finally inside the building, the commander called out, "My name is Denny Behringer. I'm the DMORT commander here at St. Gabriel, and I'd like to welcome you all to beautiful Louisiana—the Pelican State, in case this is your first time here. Before we go any further, are there any members of the press present? I want to reiterate what I said outside: This DPMU will be closed to both the press and the public. At DMORT we do everything we can to treat victims and their families with the utmost dignity and respect. Please understand: This is not about secrecy; it's about privacy. I want you all to take a look at the person standing beside you; if you don't recognize him or her, ask to see an ID."

Denny waited. Apparently there were no infiltrators in the group.

"I know it's late," he continued, "and I know you've all had a very long day already, so I won't keep you any longer than I have to. I want to give you a quick tour of the DPMU, just to make you all familiar with our basic function and layout. If this is not your first deployment, please be patient—our newcomers need to hear this. After the tour, we'll hold a quick incident briefing. I know you're all just dying to sit through a meeting right about now, but hey, what can I say? You're federal employees now."

The last remark garnered a laugh from almost everyone. When a DMORT team is activated, its members become temporary employees of the federal government, with all the accompanying rights and privileges—including a mountain of required paperwork and a substantial reduction in pay. Some members of Nick's DMORT team were highly paid professionals back home—physicians and dentists among them—and volunteering with DMORT involved considerable financial sacrifice.

No one complained. Many of these people were veterans of several past DMORT deployments, yet here they were again. As any of them would tell you: It's not about the money. Some of them were there for the adrenaline; they were used to weekends on call or sleepless nights in the ER, and they loved the demanding pace. Some simply loved their profession, and DMORT gave them a chance to do more in two weeks than they might in six months back home. Others, like Nick, were there to serve the living by doing what they loved most—studying the dead—and there was no better place than DMORT to do it.

Nick loved the DPMU. Permanent city morgues were usually relegated to some isolated, subterranean corner of a crumbling municipal building, but the DPMU was always brand-spanking-new, bright and aboveground, and, once up and running, bustling with activity. The cavernous warehouse was divided into two major sections, the largest reserved for storage, office space, and casketing operations. The remainder of the warehouse housed a series of long carnival tents, some an ordinary canvas color, while others sported colorful striped canopies complete with scalloped trim. Each tent contained a different forensic station, and each station was further divided into separate postmortem bays to allow three or four forensic specialists to work simultaneously. Each man or woman worked a twelve-hour, seven-to-seven shift, ideally rotating out of the disaster site after two exhausting weeks of duty, though the tour of duty depended entirely on the nature and scope of the disaster—and every disaster was different.

"This is the admitting area," Denny began. "Whenever a body is admitted to the DPMU, a rigid protocol will be followed. The body will first be decontaminated with a chlorine solution, and then assigned a number, a folder, and a personal escort who will accompany it throughout its examination. The escort will not only ensure that proper procedures are followed, but he will also establish a chain of evidence in the event that any criminal activity is indicated."

Denny motioned the group into the first tent. "The first forensic station will focus on victim identification. Personal effects such as jewelry and watches will be collected and inventoried here. Fingerprints will be taken—if there are fingers still present and if the condition of the tissues allows it. One of our pathologists will then make a cursory examination, searching the body for scars, tattoos, or other identifying marks. In the absence of these, the body might be x-rayed or even autopsied to search for orthopedic devices or surgical implants. As some of you know, newer devices bear serial numbers that can be tracked through manufacturers' records. In cases of severe decomposition, a forensic anthropologist will be called in to examine fragments of bone. This should allow us to at least determine age, sex, stature, and ethnicity."

A hand went up in the back. "Will every body be autopsied?"

"Not necessarily," Denny said. "DMORT autopsies have a different purpose than those conducted under normal circumstances. The goal of our procedure is simply to identify the victim, not to determine the cause of death. However, if foul play is indicated, the body will immediately be turned over to the jurisdictional coroner for a more thorough autopsy."

He moved the group forward into a second tent. "Next comes the dental examination station. Here, X-rays will be taken to check against existing dental records. The problem in New Orleans will be finding those existing dental records. For the old, the homeless, and the disabled, regular dental care tends to fall low on the priority list. For many of them there might be no records to find. And there's another complication we might have to contend with: Dental records are very hard to locate when they're underwater."

Denny motioned the group into the final tent. "At the final station, a DNA sample will be extracted from bone—which might still give us a viable sample even if the softer tissues have decomposed. The right tibia is the bone of choice; the sample will then be labeled, frozen, and stored for later identification."

Nick shook his head; it sounded so simple, but the reality was something else. Thanks to the media, DNA identification was familiar to everyone by now—but so much had been said in its favor that the public now expected almost magical results. Nick knew that in the real world, DNA identification was a long, slow, and expensive process. Nick and Jerry had both worked the 1996 crash of TWA Flight 800; all 230 victims were eventually identified through DNA, but the process took thirteen months.

"Finally, when every station has completed its examination, the body along with its personal effects will be placed in a fresh body bag and returned to refrigeration await to formal identification. The body, once identified, will be referred to by name. Our newcomers will please take note of this—this is a personal touch that DMORT prides itself on. Once identified, the remains will hopefully be released to a waiting family. If no family can be located, then the body will be buried or cremated by DMORT itself. Are there any questions about our facility or procedures?"

There were none.

"In that case, this completes our tour of the DPMU. Please help yourselves to some water—do your best to stay hydrated."

The group now gathered in a large, open meeting area and spread out a bit to allow the stagnant air to circulate between them. The air-conditioning still wasn't working, but at least the high warehouse roof allowed the heat to rise away from them. Along one side of the room was a table covered with water bottles; first in line were the sweat-soaked members of Region IX, who were forced to make the sudden transition from the bone-dry climate of Arizona or Nevada to the oppressive humidity of Louisiana.

"Not a bad tour," Nick said. "It was informative, it held my attention, and it kept moving. We've had better—I still like the '99 Amtrak derailment best. Overall, I give it one thumbs-up."

"Thanks for the review," Jerry said.

"Let's get the briefing started," Denny called out. "As I said, I don't want to keep you any longer than necessary—but I've got a few things that you all need to know."

4

Nick and Jerry took seats in the back of the room, and Denny stepped in front of a small podium.

"First of all, you're probably wondering about sleeping arrangements. As you may have noticed, our facility is still under construction. There's an unused elementary school nearby, and we also have an unfinished condo unit available to us; we'll provide cots or air mattresses for many of you there. I'm afraid some of you will have to sleep in your cars at first—sorry about that. I should also mention another option: We have a few refrigerated tractor trailers outside, which will be used to transport bodies from New Orleans and then to store them again after processing. Some of them are FEMA trucks, but the good folks at Wal-Mart and Ben & Jerry's were nice enough to donate a few too. The trucks sleep twenty-four each—or I should say, they're each capable of transporting twenty-four bodies. Don't worry, we promise not to keep the thermostat at 38 degrees."

The group laughed, but Jerry whispered, "It's okay by me. I'll take the air-conditioning."

Nick nodded. "Yeah, me too."

"As I said before, the DPMU will be a secured area beginning immediately. I'm sure you've all noticed that the compound is surrounded by fence and razor wire. A guard will be posted at the gate at all times, courtesy of the St. Gabriel Police Department. You'll need your credentials to get in or out 24/7—so be sure to keep them with you.

"As for meals, if you've been on a DMORT deployment before, then you're familiar with our executive dining plan: The National Guard has been kind enough to provide us with their mouthwatering meals ready to eat. Just stop by our cafeteria, affectionately known as the 'McDMORT Café,' and see what you can find. Our menu features everything that can possibly be freeze-dried or crammed into a brown Mylar bag. If you get sick of the MREs, I've been told that at the St. Gabriel Truck Stop the crawfish omelet comes with hash browns and a biscuit. You might want to have your cholesterol checked at the end of your deployment."

"I love Meals Ready to Eat," Jerry said. "Especially the Chili with Macaroni."

"They definitely beat the NC State dining halls," Nick said.

The MREs were a constant source of derision for DMORT members, but Nick and Jerry never complained. They were both single men, and both found the MREs to be a big improvement over their usual fare of Tuna Surprise or take-out Chinese.

"Now I want to say a few words about the situation facing us," Denny segued, and the tone of his address began to change. "I see a lot of familiar faces out there; many of you have been with us before. Some of you were there after 9/11. You were with us at the DPMU in Hangar 7 at LaGuardia Airport, and you probably thought that was as bad as it gets—we all did. But I want you to know that we've never faced anything like this before. New Orleans represents what we call an 'open system.' In a situation like an airline crash—even in the case of the World Trade Center—we've usually got some kind of passenger manifest or occupant list to work against. Not in New Orleans; we have absolutely no idea how many people are still there or where they're located. At other mass-casualty sites, the victims are usually confined to a limited area—say, a field or a building site. In New Orleans, the victims could be dispersed all over the city. That's not going to make it easy for us.

"You're all probably wondering, 'How bad could this get?' The storm is still predicted to make landfall early this morning; what will happen when it does, nobody knows for sure. The National Weather Service issued this warning earlier today; let me read you a few excerpts:

'Hurricane Katrina . . . A most powerful hurricane with unprecedented strength . . . Devastating damage expected . . . Most of the area will be uninhabitable for weeks . . . perhaps longer. At least one half of well-constructed homes will have roof and wall failure . . . leaving those homes severely damaged or destroyed. The majority of industrial buildings will become nonfunctional. Partial to complete wall and roof failure is expected. All wood-framed low-rising apartment buildings will be destroyed. Concrete-block low-rise apartments will sustain major damage . . . including some wall and roof failure. High-rise office and apartment buildings will sway dangerously . . . a few to the point of total collapse. All windows will blow out. Airborne debris will be widespread . . . and may include heavy items such as household appliances and even light vehicles . . . The blown debris will create additional destruction. Persons . . . pets . . . and livestock exposed to the winds will face certain death if struck. Power outages will last for weeks . . . as most power poles will be down and transformers destroyed. Water shortages will make human suffering incredible by modern standards.'"

Denny stopped reading and looked at the group. From the back of the room, someone let out a low whistle.

"Are there any predictions about casualties yet?" Nick asked.

"There's just no way to tell," Denny replied. "All we can do is prepare for the worst. They estimate that about a million people have left the greater New Orleans area so far; nobody knows how many have chosen to remain behind. Mayor Nagin has opened up ten emergency shelters for them, including the New Orleans Superdome. I've been told that facility stocks thirty-six hours' worth of food in reserve. The city is surrounded by water on three sides, and 70 percent of it is below sea level. Our DPMU is capable of processing 140 bodies a day for as long as we have to be here. We brought twenty-five thousand body bags with us; let's just pray we take some home."

"What about the levees?" someone asked. "Are they expected to hold?"

"The Army Corps of Engineers tells us that the levees were only designed to protect against a Category 3 hurricane. At the lowest points, the levees can only hold back a storm surge of about fourteen feet. Some say Katrina might double that; if that happens, the entire city will be underwater."

There was a pause, and then a lone voice spoke for everyone in the room: "The *whole city*?"

"That's what they tell us. If there is significant flooding in the city, then there are going to be casualties—a lot of them—and they're not going to be easy to identify. It happens in every flood: People get separated from their identifying documents—wallets, purses, that sort of thing. Bodies get washed around by the currents, too, so we might not even know what neighborhood the victim came from.

"What I'm trying to say is that we're not really sure what we're up against yet; the next twenty-four hours will tell. As always, DMORT will be functioning under the authority of FEMA and the Department of Homeland Security, and alongside local relief and law enforcement agencies. This is a team effort, everybody, and we play just one part. The first thing I want everybody to do is get a good night's sleep—as good as you can, under the conditions. We'll spend tomorrow getting the DPMU in shape; then, as soon as the storm has safely passed, all nonadministrative members will be transported to New Orleans to assist in rescue efforts. You are to report to the agency in charge of the rescue efforts in that area and follow their instructions. Are there any questions?"

Nick frowned, then slowly raised his hand.

"Yes. Nick."

"Did you say, 'Assist in *rescue* efforts'? I assume you meant *recovery* efforts."

"No, you heard me right. If there is extensive flooding across the city, tens of thousands of people are expected to be trapped in their homes or on rooftops. As I said, this is a team effort; the decision has been made by FEMA to focus all available resources on rescuing the living first."

"Instead of recovering the dead?"

"At first, yes. I think you'll agree, Nick, that it's a lot more important to rescue the living than it is to recover the dead."

"I'm not sure I do," Nick said, rising to his feet.

"Fasten your seat belts," Jerry mumbled. "Here we go."

"We stopped for gas on the way down here," Nick said. "A little station just north of Baton Rouge—some of you were with me." He glanced around the room and a few heads nodded. "There was a line a mile long waiting for gas—it took us an hour to get through. While we were there, two men pulled up to a pump at the same time. They began to argue about who got there first. The argument got heated. I thought there was going to be a fight—until one of them pulled up his shirt and showed the other guy a gun."

Nick paused to allow the point to sink in.

"That's what stress does to your species, Denny. Those two men were on their way *out* of town—what about the people who stay behind? What sort of stress will they be under? Hunger, fatigue, competition for available resources—and I'd like to remind everyone that New Orleans holds the record for the highest murder rate ever recorded, and that's *without* a hurricane. Human nature isn't going to improve after a major disaster; it's going to get worse—maybe a lot worse."

"What's your point, Nick?"

"You say we're looking at a lot of casualties here. All I'm saying is that some of them won't have died from natural causes—you can count on that. We owe something to those people too."

"So what are you suggesting?"

"That we divide our resources. Surely at least a few of us could be assigned to the recovery of the dead."

Denny shook his head. "FEMA estimates that one out of four residents of New Orleans has no access to an automobile. There's no way to estimate how many people have stayed behind—it could be in the hundreds of thousands. And if the city floods, there's no telling how many people will be in need of rescue. Nobody knows if all the government agencies combined can handle it; that's why FEMA wants all available personnel to focus on rescue first."

"Why was DMORT created?" Nick asked. "To help family members identify and recover the remains of their loved ones."

"Thanks, Nick, I'm familiar with the training manual."

"Murder victims have families too," Nick said, "and they want more than that—they want the murderers brought to justice. That's why the bodies can't wait, Denny. This isn't just about recovery; it's about preserving forensic evidence. You said yourself that this is a unique situation; let's not forget the problems posed by the water. Any pathologist here will tell you that a body decomposes much faster in water than it does on land—but in this case it'll be even worse. The water will be hot, and it will be filled with who-knows-what: bacteria, toxins, sewage, chemicals, pesticides—just to name a few. If the city does flood, we're going to have bodies floating in a toxic brew—"

"Nick—"

"—and it won't just be a problem for visual identification. I'm talking about major decomposition of tissues, even degradation of DNA. Nothing will last long in that soup; by the time we get around to recovering bodies, there'll be nothing left to find."

"Nick—"

"We're working against the clock here, Denny. This may be an open system, but time is the one thing that's not open. In Somerset County we had all the time in the world to collect the remains from United 93. We had time to mark off the whole field, and walk the grid, but if we take that long here—"

"First the living!" someone shouted from across the room.

"That's incredibly shortsighted," Nick said. "How many of you have actually viewed a cadaver recovered in water? Let me tell you, it's an evidential nightmare. The tissues soften; the fingers swell until the fingerprints disappear; the hair is lost; the face becomes bloated and unrecognizable—at some point even gender becomes difficult to distinguish. I'm talking about complete loss of forensic evidence: knife wounds, contusions, bullet tracks—all of it disappears. Are we really willing to let that happen?"

The room began to stir; Denny gestured for everyone to quiet down. "Nick, if you want to talk more about this, then see me after the meeting. I'm sure the rest of the team would like to get some sleep. I've scheduled our next briefing for 7:00 a.m. I know, that's awfully early—welcome to DMORT.

"There is one more thing I want to cover tonight. I'd save it for tomorrow, but I think it's that important. If you've been with us before, you know this kind of work can take a lot out of you. The hours are long, nobody gets enough sleep, and then—well, there's the nature of the work itself. That's why DMORT always includes mental health professionals on every deployment, and this time is no exception."

"Uh-oh," Jerry said. "I smell trouble."

"Some experts are predicting that Hurricane Katrina will be the worst natural disaster in our nation's history. If they're right, we'll be working longer hours and we'll be under more stress than ever before—and we need to make sure that we're dealing with that stress in a healthy way. To make sure we do, we're fortunate to have here with us Dr. Elizabeth Woodbridge."

"I knew it," Jerry said.

Nick let out a groan.

"Dr. Woodbridge is a distinguished psychiatrist in private practice in the San Francisco area. She is a longtime member of DMORT Region IX, and she's been with us on several prior DMORT deployments. Since Dr. Woodbridge will be serving such an important role here in St. Gabriel, I've asked her if she would close our briefing with a few introductory comments. Dr. Woodbridge?"

The woman who stood up looked strangely out of place. She was unusually pretty—not that the other women present weren't attractive, but the physical demands of DMORT required a what-you-see-is-what-you-get approach: Pull your hair back in a ponytail, scrub your face, and forget the makeup. But this woman looked as if she had just stepped out of a corporate office—which she probably had, just a few hours ago on the West Coast. Her hair was blonde and shoulder-length, cut in a trendy style, with a long straight wisp that crossed her forehead from left to right, causing her to forever brush it back. Her skin was fair and smooth and her eyes were unexpectedly dark and almond-shaped. Her face was beautiful but her eyes were piercing, like thorns on the stem of a rose. It was a quality that Nick found especially annoying—among others.

"I still say she's the hottest babe in DMORT," Jerry said.

"Good evening and welcome," Dr. Woodbridge began. "Or should I say, 'Welcome back.' I see a lot of familiar faces out there." As she said this, her eyes scanned the audience; when she came to Nick, she hesitated for a split second.

Jerry leaned over to Nick. "I saw that."

"Shut up," Nick said.

"As Denny told you, this deployment could pose unique challenges for all of us—including challenges of a psychological nature. Traumatic stress, sleep deprivation, insomnia, nightmares—these are things we're all susceptible to. My job, to put it simply, is to help you avoid these things—or to help you through them if necessary. If you'll allow me to be a bit pedantic for a moment, I'd like to read to you from the DMORT Field Operations Guide."

Jerry leaned in again. "What does 'pedantic' mean?"

"It means you went to a community college. Shut up."

"'Description of Duties of the DMORT Mental Health Officer,'" she read. "'(1) Monitors incident stress levels of all personnel and implements stress reduction measures as necessary. (2) Identifies appropriate assessments, interventions, prevention techniques, and counseling for early identification of personnel at risk of mental health and related problems.' That pretty much says it all: My job is to help each of you assess your individual stress level and keep it at a manageable level."

"I came here for the stress," Nick said. "Why can't she mind her own business?"

"Now, how will this happen? First of all, there are things you can do to help. I'm reading again from the Field Operations Guide: 'Be responsible for your well-being and keep in touch with your family. It is important that you monitor and maintain yourself in areas such as: stress levels, medical fitness, physical fitness, proper hydration, proper foods, and regular bowel movements.'"

"Freudians," Nick said. "She's been here for five minutes, and she's already talking about bowel movements."

"Those are things that you can do," she said. "What I can do is listen. As in all past DMORT deployments, each team member will be required to undergo an exit interview when his or her rotation is completed. But here in St. Gabriel, due to the extreme pressures we may all be forced to work under, I'll also be conducting informal interviews along the way just to keep an eye out for unhealthy coping mechanisms. So if I ask you, 'How are you doing?' please don't brush me off—because I really do care and I really want to know. Thank you."

She concluded to scattered applause. At this point the meeting broke up and people began to slowly rise and mingle. Nick just sat there, slumped down in his chair.

"Terrific," he grumbled. "A perfectly good disaster ruined."

5

"Talk to you later," Nick said to Jerry. "I need to grab Denny before he gets away."

"Go easy on him," Jerry said. "He's got a big job this time."

Denny spotted Nick charging toward him, and he held up one hand as if to repel the advance. "Now, take it easy, Nick. I know you're upset about this, but the decision has already been made."

"What fool made that decision?"

"You know how the system works: DMORT is part of the National Disaster Medical System; NDMS is part of FEMA; FEMA is part of Homeland Security; and DHS is part of the president's cabinet. So who made the decision? I don't know—somebody a lot higher up than me. Don't shoot the messenger, okay?"

"If I did, they'd never recover your body."

"C'mon, Nick. Living people are sort of the priority, you know?"

"No, they're just one of the priorities. Look, I know we need to rescue the living—I'm okay with that—but we owe something to the dead too."

"Nick, let me fill you in on something: In case you haven't noticed, this whole setup is a logistical nightmare. Everybody knows it's going to be bad tomorrow, and everybody's ready to help—the National Guard, the Coast Guard, the Department of Transportation—and those are just a few of the government agencies. We've got a hundred parties in the private sector waiting to pitch in too. And every agency's got some grand contingency plan they worked out years ago, but nobody counted on anything quite like this. The problem is, nobody knows exactly who's in charge."

"It should be FEMA," Nick said.

"It should be, yeah. And FEMA used to be a cabinet-level position, remember? That was before 9/11. They had the president's ear back then; they had clear lines of authority. But after 9/11 they lost their cabinet seat, remember? They got shelved under Homeland Security, and now it isn't clear who's making the decisions. It's tough to know where the orders are coming from, and it's even harder to know who to complain to when the orders don't make sense."

"Then you don't think it makes sense either."

Denny paused. "I think I'm not the boss," he said, "and neither are you. But since you asked me, I agree with them—I think all available resources should be focused on rescuing the living first. Think about it: If we wait to recover the bodies, then what you said is true: We might lose a lot of forensic evidence—we might even lose the ability to identify some of them. But if we wait to rescue the living, we'll just have more bodies to deal with later. C'mon, Nick, I know you like bugs more than people, but after all—we're here to serve the living."

"I'm here to serve the living," Nick said, "but there are different ways to do it. One of them is by taking care of the dead."

"And we will—as soon as the rescue operations are finished."

"I just don't see why we can't do both. Surely they could spare a few of us."

Denny paused again, choosing his words carefully. "I don't think the decision was purely logistical. When all this is over, I think the people in charge want to be able to say that they used every possible resource to rescue everyone they could. I think there was an emotional element involved."

"That's a political element, if you ask me."

"Call it what you want; that's the way it is. This is a rescue-and-recovery effort, Nick. Got that? Rescue *and* recovery—but rescue comes first. As of tomorrow, all willing and able DMORT personnel are to assist in rescue efforts in New Orleans."

"I wasn't trained for search and rescue," Nick grumbled.

"C'mon, I've seen you recover bodies from every imaginable location—trees, cliffs, power lines, caves. Search and rescue can't be any harder than that. The only difference is that the body walks away later."

"Thanks for the tip."

"You don't have to take part, you know; it's up to you. I'm sure we could find something for you to do around here instead."

Nick glared at him. "You jerk—you know I'll be there."

Denny grinned. "Yeah, I know. You'd rather die than miss the action." He started to turn away, then stopped. "One more thing," he said. "We're a team, okay? We've been together a few times now. I really need you to be a team player this time."

Nick shrugged. "I'm a team player."

"Yeah, but there are different kinds of teams. There are ball teams, where everybody has to work together like a well-oiled machine; then there are cross-country teams, where it's every man for himself. I need you to play ball this time. You know what I'm talking about, don't you?"

"You want me to play on the Region IV softball team."

Denny smiled—but only a little. "Just think it over."

He turned and left.

"Hello, Nick."

Nick turned to find Dr. Woodbridge standing behind him. Her arms hung down with her hands folded in front of her at the waist, with her two index fingers pressed together at the tips and pointing at the floor. She stood with one foot slightly in front of the other, like a spokesperson about to demonstrate a new product. She was smiling, and the moment Nick made eye contact her eyes locked onto his.

"Beth," Nick said.

"How are you doing, Nick?"

"Fine. If you'll excuse me, I was just about to—"

"You weren't listening, were you?"

"I beg your pardon?"

"My introductory comments. You weren't listening."

"Sure I was. Bowel movements—got it."

"I said if I ask you, 'How are you doing?' please don't brush me off. So—how are you doing?"

"Oh, right, I remember now. Well, let's see: After careful consideration, I would say that I'm—fine."

She reached into her blazer pocket and removed a folded slip of paper. She opened it and held it up to Nick. On it was written a single word: FINE.

"That's amazing," Nick said. "You're like that Criss Angel guy. Can you do the levitation? I really like that one."

"I wrote it down before I came over here," Dr. Woodbridge said. "It was my prediction of what you would say when I asked you how you are."

"You've really got me pegged," Nick said, "along with about 90 percent of the other men on the planet. Maybe I should try that; maybe I should write down a word for you."

"And what would that word be, Nick?"

A few colorful possibilities crossed Nick's mind, but he thought it best to keep them to himself. He tried to maintain eye contact with her as he spoke—not because he wanted to, but because he thought she might use it as some kind of test for elusiveness or guilt. He found it almost impossible to do so; her gaze was so intense that every time he made solid contact it was like touching an electric fence. It was her most annoying habit—a skill she had probably honed through years of private therapy with evasive neurotics. She didn't look *at* him, she looked *through* him; it was as if she were an ophthalmologist peering through his pupils at his retinas, searching for some capillary that was about to explode. Maybe it was supposed to communicate interest or compassion, but to Nick it just seemed—*annoying*. That was the word that kept coming to mind; that was the one he should carry around in his jacket pocket. Then she would ask, "How are you, Nick?" and he could just flash his little piece of paper: ANNOYING.

He started to look away, but her eyes darted ahead of his like a cutting horse herding a straying heifer back into the herd. That was another annoying habit; she demanded eye contact in return. During past mental health debriefings, Nick had sometimes felt like his head was a volleyball being smacked back and forth into the center of the court. He found it exhausting and it gave him a headache. *What kind of mental health is that?* he wondered. *I can get headaches on my own.*

"I couldn't help overhearing the last part of your conversation with Denny," she said.

"'Couldn't help overhearing.' That's an interesting choice of words. How about, 'Did my best to listen in.'"

"If you wish. You do know what he was referring to, don't you?"

"Is that a question or a statement?"

"Is that an answer or an evasion?"

Annoying. "Look, are we having an interview already? I just got here an hour ago; how much stress can I be under?"

Beth smiled. "No, this is not an interview. I just wanted a chance to say hello before things got busy. It's been a long time. I've thought about you."

Nick looked at her—as if he had a choice. She was wrong; Nick had been listening closely when she had made her opening comments. He had heard every word she said; he had heard her when she said, "I really do care," and he knew that she really did. It was the *way* she cared that bothered him. He couldn't help but feel that he was some sort of case study to her: the Bug Man—the weirdest guy in DMORT—someone who might be the subject of an award-winning article in the *Journal of Personality Disorders*.

"I've thought about you too," Nick replied.

"How ambiguous."

"Isn't it? I hear women love a man of mystery."

She seemed to care about Nick the same way that Nick cared about his giant hissing cockroach from Madagascar—something that fascinates you, not something you form a genuine attachment to. At every DMORT deployment they had shared, Nick seemed to become an object of special interest to her. He didn't mind her attention—what man would? He just didn't like the X-ray burns that came with it. He could never decide whether she was a woman trying to change him or a therapist trying to take him apart. Maybe it was just his male vanity, or maybe he was just an unwilling specimen trying to wriggle off the microscope slide; either way, it was just one more thing about her that he found irritating.

"I want you to know that I plan to check up on you on a regular basis," she said.

"What makes me so lucky?"

"I think you're going to be working under a lot of pressure."

"No more than anyone else."

She paused. "*Within and without*—remember?"

Nick remembered. "Within and without" was a phrase she had coined—one of those cute clinical clichés that therapists love to drum up and tuck away for future book titles. "Within and without" was her way of saying that a man's response to stress is determined by two things: the extent of the external pressure, and the nature of his own internal wiring. With Nick, her emphasis had always been on *within*.

"Has the book come out yet?" he asked. "I sure hope I'm on the cover."

"Do you deflect everything with humor?"

"No, sometimes I just walk away. Shall I demonstrate?"

"Nick, you can't get rid of me that easily."

"How many women have told me that? But I'm still single."

"I think that's the way you want it."

"I'm just looking for the right woman—but the wrong women keep blocking my view."

"Nick, I'm just trying to do my job."

"And I'm just trying to do mine—so let me."

"I'll be glad to—as long as you do your job in a healthy way."

"A *healthy way*? What's *healthy* about any of this? Do you know what DMORT members do, Beth? We volunteer our spare time to collect human remains at mass-casualty sites—does that sound healthy to you?

We do it so that some grieving widow can gain a sense of closure by burying a bone fragment from her husband's ring finger—is that healthy? Nobody around here is healthy, Beth. We're all a little crazy in our own way."

"I never said you were crazy."

"No, that would be bad clinical technique—but that's what you're thinking."

"Would you like to know what I'm really thinking, Nick?"

"No, I wouldn't. Look, I'm not crazy, I'm *special*—my mother told me so. The whole world is crazy, and it takes a lot of special people to keep it running smoothly—that's just the way it is. I like myself the way I am, okay? And if I work a little harder than most people or stay up a little longer, well, that's just dedication to my work."

"You're sure that's all it is?"

"Trust me, I'm a specimen of good mental health—and if I do decide to go postal, I promise not to do it on your watch."

She just eyed him for a moment, considering; then she turned and walked over to a briefcase lying open on a folding chair. She returned and handed Nick a document in a clear plastic cover.

"Do you remember our last deployment?" she asked.

How could he forget? This was their sixth deployment together, and each one seemed to end a little worse than the one before. Dr. Woodbridge first joined the ranks of DMORT in 1999, at the site of the Egypt Air disaster near Nantucket Island in Massachusetts. Nick didn't trust her from the start; she seemed to show a little too much interest in the mental motivations and inner drives behind these strange people who willingly gave up their spare time to collect the dead. When she was finally introduced to Nick, the one his colleagues mysteriously referred to as the Bug Man, it was as if her entire focus shifted to him—as though she had found the Prince of Darkness himself, someone twisted enough to supply a lifetime of fascinating study and analysis. Nick resented the extra attention; there was nothing wrong with being fascinated by insects—or by their forensic application. More than 90 percent of all animal species on earth are insects, and Nick could never understand how some people seemed to find nine-tenths of the world disgusting or scary. *They're the ones who need a psychiatrist*, he thought.

The trouble began with more and more frequent "debriefings," during which Dr. Woodbridge attempted to probe deeper and deeper into the machinations of Nick's mind. At first, Nick resisted. "Have you ever witnessed the death of a family member?" she asked. *No, but I can think of a couple I'd like to*. "When did you first show an interest in insects?" *It was in my baby crib—my mobile had blowflies instead of canaries*. "Would you say you have fulfilling relationships with the opposite sex?" *The living ones or the dead ones?*

But she wasn't deterred, so Nick devised a different strategy: He thought that if he answered all her questions completely and forthrightly, it might satisfy her curiosity and get her off his back. *Fool*—he knew better now. During this phase he made some regrettable admissions: He told her that he liked insects more than people; he told her that he found the human species, as a whole, irrational and disappointing; worst of all, he told her that he preferred not to think of himself as a human being at all—that he preferred to think of himself as a bug. From that point on, Dr. Woodbridge welcomed Nick into her office with special eagerness—like a biologist receiving a specimen of bubonic plague.

It was on their third deployment that Nick made his big mistake.

The simple fact was that Dr. Woodbridge was a very attractive woman, and not all of Nick resented her special attention. They sat hour after hour in her little office, seated close and staring face-to-face, talking intimately and openly about feelings and families and stress. At one point Nick thought he detected something different in Dr. Woodbridge's eyes; he wondered if her interest in him was becoming more than professional. But he had no way to be sure; he had proven himself thoroughly inept at reading signals from the opposite sex in the past, and he could think of no way to come right out and ask. So instead he improvised a simple experiment: Midway through a lengthy analysis of Nick's attachment issues, he suddenly leaned forward and kissed her—and sure enough, she kissed him back.

Hypothesis confirmed.

At that point their relationship became something more. That's when Dr. Woodbridge became Beth—and that's when the trouble began.

Nick began to have second thoughts almost immediately. They lived on opposite coasts, so their relationship would be relegated to DMORT deployments—an atmosphere hardly conducive to romance. To make matters worse, his significant other was also his psychiatrist. He had been required to expose the workings of his mind to her, and he regretted that already—was he now supposed to open his heart too? He found himself revisiting his basic motivations for involvement with DMORT, and romance simply wasn't one of them—it would only make things more difficult.

Nick decided that he'd better cut bait before things got any more complicated. He had no idea how to explain this to Beth—how to tell her that he wanted to end the relationship, even though he was the one who made the first move—so he didn't tell her. He took a more traditional male approach instead—he just went back to work. After that, their debriefings became less frequent and more confrontational. Beth seemed to keep waiting for Nick to say something, but Nick had nothing to say. By their next deployment, Beth was once again nothing more than Nick's psychiatrist—with a lot less compassion for his eccentricities and quirks.

"Nick? Did you hear me? I asked you if you remember our last deployment."

Nick blinked. "How could I forget? The voices in my head keep reminding me."

"This is the report I wrote after our last exit interview. I brought you a copy."

"Thanks, but I'm waiting for the film version."

"I want you to read it. It contains some therapeutic terms—things like 'hypervigilance' and 'depersonalization.' If you need me to define any of them for you, let me know. You're an amazing man, Nick; I've never met anybody like you. You're right, you know—the whole world is crazy, but for most people their craziness is mostly harmless quirks and eccentricities. Yours is different; yours could destroy you. Read the report when you get a chance—sooner rather than later. These are things I saw in you during our last deployment. Think of it as a list of things you should be watching for. I know I will."

She left Nick staring at the cover of the report.

A moment later, Jerry approached. "I'm telling you, buddy, the woman's got a thing for you."

Nick looked at him. "'The hottest babe in DMORT?' Who talks like that? No wonder you're still single."

Two hours later, Nick sat cross-legged in the open doorway of a refrigerated semi. Cool air poured over him from behind. It felt good, and he wished he could absorb the coolness and store it away; he wondered how long there would be air-conditioning anywhere in New Orleans. He arched his back and felt his shirt lift away from the skin; it was already dry. Behind him he could hear the low rumble of the diesel engine, which would idle all night to keep the refrigeration unit running. Inside the long trailer, six bodies of average height could be lined up end to end along each wall. A crude bench made from two-by-fours sat along each, adding a second level and doubling the sleeping capacity. Jerry lay in a sleeping bag under one of the benches; he had apparently thought it best not to test the construction with his considerable weight. Jerry was an easy sleeper, and he had dropped off in seconds; he lay on his back with his mouth open, snoring like a diesel himself.

Nick couldn't sleep. He felt the wind increasing, rocking the trailer with sporadic gusts. The rain came harder too; the drops no longer fell vertically but dashed in all directions like angry bees.

Nick kept thinking how strange it was: In each of his other deployments, the disaster had already happened, and DMORT had been called in after the fact to help pick up the pieces. Here, they were waiting for the disaster to occur. The DPMUs were on-site and assembled, and twelve hundred DMORT volunteers from all over the United States were ready and waiting—and all they could do was sit and watch the disaster happen right before their eyes, like a bomb exploding in slow motion.

The Big Easy, they called it. Nick had a feeling that, after tomorrow, nothing would be easy in New Orleans for a long, long time.

6

Monday, August 29

The hurricane ripped into the Gulf Coast like a massive buzz saw, devastating everything in its path. It came ashore exactly where predicted, at the little town of Buras-Triumph about sixty-five miles southeast of New Orleans—and instantly removed it from the earth. The storm smashed into the shore as a Category 4 hurricane with winds of 140 miles per hour, enough force to strip the roof from a warehouse like aluminum foil or toss a mobile home through the air like an empty shoebox. Century-old oaks and chestnuts were downed in an instant, leaning over onto their sides like tired old men; power lines draped everywhere, crossing with a loud crack and sending showers of sparks sizzling into the sky; glass blasted from window frames, streaking through the air like shrapnel; corrugated sheeting ripped away from sheds and walls and sailed through the air like giant razor blades.

The hurricane plowed inland, driving an eighteen-foot storm surge ahead of it, thundering up the Mississippi River-Gulf Outlet and into the narrow Industrial Canal, where it poured over the levees like an overflowing sink and into the streets of the Lower Ninth Ward. Manhole covers rocketed into the sky and came crashing down with a deafening clang; geysers of water gushed from the storm sewers and shot into the air; abandoned boats sat like houses on city streets, and severed houses floated like boats.

And still the water kept coming.

Inside one of the thousands of houses being slowly submerged, a man struggled frantically to reach a six-inch length of cord dangling from the hallway ceiling above him—but every time he went up on his tiptoes, the black water swirling around his legs knocked him off balance. Twice he had fallen headlong, and each time he struggled to his feet again the water was even deeper.

He could feel his heart in his throat, pounding like a fist on a steel drum.

Maybe Mandy was right, maybe he was a fool to stay. The storm would be a big one, everybody said so—but that's what they always said, and he'd always come through it before. He had made it through Camille as a boy back in '69—and Betsy four years before that, sitting right here in this very room. Why should this one be different? It was his house now, and a man doesn't just up and leave his house in the middle of the night—not in this neighborhood. That's what some folks wanted you to do—that's what they were waiting for. If he headed off with Mandy to the Superdome, what would he find when he came back the next day? Nothing, that's what—no TV, no liquor cabinet—and what about the stuff? What if they found that too? The stuff was worth a lot more than any TV. No, sir, it would take more than a hurricane to make him leave.

He was a fool. He knew it now—but now it was too late.

It would be dawn soon, but he looked out the window and saw nothing but blackness; he could hear the wind shrieking and howling, stripping the house apart piece by piece. The rain was no longer liquid; it blasted the roof and walls like handfuls of nails. When the lightning flashed he could catch a fleeting glimpse of his living room—a room he no longer recognized, half submerged in debris-covered water.

And it was rising fast.

He needed a chair, a step stool, anything—but everything was underwater. He remembered the dresser at the end of the hall, not more than twenty feet away. He started toward it in the darkness, but his left leg bumped something large and heavy drifting just above the floor like a sunken log. He fell forward with both arms extended, crashing into the water and sending a wave splashing out ahead of him. He struggled to his feet, grabbed the top of the dresser, and tried to wrench it away from the wall—but the sheets and blankets that filled the drawers were sodden and heavy, and the piece was impossible to move.

He turned and felt his way back down the hallway to the living room. There was another flash of lightning, and he saw the silhouette of an upholstered armchair bobbing like a slab of salt pork in a vat of beans. He grabbed the chair and pulled, but the waterlogged fabric ripped away in his hands; he grabbed the wooden frame instead and dragged the chair backward, positioning it under the dangling cord. He tried to climb onto the chair, but it threw him off, turning and sinking under his weight.

He looked at the window—the lightning flashed again, but not as brightly as before. The water was just a foot from the top of the window now, and he knew that once the water covered the window, the room would go completely black. When the water reached the ceiling, the whole world would go black—forever.

The room grew quieter. His breathing sounded tinny and thin.

He shoved the heavy chair aside. He took a deep breath and squatted in the water, gathering all his strength; he could feel bits of debris tapping and touching him everywhere like little strands of seaweed. He shot up again, using the water's buoyancy to propel him toward the ceiling. It worked—he could touch the ceiling with the palms of both hands, and he used the split second to grope furiously for the nylon cord. He did not find it, but he could feel the wooden frame that surrounded the door. He dropped back into the water and tried again; he found the frame again, and this time he tried to quickly wedge his fingertips into the narrow opening.

He couldn't do it.

He stood in the darkness, panting; the water was up to his chin now. He wiped his face; he tasted salt. The water was hot, wrapping around him like a rubber raincoat, sucking out the last of his strength.

Behind him, he could hear the water lapping at the top of the window frame. He stared up into the darkness, praying for one last chance—and then the lightning came again. In the sliver of blue-white light that flashed across the water, he saw the position of the cord—then the room went black, sealing the door to his tomb.

He continued to stare at the ceiling, searing into his mind the position of the cord—then he took a breath, squatted down into the water, and jumped for the last time.

He felt the cord brush the back of his left wrist; he twisted and grabbed it with both hands, allowing his weight to pull the attic door down and open. He heard the creak of the spring-loaded hinges and he felt the door begin to descend—but then it slapped against the surface of the water and stopped.

Even in normal circumstances the attic door took a hefty tug to open; but he had nothing to pull against now, and the water took away his weight. He worked his way around to the narrow opening and thrust his arms and head inside; he grabbed a rung of the ladder and pulled himself up, forcing the door open with his body until the springs began to moan and the door swung down into the water.

At the top of the ladder he shoved aside some boxes and rolled over onto his back, exhausted. Up here the storm was deafening; he could feel the entire attic groan under the powerful gusts of wind. He heard sections of shingles slapping against the roof, then suddenly grow quiet as they ripped off and flew away. He felt water drizzling onto his face, telling him that the tar paper was gone, too, and all that remained of his roof was a three-quarter-inch sheath of flimsy fir plywood.

He tried to catch his breath but couldn't. The attic was like an oven, and he found himself sucking at the air like a baby with an empty bottle. His lungs were on fire, and he felt a searing pain in the center of his chest.

Then, he felt water lapping at his back.

He sat up in the darkness and felt the floor; the water had already covered the plywood subflooring—and it was still rising fast.

He scrambled to his feet, banging his head on a slanted rafter. He shoved hard against the plywood roofing, but it wouldn't give way. He felt around among the boxes for anything hard or sharp—a tool, a saw, anything that might be able to penetrate the wood—but all he could find was a foot-long scrap of two-by-four left over from construction decades ago. He hammered it against the plywood again and again, but it had no effect. He began to feel light-headed and he stopped.

When he did, he heard a voice calling from somewhere outside.

"Tommy Lee Batiste!" the voice shouted. It was barely audible over the wind.

He held his breath and listened. There it was again.

"Tommy Lee Batiste!"

"In here!" he shouted back. "Hey! I'm in here!" He took the two-by-four and pounded it against the roof again, screaming at the top of his lungs.

A minute later, he saw the beam of a flashlight streaming through the slats of the roof vent at the far end of the attic, and he heard the sound of metal rubbing up and down against the side of the house.

"Tommy Lee Batiste!" the voice shouted through the slats.

"Yes! I'm here! I'm coming!" He started toward the roof vent but forgot that the plywood flooring extended only a few feet beyond the attic door. He stepped off the plywood and into the space between the floor joists. The insulation and drywall instantly gave way beneath him, causing one leg to sink into the saturated mass as if it were a cypress swamp.

"Wait!" he pleaded. "Don't go! I'm coming!"

He sucked his foot out of the muck and struggled to his feet again, steadying himself with the roof trusses and feeling his way over the floor one joist at a time. He finally reached the roof vent and collapsed against it, pounding his fist against the wood.

"Step back!" the voice commanded.

The man moved back onto the nearest joist and waited. Seconds later, an ax head crashed through the thin wooden slats, sending splinters flying everywhere; the man didn't even bother to close his eyes. His skin felt cold and clammy, and he felt as if his whole body was pulsing to the beat of his heart. His legs shook so violently that he wasn't sure how much longer he could stay on his feet; he gripped the roof truss with all the strength he had left, terrified that his legs would give out and cause him to fall through the floor joists and into the watery crypt below.

The ax crashed down again and again.

The instant there was an opening as large as his body, the man threw himself into it—and then his strength failed him. He lay over the splintered edge of the roof vent like a doll on a handrail, unable to move any farther.

Then he felt two powerful hands seize him by the arms and drag him through the opening. He felt his legs hit the water and then he was hauled toward the boat, where the two hands hooked his arms over the sides of the boat and then released him.

The man lay clinging to the side of the boat, bobbing in the waiter, waiting for his strength to return to him. He lifted his head and looked up at the face of his rescuer, silhouetted against the raging sky.

"Thank you," the man gasped. "I'll never forget—"

"Are you Tommy Lee Batiste?" the voice demanded.

"Yes—I'm Tommy Lee Batiste."

The figure in the boat lifted a thick section of tree branch over his head and brought it down hard on the center of the man's forehead.

He saw a flash of light, and then his arms went limp.

Tommy Lee Batiste slipped silently away from the side of the boat and disappeared into the churning black water.

7

Tuesday, August 30

Nick and Jerry stood at the eastern end of the St. Claude Avenue Bridge, surveying the flooded neighborhood in front of them. Three blocks ahead, the four-lane highway dipped and disappeared beneath a greenish-brown cesspool of floating debris. As far as the eye could see, only rooftops remained above the water, like little black and brown and orange playing cards folded in half on a sheet of glass. Only the top halves of trees protruded, looking more like sprawling bushes than crepe myrtles or oaks; electrical wires hung tangled in their branches like strands of silken web. Objects drifted everywhere—sofas, refrigerators, mattresses, ovens, things that Nick would have sworn were too large or too heavy to ever float. There was even an entire trailer home that bobbed in the water like a giant slab of ice cream, buoyed by some air pocket still trapped inside.

Nick wondered what else might be trapped inside.

"So this is the neighborhood you volunteered us for," Jerry said.

"This is it—the Lower Ninth Ward."

"It's underwater."

"That's sort of the point, Jerry."

"How come this neighborhood?"

"Low income, substandard housing, single-floor dwellings, low-lying area—high crime rate too. Great place to look for bodies."

"I thought we were here to rescue people."

"Yeah, that too."

Hurricane Katrina was now four hundred miles beyond the city, near the Tennessee border, downgraded to a tropical storm with winds of less than 50 miles per hour—just a blustery shadow of the destructive giant she had been less than twenty-four hours ago. The National Hurricane Center's forecast had proven impressively accurate; the storm had made landfall at precisely 6:10 a.m., smashing into the Gulf Coast with winds exceeding 120 miles per hour—and pushing a massive storm surge ahead of it.

Nick had wanted to get into the city yesterday afternoon, before the storm had even passed—but Denny refused, unwilling to allow any of his team members to risk becoming casualties themselves. Nick and Jerry left the moment they had permission to do so, departing just after dawn to reach the Lower Ninth Ward as early as possible. A nine-passenger van from DMORT's motor pool had shuttled them to the outskirts of New Orleans, but there they found every major artery into the city blocked by water. They had to make their own way to the Lower Ninth Ward, partly by hitching rides on emergency vehicles and part of the way on foot.

The city was preternaturally still. The silence was eerie; it had never occurred to Nick that a lack of sound could create such a powerful impression. There were no horns, no engines, no radios or sirens. The birds were silent, if they were present at all; maybe they had all been blown away by the hurricane winds. Even the rustling of the trees had been reduced to a wet whisper. The only sound that could be heard anywhere was the periodic cry of a human voice echoing across the water from some unseen place.

Across the bridge, at the point where St. Claude Avenue now became a boat ramp, a single Chevy Blazer was backed against the water. From a trailer behind it, a uniformed man was busy unloading a black rigid inflatable boat.

"Where is everybody?" Jerry asked. "I thought there would be more people here to help. Who do we report to?"

"Beats me," Nick said. "Let's try that guy."

They hiked their canvas duffel bags over their shoulders and descended the three blocks to the water.

"Morning!" Nick called out as they approached.

The man answered without looking up. "Yeah, how ya doin'."

His shoulder patch bore the insignia "NOPD," and his nameplate said "LaTourneau." He was of medium height but lean, which made him look taller than he really was. His hair was black and coarse, wavy on top and short on the sides, just beginning to show gray around the temples. He was clean-shaven, something Nick found odd given the circumstances, and his NOPD uniform was crisp and starched tight.

The man worked quickly and deliberately, sliding the sleek black rescue craft off its trailer and into the water. The boat was little more than an oversized inner tube bent into the shape of a horseshoe, with cone-shaped caps covering each end. A rope handrail ran along the top of the tube, attached every couple of feet and lying in a scalloped pattern like icing along the rim of a cake. A single bench spanned the back of the boat, and behind it a Johnson RescuePro motor angled forward with its shielded propeller pointing into the air. On each side of the craft, in giant white letters, was the word *ZODIAC*.

"Cool boat," Jerry said. "What kind is it?"

The officer didn't bother to answer.

"Just a wild guess," Nick said. "It might be a Zodiac."

"I'm in kind of a hurry here," the officer said. "The sun's coming up, and it gets pretty hot on an asphalt roof."

"Are you working alone, Officer LaTourneau?"

"Not much choice."

It suddenly occurred to Nick that, in their civilian clothes, he and Jerry might look like nothing more than a couple of curious onlookers. "I'm Dr. Nick Polchak," he said. "My colleague here is Jerry Kibbee. We're with DMORT up in St. Gabriel."

The acronym didn't seem to ring a bell.

"Disaster Mortuary Operational Response Team," Nick explained.

"You boys here to collect bodies?"

"Eventually, yes. They sent us down to help with the rescue efforts first. Where is everybody?"

"Who?"

"FEMA, Urban Search and Rescue, the National Guard. DMORT told us there would be half a dozen agencies pitching in."

"Well, if you see any of those boys, tell 'em I could use a hand."

Nick and Jerry watched as the officer loaded his equipment into the boat and climbed into the stern, lowered the motor into the water and checked his fuel.

"So," Nick said, "what's the plan?"

"Plan?"

"The strategy, the order of events. What do you want us to do?"

The officer stopped and looked up. "You got me confused with somebody else. I'm with the New Orleans Police Department. We're not in charge here."

"It's your city."

"Yeah, well, our city is underwater right now—about 70 percent of it, from what I've been able to piece together."

"Don't you know?"

"The power's off; the phones are out; even the cell towers are down. We're completely cut off. The only way we can talk is by radio, and every emergency service in the city has to share one frequency. You can't get a word in edgewise, so I just listen in and try to figure out what's going on—as long as the batteries hold out, that is."

"What have you heard?"

"Do you know the city?"

Nick shook his head. "We're from out of town."

The officer pointed up the road. "You came across the St. Claude Avenue Bridge. It crosses the Industrial Canal—that's a shipping channel that connects Lake Pontchartrain with the Mississippi. There are neighborhoods all along the canal, and there are concrete levees on both sides to keep the water out."

"They're not doing a very good job."

"Nobody counted on this much water; the levees gave way sometime yesterday. The storm came in about 6:00 a.m. By 9:00 a.m. there was eight feet of water here—ten over there in St. Bernard Parish. The levees on the Seventeenth Street Canal failed too; that's flooding the rest of the city, from what I hear. I came out here yesterday as soon as the storm passed, but the wind was still pretty rough. I only had a few hours before dark, but I started pulling people out of trees and such."

"You were the only one out here?"

"Me and a couple of locals."

Nick paused. "There must be some kind of plan."

"Look—nobody can call in and nobody can get to the station, so NOPD has no way to coordinate efforts. FEMA, the National Guard—they've all got the same problem we do: Communication is out, the roads are blocked, there's no infrastructure. The only reason I'm here is because my house didn't flood—not yet, anyway. I just grabbed a boat and headed over—I know this neighborhood like the back of my hand. There are fifty-six hundred homes in the Lower Nine, and the water came up fast—no telling how many are trapped here. There are folks on rooftops, folks in attics—"

Nick looked across the neighborhood at the low-pitched rooftops, their attics vented by only a few narrow rows of slats at each end. It was August in New Orleans, with the temperature over ninety degrees and humidity to match; by afternoon the attics would be little more than slow-cookers.

"How can we help?" Nick asked.

The officer looked over Nick's shoulder at the empty road behind him. "You boys got a boat?"

Nick turned and looked, too, as if he somehow expected a cabin cruiser to have magically materialized behind him.

"How did you figure you'd help without a boat?"

"I guess we figured you guys would have boats."

"You don't say."

"Where'd you get yours?" Jerry asked.

"NOPD has seven. I grabbed one; the rest are all out."

"That's not a lot of boats for a whole city."

"I hear the Guard has more."

"Where are they?"

"They can't get to them—they're surrounded by water."

"Imagine that," Nick said under his breath. "No offense, but . . . didn't you people ever think about this possibility? I mean, if you live in a bathtub, sooner or later you're going to get wet."

"*Plan ahead*," the officer said. "Thanks for the advice. Here's some advice for you boys: Next time, bring a boat."

"Where can we get one?"

"Why don't you ask DMORT? Sounds like they've got everything figured out."

The officer pushed away from the pavement with his oar until the propeller had safe clearance; then he started the motor and raced off into the Lower Nine.

"Hardworking guy," Jerry said. "FEMA should put him in charge."

"They better put somebody in charge fast," Nick said, turning back toward the bridge. "Come on."

"Where are we going?"

"To find a boat."

The St. Claude Avenue Bridge was an old bascule-type drawbridge, counterweighted at the near end to allow the span to swing up and out of the way of passing ships; the lumbering metal structure towered over Nick and Jerry like a rusted dinosaur. At the foot of the bridge they left the roadway and turned right, following the earthen levee north along the Industrial Canal. In the canal to their left, they could see the massive locks that lifted ships and barges from the lake up to the level of the Mississippi River. The locks were empty; there were no vessels in sight, except for one long barge half a mile ahead that had smashed through the levee and rested among the houses in the Lower Ninth Ward.

"Look up ahead," Nick said. "We might be in luck."

A hundred yards ahead of them, an old man sat parked along the grassy levee in an old Dodge pickup. Behind him was a trailer towing a flat-bottomed silver boat. As they approached the truck, the door creaked open and the old man stepped out to greet them.

"Morning," Nick said. "Going fishing?"

"Wish I were," the old man said. "Thought I might see if I could help out."

"That's nice of you. We heard there were some locals out here yesterday. Thanks for pitching in—we could use a lot more like you."

"Who're you boys?"

"We're with—the federal government. Is this your boat?"

"What's the government doing about all this? We got people who need help here."

"That's why we're here, sir. Nice boat you got there. Is it an eighteen-footer? I love these old aluminum johnboats. Nowadays they're all fiberglass—I hate fiberglass, don't you?"

Nick's tongue was on autopilot; his mind was racing, trying to concoct the Big Lie that just might win him a boat. He could try the patriotic approach: *Your government needs your sacrifice*; or maybe an appeal to pride: *You and you alone can make the difference*; and, if all else failed, there was always power: *By authority of the federal government, I am authorized to commandeer this vessel.*

But while Nick was still formulating his strategy, the man said, "Take 'er."

"Excuse me?"

"I figure you boys need a boat. That's what you're hinting at, ain't it? Seems like everybody got caught with his pants down this time."

"You got that right."

"Know how to run 'er?"

"No problem," Nick said. "I grew up in Pittsburgh, right along the Allegheny River. I used to have a skiff a lot like this one, only not quite as big. You've got an Evinrude, I had an old Mercury—only mine was a lot smaller. I have to say, that's a lot of muscle for an eighteen-foot johnboat."

The old man grinned. "Can't make much use of it in the bayous, but when I get out a ways I like to open 'er up from time to time."

The old man backed the trailer down the levee to the edge of the water. Nick and Jerry helped him offload the johnboat, then listened as he reviewed the workings of the boat and the peculiarities of the aging motor.

"I sure appreciate this," Nick said. "When do you need it back?"

"I'll give you my number," the old man said. "Just call me when you're done; I'll come and get 'er."

"It might be a while. That okay with you?"

"Like I said, I'd like to help out. You'll find a lock and chain in the bow—just lock 'er up at night."

"You made this awfully easy," Nick said.

"You boys can use it better'n I can," the old man said. "Besides, I've got Cajun blood—we're known for our generosity."

Fifteen minutes later, Nick and Jerry were motoring across the water, headed into the center of the Lower Ninth Ward.

Jerry sat in the bow, glaring at Nick at the tiller. "I've got a bass boat back in Fort Wayne. I'm out on the lake every weekend. How come you get to drive?"

"Physics," Nick said. "You're the only thing we've got that's as heavy as this motor; if we put both you and the motor back here, we'll be standing on end."

"Physics," Jerry grumbled. "What happens when we find somebody to rescue?"

"What do you mean?"

"This isn't like collecting bodies, Nick. These are real people we're dealing with—neither one of us was trained for search and rescue."

"Denny explained it all to me," Nick said. "It's just like recovering bodies, only the body walks away later."

"Let's hope so," Jerry said.

Nick guided the boat down the center of a main street, trying to imagine what the Lower Ninth Ward must have looked like before it was cut off at the knees. Nick's head was almost even with the streetlamps; street signs were completely underwater, making it almost impossible to follow a road map—even if they had one.

"You think any of these electrical wires are live?" he called up to Jerry.

"Could be. Better steer clear of them, just in case."

The water looked even higher than it had just an hour ago, rising just to the soffits of some houses and overlapping the lowest shingles of others. Nick wondered how long it would take the Corps of Engineers to repair the breached canals; he wondered how long it would be before the water reached an equilibrium and stopped rising; he wondered what would still be visible when it did.

"Looks like we've got customers," Jerry said.

One block to the north they spotted two men stranded in the top of a tall chestnut tree. They were smiling and waving and appeared to be shouting, though their voices couldn't be heard above the engine's drone. Nick steered down an alley and approached the tree; as he drew closer, the two men stopped smiling.

Jerry turned to Nick. "They don't look too happy to see us."

"You don't make a very good hood ornament," Nick said. "It's like being charged by a hippo."

Jerry looked at the two men. "I don't think that's the problem."

Nick looked up into the tree. The two men staring back at him were African-American—a high statistical probability, since 80 percent of the residents of the Lower Ninth Ward were black. Maybe that was the problem; maybe these men were expecting someone a little more familiar to come to their rescue—a neighbor, a friend, even parish police.

"Good morning!" Nick called up in his friendliest voice. "Can we help you gentlemen?"

There was a long pause. "Who're you?"

"We're with DMORT."

"Who?"

"The Disaster Mortuary Operational Response Team."

"Say what?"

"We collect—we're a part of—"

Nick stopped to reconsider; Jerry took over. "We're here to get you guys out of that tree."

"What for?"

"You don't want to stay up there, do you?"

"That depends. Where you planning on taking us?"

Jerry turned to Nick.

"Beats me," Nick said. "They told us to report to whoever was in charge and get further instructions here. I'm not sure where to take them; let's just get them to dry ground."

Jerry looked up into the tree. "Let's get you out of that tree first. We'll figure it out from there."

"We're staying," the man said.

"C'mon now, you can't just stay up there."

"It's my tree," the man said. "I can stay up here if I want to—and he can stay with me."

"We'll take you anywhere you want," Jerry said. "Back to the levee, over to the bridge—"

"You go on now," the first man said. "We'd just as soon wait for another boat."

Nick watched the two men; they kept slapping at their arms and legs as they spoke. He used an oar to bring the boat in closer and reached for one of the tree's lower branches.

"You just keep your distance now!" one of the men shouted down.

Nick adjusted his glasses and studied the tree branch closely. "*Solenopsis invicta*," he announced. "You can tell by the single median seta on the anterior clypeal margin."

"What's that?"

"Fire ants—and not just your run-of-the-mill domestic variety either. These are red imported fire ants, introduced from the jungles of Brazil back in the 1930s. You guys better come down from there right now."

"Fire ants don't live in no trees."

"Neither do people, but you're up there. The ants are trying to escape the water—they don't want to drown any more than you do."

"What's he talking about?"

"Look—other *Solenopsis* species just bite and then spray the wound with formic acid. Not *invicta*. They only bite so they can hold on while they inject an alkaloid venom. The venom burns like fire—thus the name."

"I don't like the way he talks," one of the men said.

"Guys, I'm not kidding. *Invicta* can kill small animals. Come on down now."

Neither of them moved. Nick and Jerry just sat there, staring up at the two men, wondering what to do next.

"We don't have time for this," Nick grumbled, then called up to the two men: "We're leaving now, but we'll swing by again a little later to see if you've changed your minds. At least climb down from there and get onto a rooftop. I know it's hot, but believe me, 'hot' is better than 'on fire.' By the way, you'll feel them bite first. Try to brush them off before they sting—otherwise you'll get little white pustules."

Nick revved the motor and steered the boat away.

Jerry waited until they were well out of earshot before he said, "*Pustules?* Are you out of your mind?"

Nick shrugged. "I'd want someone to tell me."

"Those guys would rather sit in a tree with a bunch of fire ants than be rescued by us. Man, we *suck*."

"We just need practice," Nick said. "We'll be pros by this afternoon."

A few minutes later they spotted a man standing on a rooftop between two gables with open windows; he was flagging them down with a red towel.

"Easy pickings," Nick said. He eased off the throttle and brought the boat up alongside the house. As they approached, they saw a woman step out one of the gable windows and onto the rooftop; she turned and reached back inside, and someone handed her a small child. An older woman climbed out after her, followed by a girl of about eight or nine, then a younger boy . . .

Soon there were nine people crowded together on the roof.

"Thank the Lord," one of the women said to the sky.

"The Lord needs a bigger boat," one of the boys mumbled—earning him a swat on the back of the head.

"We sure can't take all of you at once," Nick said. "We'll have to take you in shifts."

"We go together or we don't go at all," the woman holding the child said.

Jerry looked at Nick.

"It's physics, Jerry," Nick said. "Even if I left you here, this boat wouldn't carry ten people—not safely, anyway."

Jerry turned to the group. "Folks, listen to me. We can take all of you to safety, but we can't take all of you at once. We can take the women and children first, or you can divide up any way you want. We'll take a group of you over to the levee, then come right back for—"

"We go together or we don't go at all," the woman said again. "Ain't no use talkin' about it."

"Ma'am, be reasonable," Jerry said.

"I am being reasonable—don't tell me I'm not. This is my family. You boys got family back home? A wife? Babies?"

"I'm not married," Jerry said. "Neither is he."

"Then you don't know. Lots of folks, they headed off to the Superdome—they say they got buses there to take people to other places—Houston and Baton Rouge and such. What if the bus is like your boat? What if they can't take us all at once? Then we get split up, that's what. Maybe we don't find each other again."

"Ma'am, that doesn't have to happen."

"Don't have to, but it might. Where you want to take us?"

"To a rescue shelter—a safe place with food and water for your kids—maybe a place to sleep too."

"Where is this place?"

"I honestly don't know."

"Have you seen it? With your own two eyes?"

"No, ma'am, I haven't."

"Who are your people, young man?"

Jerry looked confused, so Nick took the question. "He's from Indiana, ma'am—that's where his people are. I came down from the Carolinas."

"Well, you boys are in Louisiana now, so let me tell you: They promise us all kinds of things down here—schools, jobs, roads—and we don't see much of it. So maybe this place of yours is real and maybe it's not. We'll stay and wait for a bigger boat. We'll do what we have to, but we'll do it together. We don't mean no disrespect."

"None taken," Jerry said. "To tell you the truth, I'd probably do the same."

The two men managed to scrounge half a dozen water bottles from their equipment bags and handed them across to the family.

"Drink all you can," Nick said, "especially the kids—they'll dehydrate faster than the adults will. Stay in the shade as much as possible; you can use the floodwater to cool your skin, but whatever you do, don't drink it—and I wouldn't get it in my eyes either."

"Thank you. God bless you."

"I have to tell you, we've only seen one other boat on the water this morning. It's bigger than this one; maybe he can take your whole group. If we see him, we'll try to send him over, but I can't promise you when that will be."

Nick opened his equipment bag again and took out a black-and-yellow

GPS receiver. He held it level and switched it on; he waited for the screen to illuminate, then for the unit to make contact with the satellites in stationary orbit overhead. He hoped that at least one technology was still working. It was—he jotted down the coordinates.

Jerry watched the house as it receded in the distance. He turned to Nick: "Still think we'll be pros by the end of the day?"

Nick didn't answer.

"Maybe we should turn the boat over to somebody who knows what they're doing."

"Good idea," Nick said. "Maybe somebody in that big crowd back on St. Claude Avenue. Sorry, Jer, we're the only ones out here. We're stuck with this job; we just need to figure out how it works."

Neither of them said much for the next few minutes. Jerry just stared ahead of the boat, looking despondent, while Nick kept thinking how much easier it was to collect people's remains than it was to collect people. *What strange creatures human beings are*, he thought. An insect responds to immediate stimuli; *Solenopsis invicta* is smart enough to flee rising floodwaters—but the instant the water recedes it will return to the earth. It never wonders if some greater danger might be waiting for it there—it simply knows itself to be a creature of the earth. But the human species is different—the human species will climb a tree and refuse to come down, for no other reason than a vague imagination of what might happen if they do. *What a strange species they are*, he thought, and he was glad he wasn't one of them.

A hundred yards ahead they spotted a lone figure standing on the very peak of a rooftop, silhouetted against the morning sky. From a distance the figure appeared to be an adult male, but as the boat drew nearer Nick could see that he was younger than he first appeared. The boy was facing in the opposite direction, seeming to search the horizon for some unknown object or person. He apparently heard the sound of the boat's motor and slowly turned to face Nick and Jerry as they approached.

He appeared to be around ten years old, just on the verge of his adolescence. His shoulders were already broadening and his hands seemed a bit too large for his arms. His skin was the color of black walnut, still smooth and rounded from the underlying layer of childhood fat cells, still a year or two from the day when testosterone would bind his muscles into taut cords and plow his perfect skin into sinewy furrows. His hair was black and closely cropped, glistening at the tips against the sun; his eyes, oddly enough, were blue, and they made Nick wonder about the boy's ancestry. He was shirtless and shoeless, dressed only in a pair of dark crew shorts tied off at the waist.

The boy didn't throw his shoulders back as the boat approached, and he made no effort to flatten the slight S-curve of his belly; he stood with a complete lack of self-consciousness—something else adolescence would rob from him. The boy reminded Nick of a black statue of David, teetering between boyhood and manhood, with all the strengths and vulnerabilities of both.

Nick killed the motor and let the boat cruise silently up to the house. Neither man said anything; after their last feeble attempts at rescue, Nick was hoping that Jerry might make the first attempt—but apparently Jerry had the same idea. To their surprise, it was the boy who spoke first.

"My name is James Terrebonne Walker," the boy said. "I want you to help me find my father."

Nick and Jerry just stared.

"What?"

"I want you to help me find my father. I'll come with you, but you got to promise."

"Where did you last see him?" Nick asked.

"We got separated in the flood."

"Is this your house?"

"No."

"Do you live around here?"

"This is my neighborhood."

"Can you take us to where you live?"

The boy looked around. "It's kind of hard to find."

"Yeah, I can imagine. How long have you been up there?"

"Since the hurricane."

"Have you had anything to eat? Anything to drink, any food or water?"

The boy shook his head.

"I want you to come with us," Nick said. "Come on down and climb into the boat."

"Not until you promise."

"Look, we'd like to help you," Jerry said, "but right now our priority is to—"

"I promise," Nick said. "I'll help you find your father."

Jerry turned to Nick and leaned in closer. "What are you doing? You can't go throwing around promises like that."

"They sent us down here to rescue people, Jerry. I'm not going to spend the rest of the day arguing with people in trees. Have you got a better idea?"

"You'll get his hopes up."

"He could use a little hope right now."

"That's false hope. What happens when you don't find his father?"

"I'll find his father."

"How?"

"I have no idea."

Nick looked up at the boy. "Well, Mr. James Terrebonne Walker, are you coming or not?"

"J.T."

"What?"

"I go by J.T."

"Good, that's a real time-saver. My name is Nick—the big guy there is Jerry. Now, J.T., are you coming with us or not?"

"You promised," the boy said.

"Yes, I did. I'll try to find your father."

"No, you changed it."

"Okay, okay," Nick said. "I will do everything in my power to help you find your father. Satisfied?"

The boy nodded and started down the rooftop. He stepped over the edge of the boat without hesitating and up onto the center bench; he jumped off with both feet at once, plopping down on the bench facing Nick.

"Can I drive?" he asked.

Nick raised one eyebrow. "Do you know how?"

"You're doin' it—how hard can it be?"

"I drive. You ride."

"What's *he* do?" J.T. asked, jabbing his thumb back at Jerry.

"Jerry? He's the anchor."

"Thanks a lot," Jerry said.

"Actually, Jerry is a highly trained search-and-rescue professional. He's famous around these parts."

The boy squinted at Nick. "*Man*, you've got big glasses."

"What glasses?"

He paused. "You're shinin' me."

"I think you could use some shinin'," Nick said.

J.T. lifted both legs and twisted around on the bench. "Okay—let's get goin'."

"Aye, aye, sir." Nick twisted the throttle and the boat started forward.

As the boat churned through the debris-choked water, Nick found himself staring at the back of the boy's head. *The kid's got guts, that's for sure.* He wondered how the boy got up on that rooftop all by himself. It wasn't even his house—did his father help him? Were they together when the storm first struck? Was it the hurricane that separated them? If so, Nick had a pretty good idea where he would find the boy's father: on a gurney at the DPMU in St. Gabriel a couple of weeks from now.

Jerry seemed more interested in the floodwaters surrounding the boat. The water was completely opaque, and when Nick angled the bow of the boat into the sun, they could see a rainbow film of oil shimmering on the surface. There was debris floating everywhere; when they rounded some corners, their little johnboat was like a Coast Guard cutter plowing through an ice floe of disposable diapers, garbage bags, and broken tree limbs.

"This has got to be the most polluted water in the world," Jerry said. "No telling what's in it."

"Oil and gasoline from the refineries," Nick said. "Raw sewage from the water treatment plants; chromium and copper and zinc from metal plating plants; herbicides like 2,4-D and atrazine; residues from banned pesticides. How's that for starters?"

"I thought we'd see more you-know-whats," Jerry said.

"What?"

Jerry nodded at the boy. "You know—*people*."

Nick shook his head. "We shouldn't see them for a couple of days."

"Why not?"

"I'll explain it to you later."

The boy turned and looked at Nick. "You talkin' about dead folks? I seen one."

Nick looked at him. "Where? On a rooftop?"

"Floatin' in the water. Saw it yesterday, once the rain quit."

"Are you sure it was floating? It wasn't lying on top of something?"

"Floated right by me—I guess that's floating. He was sort of blowed up, like a carnival balloon."

Nick paused. "You don't mind talking about this stuff?"

"I seen lots of dead stuff: frogs, possums, canal rats—they fall off the ships and I find 'em along the levees by the river. Dead stuff always floats."

Nick wasn't sure whether to pursue this conversation with a boy his age. He looked over at Jerry for guidance, but Jerry just shrugged.

"Dead stuff doesn't always float," Nick said. "Suppose Jerry there fell off one of those ships. At first he'd float—that's because he eats too much bratwurst and potato salad, and fat has a lot of air in it. But once Jerry drowned, his lungs would fill with water and he'd sink. He wouldn't float again for a couple of days—maybe even a week or two. It all depends on the season and the temperature of the water."

"What makes him float again?"

"Do you know what bacteria are?"

"Sure. I'm a smart guy."

"Well, smart guy, you've got about a hundred trillion bacteria living in your belly—that's ten times the number of cells. There are good bacteria and bad bacteria, and they sort of keep each other in check—until you die, that is. Then it's like Mardi Gras, and they all run wild and start eating everything in sight. When they do that, they make gas—just like Jerry does. A hundred trillion little Jerrys inside you, each producing a tiny bubble of gas. It all collects, and when it finally does it's just like you said: You blow up like a carnival balloon. It just takes time."

Nick looked at Jerry. "That's the problem."

"What problem?"

"Time. A body in water decomposes in six stages. The first stage is called *submerged fresh*; that's the period of time from when the body is first submerged until it bloats and rises to the surface. Then comes the second stage: *early floating*. We've done studies on pig carcasses submerged in water; in northern latitudes it takes eleven to thirteen days to reach the second stage—in the midlatitudes it takes less than a week. This water is like soup; it would accelerate the process even more, but it should still take a day or two for a body to float."

Nick looked at J.T. "You're sure you saw this body yesterday?"

"You think I'd forget yesterday?"

"Do you think you could take me there—to the place where you saw this floating body?"

"Nick," Jerry said.

"The body has probably moved since then, but we could let the boat drift to see which way the current is flowing, and then we could—"

"*Nick*—that's not why we're here, remember?"

Nick settled back like a deflating air bag.

Suddenly, J.T. jumped up and stood on the center bench.

"Hey, be careful," Jerry said.

"Over there—on that rooftop. See them? Head over that way."

Nick looked where the boy was pointing but saw nothing. He slid his glasses back and forth on his nose; the thick lenses provided him with almost microscopic vision up close, but at distances they were almost useless. He looked over at Jerry for confirmation, but Jerry just held up both hands and shook his head; apparently his distance vision wasn't much better.

"You've got eyes like the *Salticidae*," Nick said to the boy.

"Like what?"

"Jumping spiders—they've got the best eyes of all the arthropods. Little black eyes that—forget it, just tell me where to turn."

J.T. perched on the center bench as if it were a crow's nest, pointing out upcoming turns and barking orders like a ship's master. He guided the boat down a series of narrow alleys and across three major streets to a rooftop with a large chestnut tree behind it. As the boat drew nearer, Nick and Jerry both recognized it.

"Uh-oh," Nick said. "Been there, done that."

Nick swung the boat around in front of the tree, but this time there was no one in the upper branches. He circled around to the rooftop behind the tree and found the two men sitting side by side on the asphalt shingles. Nick had no idea what to say that he hadn't said before, and apparently the men didn't either; they just sat there, glaring back and forth between Nick and Jerry.

It was the boy who broke the silence. "We're here to rescue you," he announced.

All four men looked at him.

"I was on a rooftop just like this one," the boy said. "These men came along and rescued me, and now we're here to rescue you."

"Where they takin' you?" one of the men asked.

"To find my father."

"Where's that?"

"Wherever we need to go—and I'm in a hurry, so if you don't mind—"

"We don't know these boys," the other man said.

"You know me," J.T. said. "You know my people. Now come on, get in. There's folks on rooftops all over the place, and we got to go. You makin' 'em wait, and that's not right."

J.T. planted one foot on the edge of the boat and leaned out, extending his hand. The two men hesitated for only a few seconds before relenting.

Jerry shifted to the opposite side of the boat to offset the weight. Nick took one of the men by the elbow to help steady him; he looked at the man's forearm as he climbed aboard.

"Pustules," Nick said. "I told you so."

Two minutes later, they were moving again.

Nick looked again at the young boy, still standing on the center bench between the two seated men. *We might be on to something here*, he said to himself.

Half an hour later, the passenger list included three additional travelers. The boat sat low now, with water almost up to the gunnels in the rear. The wake of a passing boat might have swamped them, but there were no other boats; they were alone on the water, and the water was almost perfectly still. Slowly, cautiously, they motored west toward the earthen levee that separated Surekote Road from the Industrial Canal.

"Over there!" the boy suddenly announced.

"Are you crazy?" one of the female passengers said. "This boat is full—one more and we'll sink."

"She's got a point," Nick said. "We'd better drop these folks off first, then come back."

"Over there," J.T. said. "That's the place."

"What place?"

"The place I told you 'bout—the place where I saw the floater."

"Where?"

"Go left after this house, then straight. I'll show you."

Nick paused—then pushed the tiller away from him and slowly brought the boat around.

"Where we goin'?" another passenger demanded. "Didn't you hear the woman? This boat is *full*."

"Relax," Nick said. "We're only taking a look."

In a large, open area created by the intersection of two streets, the body of a man floated faceup in the water. Nick killed the engine well short of the body to keep from disturbing it and let the boat drift slowly forward.

"What are you doing?" someone asked in horror.

"What *is* that thing?"

"Man, get us *out* of here!"

In the watery stillness the body looked like a man trapped beneath a sheet of glass. It drifted just below the surface, as though it couldn't quite decide whether to rise or fall; only the abdomen protruded above the water. The hair drifted out from the head, but didn't wave; the clothing billowed out around the arms and legs, but didn't move; it was like a photograph of a man falling through space, captured by a shutter flashing at a thousandth of a second.

It appeared to be the body of a Caucasian male, but at a distance it wasn't easy to tell. The tissues had already begun to turn a greenish-blue, and under the brackish water the color looked even worse.

Nick turned to the group. "Folks, I need to explain something to you. I'm Dr. Nick Polchak; I'm a forensic entomologist from North Carolina State University. This is Jerry Kibbee; Jerry and I work for an organization called DMORT—the Disaster Mortuary Operational Response Team. Our job is to collect bodies—that's what we normally do, only there are so many people trapped on rooftops right now that we've been asked to help with the rescue efforts first. That's why we're here today, and that's why you're all in this boat with us; but sooner or later we'll have to come back for the bodies, and that happens to be one of them right over there. So if you'll bear with me for just a minute, I need to take a closer look."

When they reached the body, Nick stuck an oar deep into the water and pushed forward, causing the boat to come about in a tight J. He leaned over the port gunnels and looked down at the body; he saw a deep, jagged gash down the center of the forehead and a line of plump white maggots wedged into the wound like pebbles in a sidewalk crack.

"I need to look closer," he said.

"Closer than *this*?"

He handed the oar across to Jerry and opened his equipment bag. He took out what appeared to be a tool kit or tackle box. He opened it in his lap and removed a long, slender pair of forceps and a small glass jar filled with a colorless liquid.

"Get me in close," Nick said to Jerry.

Jerry brought the boat around until it was almost touching the head.

"I need a couple of you to shift to your right to keep us balanced," Nick told the group. "I need to collect a few maggots."

The entire group scrambled to the opposite side of the boat, which lurched precariously to starboard. Two people shouted in alarm; one of them was Jerry.

"Easy, folks," Nick said. "Jerry, get a grip—I could use your help here."

Jerry shifted his considerable mass around to the port side. The boat struck a tenuous balance again, with five horrified passengers on one side and Nick and Jerry on the other—with J.T. sandwiched between them. Together they slid onto their knees and leaned out over the water and the body just below.

Nick looked over at the boy. "You okay with this?"

"Cool," he said with a grin.

Nick removed the lid from one of the jars and handed it to J.T. "Hold this," he said. "Don't spill it."

"What is it?"

"It's called Kahle's solution. It's sort of a preservative."

Nick took the silver forceps and flexed them a few times.

"What's that?"

"A light-tension larval forceps—it lets me pick up maggots without squashing them."

He reached down to the body and began to pluck maggots from the center of the ragged wound. He held the first one up close to his enormous lenses and rotated it back and forth, studying it.

"I thought so," he said.

He removed several more maggots and dropped them one by one into the waiting jar.

"See how the wound looks kind of ragged? That means the tissues were torn, not cut. That's what they call a 'blunt-trauma' wound."

Nick twisted the lid back onto the jar and turned to the other passengers. "That's all I needed," he said. "Thanks for your patience. There's just one more thing: I need to bring this body with us."

"Say *what*?"

"We've got plenty of room if we lay it along the left side. I've got a body bag right here."

"Lord have mercy," someone groaned.

Even Jerry looked astonished. "Nick, what are you doing? You know what DMORT told us: *first the living*."

"This can't wait," Nick said. "It's the water, Jerry—it's speeding up decomposition."

"We should at least come back for it. These people have a point. Let's take a GPS reading and come back later."

"It *can't wait,*" Nick said. "Those are third-instar maggots, Jerry—that means they've been there for a while, and there should be a lot more of them. They're dying off in the toxic water, or maybe they've just washed off—either way, we're losing forensic evidence by the minute. The body has to come with us."

One of the men glared at Nick. "You ain't haulin' that thing in the boat while I'm sittin' here."

"It's just a body," Nick said. "That 'thing' was one of your neighbors just a few days ago."

"Well, it ain't my neighbor now! Now, you take me to that levee, or you take me back to my roof—but I ain't sharin' this boat with no dead man. That's moodee, man—that's bad mojo."

Nick considered his options.

A few minutes later, they were slowly motoring toward the levee again. Behind them, a black body bag rode like a surfboard in the boat's gentle wake, tethered to the stern by a length of nylon cord.

"I don't get it," J.T. said.

"Get what?"

"You said it takes a couple days before a body floats."

"That's right."

"Couple days ago, there was no water here."

Nick nodded. "You really are a smart guy."

10

"You disobeyed my direct orders," Denny said, glaring across the desk at Nick. "What did you think you were doing?"

"I was doing what we came here to do—collect bodies."

"You're not here to collect bodies, Nick. You're here to do whatever DMORT tells you to do—whatever *I* tell you to do, because I'm the boss."

"Come on, Denny, the body was sitting right there in front of me."

"According to Jerry, you went out of your way to find it."

"A couple of blocks, that's all. I only wanted to take a closer look."

"You weren't supposed to be looking."

"You didn't say we couldn't look."

"Stop acting like my six-year-old, will you? You know what I meant—you were supposed to be assisting with rescue efforts."

"We were! We had a whole boatload of people—you can ask Jerry. But there was this kid in the boat, and he happened to mention a floater he saw yesterday."

"So?"

"Think about it, Denny: Katrina didn't hit until yesterday morning—and just a few hours later there's a body already bloated enough to bring it to the surface? There's no way—not even in this water. That body's been decaying for a few days at least. That's what I wanted to check out, and it's a good thing I did."

"You disobeyed my orders: *first the living*."

"What was I supposed to do, just sail off and leave it there?"

"That's exactly what you were supposed to do—that's what I told you to do, remember?"

"That makes no sense."

"I don't care if it makes sense to you, Nick. I care about your following orders—my orders."

"Other bodies have been collected. I've seen them here at the morgue."

"Those are bodies that were turned in to us, not bodies we collected ourselves."

"What difference does it make?"

"It makes a big difference. You have no idea what's going on here, do you? Not just in the Ninth Ward, or even in New Orleans—I'm talking about nationwide. It's those fish-eye glasses of yours: You can't see a thing unless it's right under your nose. You can't see the big picture."

"Let me tell you what I can see, Denny: I see *maggots*—and not the kind that were supposed to be there. The body was still submerged, all except for the abdomen—but I found the maggots in the head area, under an inch or two of water. They were infesting a blunt-trauma wound—the kind that might have been made by a club or a bat."

"Or a falling tree limb or flying debris."

"Shut up and listen, will you? The maggots were *Chrysomya rufifacies*—hairy maggot blowflies. The larvae are unmistakable—they've got these little fleshy spikes all over their bodies. The hairy maggot blowfly is not an aquatic insect—it's terrestrial. The adult blowflies that laid their eggs in that wound found the body on land, not in water."

"So maybe this guy died on land but the rising water just carried his body away."

"That's possible," Nick said. "But *when* did he die? That's the issue here. A maggot passes through three stages of development before it pupates into an adult—three *instars*, they're called, and it takes a specific amount of time for the maggot to reach each instar. Those were third-instar maggots, Denny—it took several days for them to reach that stage of maturity. That guy had been dead for days before we found him, and that means he wasn't a hurricane victim. He might have died from that blunt-trauma wound—or he might have been murdered."

"Or it might have been an accidental death—or even a suicide."

"Maybe. An autopsy might tell us more—if the tissues haven't decomposed too badly. *That's why I brought the body back.*"

Denny shook his head. "Nick, you're missing the point."

"Missing the point? What other point can there possibly be?"

"Let me try to explain something to you—something you might not have thought of before: Hurricane Katrina—the city of New Orleans—it's all a kind of test."

"A test of what?"

"A test of how federal, state, and local authorities respond to a catastrophe after 9/11. Did you catch that last phrase? *After 9/11*—that means everything. For the last four years, every politician in America has been talking about homeland security and disaster preparedness and emergency contingency plans. Entire agencies have been created since 9/11; DHS didn't even exist four years ago, remember? Everybody feels like we got caught with our zipper open on 9/11, and no one wants to see it happen again. So after four years and a few billion dollars, what have we learned? Here comes Hurricane Katrina—let's find out. So everybody and his brother throws a sleeping bag in the trunk of his car and heads for New Orleans—including the media."

"The media," Nick said. "Is that what this is all about?"

"Give me a little credit, will you? This is not about trying to impress somebody. You know DMORT, you know our policy: *the utmost respect for the dead and their families*. So when the media showed up and asked to take pictures of bodies, you know what we said? We made a simple request: 'Please, no photographs of bodies. No coverage of victims.' That's all it was, a request—but they ignored us; they did it anyway. You've seen the pictures on TV: bodies on rooftops, bodies on sidewalks. So then we made it more than a request—we made it a 'zero access' policy.

"You know what CNN did? They filed suit against FEMA in federal court in Houston—they said we were trying to 'control content,' like we had something to hide. Hey, I'll let anybody look over my shoulder. I'm proud of DMORT, and I'm proud of how we do things around here. We just didn't want to see people exploited, that's all—we didn't want the suffering sensationalized. But the media—hey, they're just people like everybody else: There's good ones and there's bad ones. Some of those vultures would film the autopsies if we'd let them.

"The point is, now there's going to be a camera on every corner, watching everything we do. Whatever the camera sees, America sees—and Americans need to see us making every possible attempt to save the living. That's the test we have to pass here, Nick. Nobody's going to be satisfied if all we've learned to do since 9/11 is collect the dead more efficiently. We've got to show people that we've learned to protect the living."

Nick shook his head. "In a few days the bodies of the hurricane victims will reach a stage of decomposition known as *floating decay*. That's what Americans will see then: decaying bodies floating everywhere, because we've made no attempt to recover them."

"Fair enough," Denny said. "But right now, we want them to see rescue boats filled with grateful survivors. No bodies—not yet."

"How long will this policy remain in effect? When will we be able to start recovering the bodies?"

"The Corps of Engineers says 80 percent of the city is underwater. There are six thousand homes in your neighborhood alone; in St. Bernard Parish next door, there are forty thousand more. You tell me."

Nick took off his glasses and rubbed the bridge of his nose. "The guy was murdered, Denny. I feel it in my gut. I can smell it."

"You might be right. It's a definite possibility."

"And you're willing to let that go?"

"No—but I'm willing to place other priorities ahead of it."

"So we just let a murderer walk away."

"We're not here to solve the crime problem in New Orleans, Nick. Like you said, they've got one of the highest murder rates in the U.S. They're going to have to take care of that themselves."

"They can't do it without evidence," Nick said. "The way we're going, there won't be any."

"I hope you're wrong about that. But for now, we have to let it go."

"That goes against everything in me."

"And when you disobey my direct orders, that goes against everything in me. I told you before, Nick, I need you to play ball this time. If the coach shows you the bunt sign, you better bunt. I don't care if the all-time home-run title is on the line—*you bunt*. You do it for the good of the team, and you do it because he's the coach—that's the bottom line here. Are we clear about this?"

"Right, Coach."

"I'm not kidding around."

"I get it, Denny, I get it."

Nick stopped in the doorway on the way out. "What happens to the body I brought back today?"

"You know the process. We'll do our best to identify it."

"And the blowfly larvae I collected?"

"That's none of your business. You're doing search and rescue, remember?"

Nick reluctantly nodded. "I heard the mayor's casualty estimate on the way back up here. He figures between two and ten thousand victims. Ten thousand victims . . . it makes you wonder, doesn't it?"

"What?"

"How many of them might have been murdered."

"Get some sleep, Nick."

Nick stepped out of the warehouse and into the darkness. It was almost midnight now; he stopped for a moment to let his eyes adjust to the light. Across the parking lot, he could hear the low rumble of the tractor trailers all lined up and waiting to transport the dead—instead, they were little more than minimotels. *Like the man said*, he thought, *first the living*. At least the air-conditioning would feel good tonight.

"How'd it go in there?"

Nick turned to find Beth Woodbridge standing behind him.

"I have to stay after school," Nick said.

"You've had worse."

"I forgot—you keep the school records."

"Mind if I walk with you?"

"Well, I can't outrun you."

"What happened today?"

"I have a feeling you already know. I have a feeling everybody does."

"You make good gossip," Beth said. "You're a very interesting man."

"You said that before. I suppose I should be flattered."

"But you're not."

"It's the way you say it—sort of like when I say, 'The secondary screwworm is a very interesting maggot.'"

She paused. "What did happen today?"

"I was a bad boy—I took something that didn't belong to me."

"So I heard."

"Why don't you tell me what happened today? That'll save a lot of boring repetition."

"You were instructed to assist in rescue operations in the Lower Ninth Ward. Instead, you recovered a body."

"It wasn't 'instead'—it was 'in addition.' I guess they don't give points for extra credit around here."

"Were your instructions unclear?"

"I heard what they said. I disagreed."

"You disobeyed."

"I *disagreed*—there's a difference. I'm not a machine, Beth; I don't operate by remote control. In the field I have to make my own decisions."

"And you decided to act in violation of direct orders."

He turned and looked at her. "Look—this is not like the last time, if that's what you're thinking. I just couldn't walk away from it, okay? It was the right thing to do, and I couldn't let it go."

"I know."

They walked the rest of the way without speaking.

"Well, here we are," Nick said. "I suppose a gentleman would walk you home, but after all, the place is surrounded by razor wire."

"That's okay. I know the way back."

She started back toward the DPMU, but a few yards away she turned back again. "Will you be able to sleep?"

"The sleep of the righteous," Nick said. "No problem."

"I'm serious. Will you be able to sleep?"

"I will if you stop talking and go away."

"All right," she said. "Good night."

Nick watched her until she reached the warehouse, then swung open the trailer door and crawled inside. On the floor to the left, Jerry was already in a deep sleep. He lay on his back with his chin slung low like a hammock; a deep, moaning sound was coming from somewhere inside him.

Nick nudged his shoulder. "Hey. Jerry."

"Wha— Are we there yet?"

"Wake up, you big snitch."

Jerry propped himself up on one elbow and rubbed his face. "What'd I do?"

"'According to Jerry, you went out of your way to find the body,'" Nick recited from memory. "Thanks a lot."

"Hey, he asked me. What was I supposed to do, lie?"

"Next time, just leave out a few of the details—that's called *editing*. Where's the boy?"

Jerry pointed toward his feet.

On the floor at Jerry's feet, two equipment bags lay end to end. Nick slid one of them aside and found J.T. curled up in a tangle of blankets. The boy slept so soundly that he didn't even appear to breathe; Nick considered laying two fingers on his carotid artery just to make sure.

"Poor kid," Jerry said. "He was out cold the minute his head hit the pillow."

"Did anybody see him come in?"

"Nah—they were all asleep before we got here. Most people work normal hours."

"Most people are boring."

"He can't keep coming here, you know. It's against the rules."

"He slept on a rooftop last night, Jerry—if he slept at all. What was I supposed to do, leave him there on the levee with a bunch of strangers? I thought the kid deserved a good night's sleep."

"Doesn't everybody," Jerry said.

"Well, sleep fast. We'll need to get up early to sneak him out of here before the rest of them wake up."

"I thought the plan was to take him up to the Family Assistance Center."

"We'll do that first chance we get," Nick said. "Right now he needs to sleep."

Jerry heaved over onto his side, and Nick slid the equipment bag back in place to conceal the boy's presence. His own sleeping bag was across the aisle to the right; he didn't bother to climb into it, nor did he remove his glasses. He just rolled onto his back and lay there, staring at the bunk above him.

11

Wednesday, August 31

Nick unlocked the chain from around the trunk of the tree and tossed it into the boat; it landed in the aluminum hull with a loud clank. The old magnolia was a perfect place to conceal the boat the night before, just fifty feet from the point where St. Claude Avenue became submerged but in water still shallow enough for wading. Nick slid the boat out from under the spreading limbs and swung it around toward the street.

The old man had been nice enough to loan them the boat—too bad he didn't throw in the trailer as well. *It wouldn't have helped anyway*, Nick thought, because they had no vehicle to tow it with. DMORT maintained a small motor pool of cars and vans to shuttle team members the sixty-five miles to the city and back, but none of the cars had a trailer hitch—and none of them were scheduled to leave St. Gabriel while it was still dark. If you wanted to keep those hours—Nick's hours—your only option was to hitch a ride on one of the countless relief vehicles constantly ferrying back and forth. This morning they had shared the cab of a FEMA semi hauling pallets of water and supplies into the city. Jerry and J.T. had slept the whole way down, leaning up against each other like tent poles, while Nick learned what he could from the driver about conditions in the city.

The whole downtown was underwater, the driver told him; the Seventeenth Street Canal had a two-hundred-foot-wide breach in it, flooding the city with millions of gallons from Lake Pontchartrain. Charity Hospital needed to be evacuated, he said, and so did Tulane University Hospital just across the street, with eleven hundred patients between them. Both hospitals had been on emergency backup generators since

2:00 a.m., and the water was rising an inch every five minutes. Soon the water would drown the generators and all power would cease—lights, air-conditioning, even the ventilators of those on life support.

Jerry and J.T. waited for Nick at the edge of the water. When the boat came within reach, they both grabbed the bow and dragged it up onto the pavement with a grinding crunch that sounded especially abrasive in the morning stillness.

"Don't you get tired of doing all the work for him?" Nick asked.

"He's just a kid," Jerry said.

"I was talking to the kid."

Nick emerged from the water like a robot, growing heavier with each plodding step; on the roadway, he peeled down the heavy rubber waders and wrestled them off.

Jerry hoisted the gas can into the boat and reattached the fuel line. They had taken the empty can back to the DPMU the night before, stopping to refill it at a gas station in St. Gabriel. In New Orleans there was no fuel to be found—unless they siphoned it from the gas tank of an abandoned vehicle.

"How long you figure we'll have to keep doing this?" Jerry asked.

"Beats me," Nick said. "The driver said that FEMA Urban Search and Rescue Teams should start arriving today. I figure they'll have to set up some kind of fuel depot."

"There's a boat," J.T. said suddenly.

"Where?"

"Can't see it yet. Over that way, I think."

Soon both men could hear the high-pitched drone of an outboard motor echoing across the water. Seconds later, a sleek black rescue boat emerged from between two houses and headed toward the ramp.

"It's that LaTourneau guy," Jerry said. "Man, he's out early."

"Yeah," Nick said. "Looks like he's just getting back."

The boat was laden with seven passengers and the NOPD officer at the helm; there were no other rescue workers aboard. LaTourneau swung the boat around and lined it up with the avenue; Nick and Jerry stepped aside as he gunned the motor and drove the boat up onto the pavement, killing the engine and rocking it forward at just the right moment.

"Cool boat," J.T. said.

Jerry nodded. "That's what I said."

"How's fishing?" Nick called to LaTourneau.

"Not bad," he called back. "Looks like all you boys got is a minnow."

"Maybe—but he's a keeper."

The passengers began to swing their legs over the Zodiac's rubbery sides and slide down onto the pavement. There were men, women, and children in the group, but almost no possessions among them.

"Listen up!" LaTourneau shouted to the group. "This is as far as I can take you. The Superdome has been opened up as a refugee center; you'll find food and water and shelter there."

"What happens to us then?" someone asked.

"I don't know, sir. I imagine they'll be bringing in buses to take you somewhere else."

"What about our houses? Our things?"

"I don't know. Right now, we're just trying to keep people alive. You all know where the Superdome is: Take St. Claude Avenue as far as you can and then follow the river if you have to. That'll be the highest ground."

They all looked at one another; none of them appeared to have any better options. Some of them shook their heads, some of them joined hands, and they all slowly started up the road toward the bridge and the city beyond—all except for J.T.

Nick looked at LaTourneau. It was barely dawn, and the man was already returning with his first load of evacuees. He wondered what time LaTourneau had put in; he wondered what time he had knocked off the day before—or if he had quit at all. In the stark morning sun Nick could see dark circles under his eyes, the first telltale hint of fatigue, but the man still moved quickly, brusquely, as if there were no limit to his energy. His first boatload of grateful passengers had barely set their feet on dry ground, and LaTourneau was already standing ankle-deep in the water beside his boat, preparing to shove off again.

"Hold on a minute," Nick said. He walked over and extended his hand. "Nick Polchak—we met yesterday morning, but I didn't catch your name."

"The name's LaTourneau," he said. "You're the guys collecting bodies."

"That's right. I'm a forensic entomologist; Jerry there runs a funeral home up in Indiana. The little guy, his name is J.T."

LaTourneau looked down at him. "Run along now, son. You'd better stay with the others or you'll get lost."

"You ain't my father," J.T. grumbled, "and I ain't your son."

"We told him we'd help him find his father," Nick said. "They got separated in the storm."

LaTourneau looked at him. "How do you plan to do that?"

"We're working on it," Nick said. "By the way, I was wondering: How many officers does the NOPD have, anyway?"

"About sixteen hundred. Why?"

"This is the second morning I've seen you out here all by yourself."

"It's a big city."

"It's a big neighborhood too. How many homes did you say—about six thousand? Seems like a neighborhood this size would merit more than one officer."

"Like I told you yesterday: We have no way to coordinate."

"I was talking to a guy driving a FEMA rig this morning. He said he heard on CNN that half of your officers failed to report for duty after the storm."

"That's a lie."

"That's what he heard."

"He's with FEMA, and he's complaining about us?"

"Yeah, you've got a point there. Nevertheless, *half* of your officers—any idea what happened to them all?"

LaTourneau glared at him. "Where'd you say you're from?"

"Pittsburgh, originally. Right now I'm at NC State in Raleigh."

"How's the weather up there in Raleigh?"

"Fine, I suppose."

"Well, aren't you the lucky ones. That means your homes are nice and dry, and your families are safe, and you're free to jump in your Mercedes and drive down to help out the poor folks in New Orleans. We weren't so lucky here; maybe you've heard, we've had some rain. Our officers are a part of this city, Polchak, and we got rained on just like everybody else. We've got people up in Plum Orchard, and Gentilly Woods, and Pontchartrain Park—they're all underwater just like the Lower Nine, so we've got officers trapped on rooftops and in attics just like the people around here. They've got a right to stay alive, too, don't you think? And they've got a right to look after their families—maybe that's why some of them didn't show up. Did you ever think about that?"

"What about your family?" Nick asked.

"I don't have one—that's why I was free to show up for work. Let me tell you something about NOPD officers: They're some of the most dedicated people I've ever met; they put their lives on the line every day. I know this city; I know every alley and sewer in it. I've been with Vice and Narcotics for almost twenty years now, and believe me—our people are the only reason this place hasn't turned into a cesspool a long time ago. So if you don't mind, people are waiting—it can hit 130 degrees in some of these attics."

He shoved the Zodiac back into the water and jumped aboard. Once the craft floated free of the pavement, he started the engine and roared away.

"He thinks I drive a Mercedes," Nick said. "Welcome to public education."

"Why do you do that?" Jerry asked.

"Do what?"

"Annoy people."

"It's a gift, I suppose."

"Well, get off his back. He's trying to do his job, just like you and me."

"I didn't say those things just to annoy him, Jerry. The NOPD's got sixteen hundred men, and all they can muster is one lousy officer for the whole Lower Nine? The best thing he could do right now is round up some other guys—mobilize some resources. What's he going to do, save the whole city by himself?"

"You heard what he said: The NOPD's a part of the city too. They got socked in like everybody else. He's got no way to 'mobilize resources.' At least he's out here doing what he can."

"I've got to hand it to him, he sure puts in the hours. I hope the NOPD pays overtime."

They heard automobile engines behind them now and looked back up the road. Two vehicles hauling boat trailers were just coming across the bridge. One vehicle was emblazoned with the logo of the Louisiana Department of Wildlife and Fisheries; the other was packed with uniformed soldiers of the National Guard.

"Looks like we're finally getting reinforcements," Jerry said.

"It's about time. We better shove off and give them some room."

"Hang on a minute," Jerry said, motioning Nick aside. "What about the boy?"

"What about him?"

"Are we taking him with us again?"

"What else can we do with him?"

"Nick, this is dangerous work."

"So is standing on a rooftop in a hurricane. So is sitting in an evacuation center with thousands of angry people. I'd say he's better off with us."

"I don't get this," Jerry said. "You never liked kids before—how come you suddenly want this one around? And don't tell me it's your fatherly instincts—bugs don't have fatherly instincts."

"The kid's got great eyes, Jerry. He can spot a cat on a rooftop at three hundred yards—can you do that?"

"Nick, the kid's expecting you to help him find his father."

"And we came down here expecting to recover bodies, but DMORT has us doing something else instead. 'First the living,' Denny told us. Well, the boy's in the same boat we are, Jerry—*first the living*. I'll get around to helping him find his father, but first he has to help us."

"Help us? How?"

Nick turned and nodded to the two approaching vehicles. "That's two more search-and-rescue teams, and there are bound to be more on the way. More boats mean more people; more people mean more accountability. We'll be crossing paths with other boats now, and they'll be watching what we're doing. We're supposed to be rescuing people—how can we be doing that if our boat is always empty? Don't you see? As long as the boy is with us, it'll look like we're doing what we're supposed to."

"What will we be doing instead?"

"Looking for bodies, of course."

Jerry did a double take. "Nick, are you out of your mind? You know what Denny told you last night."

"Don't rupture a blood vessel, Jerry. By this afternoon they'll have a dozen SAR teams searching for survivors in the Lower Nine; how many people are checking for bodies? We're working against the clock, too, you know. That body we found yesterday only had a handful of maggots left on it—in another day there would have been none at all. Think about it, Jerry: The very first body we looked at turned out to be a possible murder victim—how many others might be out there? We have to look—you know we do."

"You're going to get me in trouble again, aren't you?"

"When did I ever get you in trouble?"

"Are you kidding?"

"I mean serious trouble."

"Are you *kidding*?"

"I mean bone-breaking, bloodletting, life-threatening trouble."

"You mean you haven't killed me yet."

"Now that's a more positive perspective."

Jerry shook his head. "You're using the kid. You can't do that."

"I'm helping him, and he's helping me."

"Are you really going to help him, Nick? I need to know that. You need to promise me too."

"Look," Nick said. "Tonight we'll take him back to St. Gabriel again, and we'll get a technician to come down from the Family Assistance Center in Baton Rouge. They'll take down his family information and do a cheek swab and get him into their database—that's the best way to start looking for his dad. Fair enough?"

J.T. approached them from behind. "Are we goin' or not? It's startin' to get crowded around here."

Both men turned and looked at him.

"Maybe we should let him decide," Nick said, taking the boy by the shoulder. "J.T., I'll give you a choice: You can come with me and Jerry and help us rescue people and look for bodies, or you can stay here and find your way over to the Superdome."

"I'm coming with you," he said.

"There you go," Nick said. "Out of the mouths of babes."

Jerry rolled his eyes. "Some choice."

12

Nick steered the boat back along St. Claude Avenue toward the bridge; when he came to the bridge he turned right, following the levee north along the Industrial Canal. In less than half a mile they came to a second bridge, a lift-type structure carrying Claiborne Avenue across the canal. Damaged by the hurricane, the entire center span had been hoisted high above the water and secured in place, rendering the road impassable but leaving the canal open to navigation—whenever the Industrial Lock was repaired, which had also been damaged by the storm.

Beyond Claiborne Avenue they discovered two enormous breaches in the levee floodwall, the apparent source of the water now inundating the Lower Nine. The storm surge in the Industrial Canal had overtopped the floodwalls, thundering over the ledges like a waterfall and quickly eroding the earthen levees that held them in place. Without a supporting foundation, the massive concrete slabs had been shoved aside like so many dominoes; in some places the slabs had vanished completely, allowing an unimpeded view across the canal into the Upper Ninth Ward on the opposite side.

Past the breaches Nick steered away from the canal and into the flooded neighborhood again. Since two more SAR teams were right now putting in on St. Claude Avenue, and since more were sure to come, Nick decided to head deeper into the Lower Nine—no sense covering the same ground as everybody else. Jerry sat in the bow again, serving as both ballast and figurehead, and J.T. took up his usual position—standing on the center bench with both fists on his hips, like Peter

Pan patrolling the Blue Lagoon. They talked as they motored along, raising their voices above the constant drone of the Evinrude.

"I still say it's the hands," Jerry said. "It happens every time."

"The hands? What are you talking about?"

"You tell a woman you're a mortician, and I guarantee within thirty seconds she'll look at your hands. It's like they wonder if you washed them or not—like they wonder what you've got under your nails."

"That's crazy," Nick said. "I can think of lots of reasons women don't like you."

"You know what a woman told me once? She said, 'I thought your hands would be cold.' Cold! I said, 'I run a funeral home, not the Hair Club for Men—I'm the president, not a client.'"

"There's your problem," Nick said. "You're too sarcastic."

"I'm telling you, it's the hands. It's getting so I don't even mention what I do anymore. I just say, 'I own a business,' but I don't say what kind."

"Morticians are like lawyers," Nick said. "Nobody likes them until they need one. There's nothing wrong with what you do, Jerry—it's an ancient and noble profession. I'd tell them if I were you; if they don't like it, that's their problem."

"Do you tell women you're a bug man?"

"Absolutely. I walk right up and say, 'Hi, I'm Nick Polchak. An hour ago I was collecting maggots from a decomposing corpse. May I say, you look lovely tonight.' It works every time."

Nick looked at the boy. "What about you, J.T.? You got a girlfriend?"

"Plenty," J.T. said.

"Well, help us out here. What's your secret?"

"I just act like me, that's all."

"I already do that," Jerry sighed. "That's my problem."

"You weren't listening," Nick said. "He said you should act like *him*."

"There!" J.T. shouted, pointing across the water.

"Where?" Nick straightened up and blinked. As usual, he could make out nothing but the featureless geometric shapes of rooftops and chimneys. "Just tell me where to turn."

A hundred yards ahead, at one end of a long row of carbon-copy shotgun houses, a woman's body floated near a wooden lamppost.

"How could you possibly see that?" Nick asked.

The boy just shrugged.

Nick killed the motor and they coasted forward in silence. The body floated facedown; she was more than a little overweight, and the corrosive water had leached enough cheap dye from her hair to reveal her advanced years. Nick considered the body and its position in relation to the house behind it. He wondered if the woman had tried to escape from the flooding house; he wondered how deep the water was when she decided to take a chance; he wondered if this was as far as she'd gotten before the water swept her away. Nick shook his head. Six inches of moving water can knock a man off his feet; people always underestimate its power.

Apparently the boy's mind was traveling the same path. "You think she lived here?" he asked, staring down at the body.

Nick looked at J.T. He knew he needed to be careful; the boy had thick skin, but he was still only a boy. It took forensic professionals years to sufficiently harden themselves against constant exposure to death. That's why DMORT always included a psychiatrist among its team members. Nick thought about Beth; he wondered what she would say about the boy—and the things Nick was exposing him to.

"You okay?" Nick asked.

"Sure."

"I don't suppose you recognize her."

"Want me to look at her face?"

"No," Nick said, wanting to avoid the additional trauma of a full frontal view. But what he told the boy was, "Her lungs might still have some air in them. If we roll her over it could send her to the bottom. It doesn't matter anyway; they'll figure out who she is sooner or later. Right now, we just need to keep track of her."

Nick took out his GPS receiver again and took a reading; that way, when DMORT finally returned to the business of recovering bodies, they would know exactly where to find her. To make certain that her body didn't drift with the shifting currents, he cut a length of rope and secured one of her legs to a lamppost nearby.

Nick started the engine again and let it idle, allowing the boat to cruise slowly down the row of houses; he revved the engine from time to time to send a signal to anyone trapped inside. Near the opposite end of the row they found a man and a woman sitting quietly in lawn chairs on a second-story balcony with water covering their feet. The scene was strangely surreal—a peaceful suburban image cut and pasted into a background of total ruin.

J.T. once again extended the invitation, and once again the boat took on additional passengers. An hour later, the boat was loaded to capacity again; they returned to the earthen levee and dropped them off, advising them about the damaged Claiborne Bridge and encouraging them to seek shelter in the Superdome.

Back in the Lower Nine, they entered a commercial district where houses gave way to barbershops, clothing stores, and markets. Glass was shattered everywhere, and water flowed freely in and out of storefront windows; in one window a mannequin stood up to its knees in water, as if modeling the latest fashion for flood victims. Nick noticed that the water here came only halfway up the storefronts; this section of the neighborhood must have been situated on slightly higher ground.

They rounded a corner and came face-to-face with four men standing waist-deep in the water. One of the men was pushing a grocery cart loaded with plastic-wrapped cases of bottled water; the man behind him struggled with a wavering stack of twelve-packs of Bud Light. A third man had a bulky block of Huggies disposable diapers under each arm and three pairs of tennis shoes tied together by the shoelaces and strung around his neck.

The fourth man had a rifle.

The instant Nick spotted them he shut down the engine and brought the boat to a stop—but when he saw the rifle, he regretted the decision.

The man pointed the rifle over their heads. "Get out of the boat," he ordered.

Nick said nothing, quickly considering his limited options.

The man squeezed the trigger and fired three shots into the air—one for each of them, Nick supposed.

"Get out of the boat—I ain't gonna tell you again."

"I'm looking for my father," J.T. said.

"Not now," Nick said, taking J.T. by the arm and trying to pull him down into the boat—but the boy twisted away, refusing to surrender his position on the center bench.

"You see your old man around here?" the man with the rifle asked. "Get out of there, boy."

"I'm looking for him," J.T. said. "That's why we need the boat."

"Look," Nick called out, "we're a search-and-rescue team—we found this boy stranded on a rooftop not far from here, and there's bound to be a lot more like him. C'mon, man—it's your neighborhood, not mine. We need the boat more than you do."

The man leveled the rifle at Nick's head.

Nick felt his face go red.

He knew what he would have said to this moron if he was alone—he would have held up one finger and told him to *aim at this*. He knew precisely which words he would use, and he could feel them rising up in the back of his throat even now—he could taste the acid. But he wasn't alone—he had J.T. and Jerry to think of, and he knew he had no right to make a stand—though the thought made him sick to his stomach.

"All right," he growled. "We'll give you the boat." He glanced over at J.T. "We can find another one."

Just then a fifth man emerged from the flooded store. To Nick's astonishment, he was dressed in an NOPD uniform and wearing his service sidearm. "Who fired those shots?" the officer demanded.

"They got a boat," his armed companion said.

"What'd I tell you 'bout that? Gimme that rifle—you fire a bullet into the sky, it comes down on the other side of town like a rocket. You fool, you can kill somebody that way—don't you know that?"

"We're with FEMA," Nick called out. "We're a search-and-rescue team."

"You boys go on about your business," the officer said.

How about doing yours? Nick wanted to say. He had a dozen questions he was dying to ask: *What are you doing with a bunch of looters? Why aren't you helping with the rescues yourself? Why don't you establish some order around here? Why would you let that idiot carry a firearm? Why don't you use your own?* But he had no way to know how far the officer had strayed from his duty, so he thought it best to keep his questions to himself. Right now the best thing to do was fire up the engine and get out of there.

He did.

No one said anything for the next few minutes.

Nick looked over at Jerry: "I didn't hear much from you back there."

"I know," Jerry said.

Nick wanted to rib him about it but quickly decided not to. He had felt the adrenaline racing through his body, too, and he understood the effect it had on the brain: The hormone had a way of shifting the mind into hyperdrive, making it spin like a runaway flywheel, generating a thousand possibilities but resting on none. Jerry was no coward. It wasn't a matter of courage; sometimes adrenaline takes away your ability to choose.

Instead, he turned to J.T. "I'll say one thing for you—you've got guts. I believe you would have taken a bullet back there."

"I don't care," the boy grumbled. "It's not his boat."

"We could have found another boat," Nick said.

"We already got one."

Nick started to say, "It's not as important as your life," but it occurred to him that maybe it was. The boy didn't refuse to give up the boat out of stubbornness, or because it was their property—he was using the boat to find his father, and the man was about to interfere. Nick thought again: Maybe he had taken his promise too lightly; maybe it was more important to the boy than he knew.

"Tell me more about your father," Nick said.

J.T. looked back over his shoulder. "What you want to know?"

"His name, first of all."

"Bastien Callais Augustine Walker."

"That's quite a mouthful."

"Catholics got lots o' names," he said proudly.

"Describe him for me."

"He's a big man—tall, like you. Real smart too—knows all kinds of stuff."

"Is he black, like you?"

"Sure."

"Hair?"

"Sure."

"I mean hair color. Is it like yours?"

"Sure."

Nick tried a different tack. "Where did you last see your father?"

"I told you, we got separated in the storm."

"Was he in the water? Was he trying to swim?"

Before the boy could answer, they heard the sound of an approaching boat and looked up.

"There!" J.T. said, pointing to three o'clock.

Nick slowed as they approached the next intersection and waited; three blocks away, a boat approached carrying four National Guardsmen. The boat was large and solid-looking, painted in a distinct camouflage pattern that made it stand out more than conceal it in the suburban setting. In the bow of the boat, a soldier rested the stock of an M16 against his thigh and kept the barrel pointed into the sky. It was a very simple and very clear symbol of authority—one that Nick's boat lacked.

"I've got boat envy," Nick said. "Everybody else's is bigger than mine."

"Afternoon," one of the Guardsmen called out.

"Welcome to the Lower Nine," Nick said.

"You fellas from around here?"

"We're with DMORT, up in St. Gabriel."

The Guardsman looked at J.T. "I thought you guys collected bodies."

"I thought you guys rescued people. Where've you been?"

"Whaddya mean? We've got eight thousand men along the Gulf Coast."

"You're the first we've seen."

"Well, transportation's a little tough around here."

"That's what the people on the rooftops tell us. What are you hearing about the rest of the city?"

"They're trying to plug the holes in the levees with big sandbags—no luck so far. The lake's six feet above sea level, so the water keeps pouring in. The pumps don't work—the motors have all been flooded."

"Any casualty estimates?"

"It's anybody's guess. Coast Guard claims they pulled twelve hundred people off rooftops yesterday, but there's a lot more out there."

"We've been sending ours to the Superdome. Is that still the plan?"

"That's what they told us—but we hear they've already got thirty thousand people there."

"Thirty *thousand*," Nick said. "The Superdome is a stadium, not a hotel. This isn't a Saints game; they can't expect people to just sit in the bleachers for a week or two—people have got to sleep, they've got to stretch out."

"I hear the place looks like a landfill," the soldier said. "Trash everywhere, the toilets don't work, and they're running out of food and water. They said they were bringing in buses, but nobody's seen any so far. We can't even get our own trucks in yet—the water comes all the way up to the ramps."

Nick shook his head. "Maybe we should start putting people back on rooftops."

"Maybe we should just follow orders," the soldier said.

"That's always my policy. By the way, have you guys spotted any bodies?"

"Sure, we've seen a few."

"I'm talking about unusual ones."

"'Dead' isn't good enough?"

"I'm looking for bodies with bullet or trauma wounds—bodies in an advanced state of decay—that sort of thing."

"We saw one like that, 'bout a quarter mile from here."

"Did you get a GPS reading? Let me have it, will you?"

The Guardsman relayed the coordinates and Nick jotted them down.

"Thanks," Nick said. "Now here's a tip for you: About a half mile down this road, you'll come to a commercial district; you'll find five guys there looting a store. One of them is an NOPD officer—see if you can knock some sense into him, will you?"

"Glad to oblige," the soldier said. He signaled to his helmsman to move on, then turned to the remaining two Guardsmen. "Lock and load," he said. They responded by checking their M16s to make sure there was a round ready in the chamber.

Jerry's eyes were fixed on the rifles as the two boats pulled away from each other. "That's what we need," he said.

"I've never been much good with guns," Nick said. "You have to be able to see the guy you want to shoot—they tell me that's an important detail."

Jerry didn't respond.

"C'mon, Jerry, lighten up—we're in the business of recovering bodies, not producing them." But he knew what Jerry was feeling.

Nick steered as Jerry directed with his GPS unit. Fifteen minutes later, they arrived at the coordinates the Guardsman had indicated and eased up alongside the floating body.

"He was right," Jerry said. "This guy's in bad shape."

Nick leaned out over the side of the boat to take a better look. J.T. once again began to do the same, but Nick pushed him back. "Not this time," he said.

"How come?"

"I need an assistant. I want you to open my equipment bag and get out the same stuff you saw me use yesterday. Can you remember it all?"

J.T. rummaged through the canvas bag while Nick examined the body.

Jerry once again had to serve as a counterweight to balance the boat. "What do you see?" he asked.

"It's already in the third stage of deterioration—*floating decay*. The skin has been thoroughly macerated by the water; it's sloughing off in some places, and it's already turning black. The abdomen has collapsed, but there's still enough gas to keep it afloat. There are some blowfly infestations on the exposed areas, but those are only a couple of days old—this man's been dead much longer than that. If only there were—"

Nick reached back over his shoulder. "Give me the forceps—the long silver things."

He plucked a single insect from the body and held it up.

"That's not like the other bugs," J.T. said.

"You're right," Nick said. "This one's different."

"You want a jar?"

"No, get me a body bag. Not like the one we used yesterday—look for one made out of mesh."

"Whoa," Jerry said. "Nick—what are you doing?"

Nick looked at him and smiled. "Jerry, how long have we known each other?"

13

"Okay, open wide."

J.T. opened his mouth, and the Family Assistance Center technician wiped a cotton swab over the inside of his cheek.

"What's that for?" the boy asked.

"DNA," Nick said. "Do you know what that is, smart guy?" Nick held out a small package.

J.T. shook his head.

"I thought you knew everything," Nick said. "Never mind—I'll explain it to you later. Are you hungry? C'mon, I'll show you what the soldiers eat—then there's somebody I want you to meet."

The boy was still sporting the same pair of knee-length shorts, but he now wore one of Nick's oversized button-down shirts and a pair of Nike's cadged from a female pathologist of similar stature. He spent a full ten minutes sorting through the selection of black-and-tan MREs before finally settling on "Cajun Rice with Beans and Sausage"—known to locals as "Bayou Beanie Weanies." Nick chose a "Chicken with Cavatelli" for himself and threw in a "Cherry Blueberry Cobbler" for each of them. Ordinarily, he would have removed the entrées from their plastic bags and microwaved them—but he thought J.T. would enjoy using a chemical ration heater instead. Ten minutes later, the boy's entrée was ready to eat; five minutes after that it was completely consumed.

"I once had a date with a woman who ate like that," Nick said. "Scary."

Nick glanced up and spotted Beth in the doorway, surveying the room. He waved to her and she approached.

"This is the lady I wanted you to meet," Nick said. "J.T., this is Beth Woodbridge."

The boy looked up and grinned. "You're pretty."

"And you're sweet."

"Forget it," Nick said to Beth. "He's already got plenty of girlfriends."

"I can imagine. May I sit down, J.T.? I'd like to ask you some questions."

She pulled up a chair on the opposite side of the table and watched the boy as he dug into his gooey cobbler. "How do you like it here at the DPMU?"

"I like the food," he said.

"I can see that. Nick likes this food, too, don't you, Nick?"

Nick had a mouthful of cavatelli at the moment. He gave the boy a big thumbs-up.

"Have you ever heard of the Family Assistance Center, J.T.?"

He shook his head.

"It's up in Baton Rouge, just a few minutes from here. We assist families there, just like it sounds. We help people get back in touch with their loved ones when they get separated, like some people have down in New Orleans. We'd like to help you find your father again."

"Nick's helping me."

"That's very nice of Nick, but we can help too. We'll put your name into a big database so everybody can see it—not just here, but all over the country. That might help your father find you."

"They stuck a thing in my mouth."

"A cheek swab? They'll take that back to Baton Rouge and keep it there. It could come in handy later, but right now we'd like to know a few things about you and your dad. Where do you live, J.T.? What's your address?"

"I forget," he said.

"Nick says he found you in the Lower Ninth Ward."

"That's right—that's where I live."

"What street do you live on?"

"It changes."

"You mean you've lived in different places?"

"Sure."

"Where does your father live? Does he live with you?"

"We got separated. I told Nick."

She glanced at Nick. "What about your mother?"

He shook his head.

"What about brothers? Sisters?"

He shook his head again.

"J.T., can you describe your father for me?"

Nick leaned in. "He told me he's tall, and—"

"I want to hear him say it. Go on, J.T."

"He's like Nick."

"Like Nick? How?"

"Tall. Smart. With glasses."

She paused. "J.T., have you ever been visited by a social worker? Do you know what that is?"

"Sure."

"Do you remember your social worker's name?"

"It changes."

"I see." She watched the boy for another minute before she rose from the table. "It was a pleasure to meet you, J.T. I hope we can talk again. Nick is going to walk me to the door now because he's such a gentleman, but he'll be right back."

She gave Nick a quick glance before she turned away.

"She's pretty," the boy said, "but weird."

"That about covers it. Finish your food—I'll be right back."

Nick followed Beth through the doorway and just around the corner, out of sight. "What do you think?" he asked.

"I'm getting some mixed signals from him," she said. "I'd like to contact the Department of Social Services in New Orleans; if I can reach them, they should be able to tell me who was working in the Lower Ninth Ward. If we can locate his social worker, we'll save a lot of time.

I'm not sure I'll be able to get through since the phones are out in the city; I may have to go through the state DSS office in Baton Rouge, and that could take a while."

"Do what you can," Nick said. "In the meantime, I'll see if I can—"

"You!" a voice said behind him.

Nick turned. It was Denny.

"In my office—*right now*." He marched by without stopping.

Beth looked at Nick. "What did you do now?"

"Later," Nick said. "Do me a favor, will you? Take the boy to Jerry—tell him to look out for him until I get back."

Nick hurried after his boss. "Denny, I can explain."

"Don't bother—I don't want to hear it."

"I had to bring that body back. It was a matter of—"

"You just don't listen, do you, Nick? I tried to tell you—we're a part of a team here. That's not just some slogan—that's the way the system works."

"Denny, if you'll just give me a chance to—"

Denny swung open his office door and stepped aside, motioning for Nick to enter ahead of him. Nick stepped inside and found a man he didn't recognize seated at Denny's desk.

He heard the door click behind him. He looked; Denny wasn't there.

"Come in," the man said without looking up. "Take a seat."

"Thanks. I'll stand."

The man didn't respond; he continued to read from a file folder open on the desk in front of him. A full minute went by.

Nick felt the hair rising like wire bristles on the back of his neck. He didn't mind getting his hand slapped—God knows it happened often enough—but he despised this kind of clumsy attempt at intimidation. "Mind if I get a magazine?" he asked.

The man didn't reply.

A chair had been set strategically near the center of the room—not so close to the desk as to suggest friendship, and not so far away as to allow detachment. It was a spot intended to provide Nick with plenty of room to squirm; all the scene needed was a bare lightbulb dangling overhead.

Nick dragged the chair closer to the desk and sat down.

The man looked up. "So, you're this bug man character."

"Is that a question?"

He paused. "I'm with the Drug Enforcement Administration here in Louisiana—the New Orleans Field Division. We cover a four-state area: Alabama, Mississippi, Louisiana, and Arkansas."

"That's a lot of ground," Nick said.

"Tell me about it."

"How'd you guys fare in the storm?"

"I'm over in Metairie—we did okay. Our office in Gulfport was wiped out."

"Sorry to hear that."

"It's just a building," he said. "What really fries me is when somebody screws up one of my investigations."

"That was a subtle transition."

"I don't have much time for subtlety. Like you said: I've got a lot of ground to cover." He looked down at the folder again. "Dr. Nicholas Polchak, PhD in entomology from Penn State University."

"Go Nittany Lions."

"Currently professor of entomology at North Carolina State University. Distinguished Member, American Academy of Forensic Sciences; Diplomate, American Board of Forensic Entomology; Member of Disaster Mortuary Operational Response Team since 1995."

"Please. I'm blushing."

The man rose from his chair and slowly walked around to the front of the desk; he leaned back against it, folding his arms across his chest and staring down at Nick. Now Nick wished he had left the chair where it was; he felt like a schoolboy in the principal's office—which, he supposed, was the intended effect.

Nick judged the man to be about six feet tall, maybe less. He appeared broad-shouldered and large-boned but slender, like an ex-ballplayer who had worked hard to stay in shape. His skin appeared weathered but not tanned, suggesting a man who had moved up to an office after long years in the field. His facial features were sharp, almost angular, with deep creases and hollows around his cheeks and mouth. He was almost bald on top; the hair on both sides had been cut to match, leaving salt-and-pepper stubble that wrapped from ear to ear. Nick wondered if the man wore contacts; his eyes were precisely the right shade of "intimidating blue."

"Yesterday you recovered the body of a man from the Lower Ninth Ward, though you were specifically instructed not to. Last night your director reprimanded you for that infraction and reminded you of your instructions—yet today you recovered a second body from the same general area. I'd like to know why."

"I'd like to know who's asking," Nick said.

"My name is Turlock," he said. "Special Agent Frank Turlock."

"Why is the DEA interested in my little faux pas, Mr. Turlock? Seems like an in-house issue to me."

"Not anymore. How much do you know about the drug situation down here?"

"Only what I read in the papers."

"We've got all the usual problems," he said. "Cocaine and crack—those are the big ones. Heroin, too, but mostly in New Orleans. We've got all the club drugs too: Ecstasy, ketamine, GHB—the college kids go in for that stuff. This is an interesting town, Dr. Polchak: The Port of New Orleans is the busiest port in the world—most people don't know that. That makes us a major drug distribution center for Colombia, Mexico, and the Caribbean. Plus we're sitting on Interstate 10—that makes us a major east-west corridor for traffickers from Miami, Houston, and the Mexican border. We've got it all here—production, trafficking, and illegal abuse. The Dominicans, the Haitians, the Jamaicans—they wholesale the stuff. The black and Hispanic gangs kill each other over turf at the local level while the whites make most of the money. It's a regular battlefield down here. My job is to put a stop to it."

"Good luck."

"It takes more than luck. It takes a lot of time and planning—two years in my case, and you were about to screw that up."

"How's that?"

"Let me explain something about drug trafficking organizations—DTOs, we call them. A DTO is a lot like any other business: Everybody has a place, everybody has a position, everybody knows what belongs to them and what doesn't. They don't want to kill each other—that's bad business. Only the gangs are stupid enough to do that, and that isn't really about drugs; that's mostly testosterone.

"And like any business, it isn't easy to keep track of where everybody is and what everybody's up to—that's what makes our job so hard. Now, along comes Hurricane Katrina, and what happens? The port shuts down, the roads are closed, distribution channels are broken, and supply lines are cut off. Whole territories suddenly become available, entire neighborhoods are up for grabs. People see opportunities to get ahead: A dealer sees the chance to become a distributor; a distributor thinks he might become a major supplier. People know the opportunity won't last, so they act—people who used to be invisible to us. This hurricane is a rare opportunity for the DEA, Dr. Polchak. When the water rises, the snakes come crawling out from under their rocks—some of them for the first time in years. They become visible, they make mistakes, and when they do we'll grab them—if somebody doesn't tip them off first."

"Somebody like me."

"Yeah—somebody like you. Tell me about the body you recovered yesterday."

"It was sighted floating on the surface, only a few hours after the storm had passed. That made me curious, so my partner and I checked it out. I found a blunt-trauma wound on the forehead infested by *calliphorid* larvae—blowfly maggots. The species is terrestrial, not aquatic—and their stage of development indicated a postmortem interval of several days. In other words, this wasn't a hurricane victim; he died on land sometime before the storm. Had he died in the hurricane, his blunt-trauma wound could have been caused by anything—a rock, a tree branch—but under these circumstances, it indicates foul play."

"And that's why you brought it back."

"Exactly."

"Even though you were ordered not to."

Nick shook his head. "Do you know what the SAR teams are calling the water in the Lower Nine? *Toxic gumbo*—that's a pretty good name for it. The water's over ninety degrees, and it's filled with bacteria and chemicals that speed up the decomposition process. Everything I noticed on that body—the trauma wound, the blowfly larvae—it would have all been obliterated in another day or two and the man would have looked just like any other hurricane victim. I didn't bag that body just to be a wise guy, Mr. Turlock—I did it to preserve forensic evidence."

"What about the second body—the one you picked up today?"

"It was in an even more advanced stage of decay. I can only guess at the time of death—at least a week ago, possibly two. An autopsy might tell us more; identification will be difficult for that one, unless they can still salvage a DNA sample from bone. The National Guard spotted the body and passed the coordinates on to me; I bagged it because of something unusual that I found."

"What's that?"

"How much do you know about forensic entomology?"

"Enlighten me."

"Well—forensic entomology is the study of certain species of insects that inhabit bodies after they die. The life cycles of these insects have been timed precisely, allowing us to use them to determine time of death—and sometimes cause of death. In the past, almost all of the species we've studied have been terrestrial; very little is known about aquatic and marine insects of forensic value."

"Aquatic *and* marine?"

"'Aquatic' means freshwater; 'marine' means saltwater; here you've got both. The Mississippi is freshwater; Lake Pontchartrain is salt. When the lake floods, salt water pours into the city; when the storm surge backs the bayous into the Industrial Canal, freshwater pours in. Like I said, you've got both. Actually, Mr. Turlock, Hurricane Katrina is a rare opportunity for forensic entomologists—sort of a large-scale field study."

"Back to the body," Turlock said. "What did you find that was so unusual?"

"I found caddis flies—they're aquatic insects, one of the few that have been shown to have forensic value. The caddis fly lays its eggs on the surface of water; the eggs then sink and hatch, and the larvae attach themselves to whatever they happen to find nearby—including a body."

"Why is that important?"

"It tells us that, unlike the first victim, this man died in water—or at least his body spent a significant time underwater after death. The general condition of the body was consistent with this—the tissues were thoroughly softened and the skin was beginning to slough."

"I'm not sure I'm following you."

"Well, think about it," Nick said. "The guy's been dead for a couple of weeks; he's been in the water most of that time—but where? Two weeks ago there was no water in the Lower Nine. That means the body was moved."

"Moved?"

"That's my guess."

"I've heard reports about bodies floating up out of cemeteries."

"Without a casket? Besides, if it came from a cemetery, the body spent the last two weeks underground; then I wouldn't have found caddis flies. No, I think somebody got the bright idea to use the flood to take care of some loose ends."

"What do you mean?"

"Bodies are notoriously hard to get rid of—ask anybody on death row. Suppose you kill somebody and hide the body as best you can, but you know someone will eventually discover it—it's only a matter of time. But then the hurricane comes along and you get a flash of inspiration: Why not dredge up the body and set it loose in the flood? That way it'll turn up along with a thousand others, and nobody will know the difference. It's pretty clever, when you think about it."

"I see what you mean."

Nick leaned forward now. "That's why we have to recover the bodies, Mr. Turlock—that's what I've been trying to tell Denny. It is pretty clever, and whoever did it just might get away with it—unless we grab the bodies before this kind of evidence is destroyed. I can prove that those two men weren't hurricane victims—but with every day they spend in the water, it will get more difficult to do. If we wait too long, it'll be impossible."

Turlock said nothing; he just continued to lean against the desk with his arms folded, staring at a point in the center of Nick's chest.

"We've got a problem," Turlock said.

"What's that?"

"These bodies that you want to recover—we don't want them brought in yet."

"Why not?"

"We've identified the first body you recovered. He was a midlevel drug dealer who worked out of the Lower Nine. We think he was trying to improve his station in life, but somebody got to him first."

"Congratulations. That should save you guys a lot of time."

"You're not listening. We don't just want him—we want the people around him. Once a body is identified, it's only a matter of time before the information goes public."

"Keep the victims' names classified. You guys ought to be able to pull that off."

"Which names? There are already thousands of people demanding information about lost family members. Which names do we keep under wraps? We don't even know who these people are yet—that's what we're trying to find out. We need time, Dr. Polchak—and right now FEMA is giving it to us. They want to rescue the living first, and that works for us. What we don't need right now is somebody dragging bodies out of the water when we're not ready for that to happen."

"I'm not sure *you're* listening," Nick said. "If you wait to recover these bodies, then whoever's doing this will get away with it."

"So what?"

"That doesn't matter to you?"

"Tell me the truth: The two bodies you recovered—can you tell me who killed them and how? Can you find me a murder weapon? Will anybody at DMORT be able to tell me, even after they do an autopsy?"

"I doubt it."

"Then I can't get a conviction—the killer will get away with it anyway. Look at it from my perspective, Dr. Polchak: All you can do is prove that a few men weren't really hurricane victims; I might be able to bring down an entire DTO. From where I stand, I've got a lot more to gain than you do."

Nick said nothing.

"You've got a problem with this, don't you?"

"I've got a big problem," Nick grumbled.

"I figured. That's why you're here, and that's why you're a problem for me. I could send you home, Dr. Polchak—I have the authority to do that—but the bodies are eventually going to come in, and DMORT needs everyone they've got. I don't suppose you'd promise not to look for any more bodies?"

"I'm a man of my word," Nick said. "I just use a lot of vague and slippery ones."

"In that case, I'd like to suggest a compromise."

"What sort of compromise?"

"I want you to find bodies—but I want you to find them for me."

"Meaning what?"

"I want you to look for bodies just like the other two you found—bodies that indicate foul play, bodies that weren't the result of Hurricane Katrina or the flooding. When you find them, take a GPS reading—but leave the bodies in place. Do you understand what I'm saying? *Do not bring the bodies back*—let's see what we can learn from them there. Then, when we think the time is right, we'll bring them in; we'll know exactly where they are. Do we have a deal?"

Nick thought for a moment before nodding.

"And just so we avoid any of those vague and slippery words, let me add one more thing: If you recover one more body without my permission, I will send you back to your classroom at NC State. Got it?"

"You really know how to threaten a guy," Nick said. "Okay, I get the point."

"Good. I'll inform your boss about our arrangement."

"Are we done here?"

"We're done."

Nick got up from his chair and smoothed the front of his shirt. He started for the door, then turned back. "What about the second body? Have they identified that one yet?"

"Sorry," he said. "It's need-to-know only."

"I have an emotional need to know. Does that count?"

"Good luck, Dr. Polchak. Keep me posted."

Nick stepped out and the door closed behind him.

When the office door clicked shut, a side door opened and another man stepped into the room. He was slightly taller than Turlock and at least twenty pounds heavier; he carried most of it around his waist. He had sandy red hair cut in a utilitarian flattop that he had probably maintained since high school. His hair was beginning to fade and thin at the same time, causing it to blend almost perfectly with his ruddy complexion. It was cut close on top, leaving an almost bald oval in the center of his head.

"Did you hear all that?" Turlock asked.

"I heard," the man said. "Do you think he'll follow orders this time?"

"He never has before."

"What do you want to do?"

"I want you to follow him, John. Take one of the boats—make sure Polchak does what he agreed to and nothing more."

"And if he doesn't?"

"We'll deal with that if we have to. We can't let him mess this up."

"Do you think he could?"

"I think he's trouble," Turlock said. "Guys like him always are."

14

The moon was almost full, giving him just enough light to navigate by—but not nearly enough light to penetrate all the darkness around him. The moon was a night-light, that's all it was—just a glowing silver disk that kept him from stubbing his toe on the way to the toilet. A stinking toilet—that's what the whole city had become, and somebody needed to shove the handle and send the whole place to the sewer where it belonged.

He knew the moon had no chance. Even the sun could only penetrate the filth a few inches, searching for something down there that might be worth saving. Even the sun found nothing—what chance did the moon have? The water around him was as black as oil; each time he lifted the oar from the water he expected the blade to be black. The water felt syrupy to him, almost solid. Maybe the city was turning into one massive tar pit, sucking down all the reptiles and rodents so that decent people could finally have a chance to live. He wanted it to happen; he wanted to help.

He looked across the neighborhood at the rooftops angling from the water, and he didn't understand. Why did the water stop rising? Why didn't it rise up over the tallest peak and finish the job? Why did it leave some of the reptiles on rooftops and in attics, where they might escape and breed? Didn't the water know the evil that the creatures did? They were the reason that his daughter was gone; they came by night and took her away.

He knew it was all his fault—he didn't do his job. He should have been watching; he should have kept the creatures away. He knew the evil that they did—he knew better than anyone else. But he wasn't watching, and the creatures came and took her from him. They came by night; it was always at night—he should have known.

"Sweetheart," he whispered, and the moon seemed to glow a little brighter. She was there; she was always there, helping him to find his way. He knew because she spoke to him. The notes, the messages scrawled on the bathroom mirror—they all made it seem as if she weren't so far away. She knew who the creatures were; she knew where they lived, because she could see everything now. She knew—and she told him.

He reached into his pocket and pulled out the note again. He unfolded it and read the address. *Thank you, sweetheart—thank you for giving me his name. Thank you for telling me where he lives.*

"Lonnie Broussard!" he shouted into the darkness. He lifted the oar from the water and listened—nothing. He rowed a few strokes farther and shouted again.

"Lonnie Broussard!"

He heard a faint reply from the rooftop to his left. He rowed up to the attic vent and tried to peer through the slats, but it was as black as pitch inside.

Of course it is. That's where the creatures live.

He jammed his oar three times against the side of the house.

"I'm in here!" said a dry, rasping voice from inside.

"Are you Lonnie Broussard?"

"Get me outta here!" The voice was closer now.

"Are you Lonnie Broussard?"

"Yeah, I'm Broussard, and I'm trapped! I been in here for two days!" Now the voice was just on the other side of the wall.

He saw fingertips wriggle out from between the wooden slats like a brood of water moccasins. He jabbed at them with the edge of his oar.

"Ow! What the—"

"Step away from the wall."

"What? Why?"

"I have to cut through the wall. Step back—do it now."

He waited until he heard a faint, "Okay." Then he took one end of a rubber laundry hose and forced it between the slats. He connected the other end to a metal pipe projecting from the side of the boat's engine; he started the engine and revved it a few times.

"How long will it take?" the voice demanded.

"Not long enough."

He stretched out in the bottom of the boat and looked up at the moon. He imagined he could see a face in it; he wanted to believe that it was her face, smiling down at him from far away. It was all his fault, and he could never change that. His daughter was gone because he didn't do his job. He didn't listen to her before, but he listened to her now. He was finding them for her, and he was sending them back into the darkness where they belonged.

15

Thursday, September 1

Nick took the boat into a more open section of the Lower Nine, where the backyards were slightly larger and tall hedges and sheds just barely poked their tops above the water. Half-starved dogs paced back and forth on some of the rooftops, whining at the boat as it passed. *They are the lucky ones*, Nick thought; a lot of animals were probably still chained to their houses when the water began to rise.

"See any others?" he shouted over the engine.

"I'll tell you," J.T. replied.

"What about you?" he called up to Jerry.

"If he doesn't see it, I won't," Jerry said.

Search-and-rescue teams were finally beginning to arrive in significant numbers. St. Claude Avenue had been crowded that morning, with SAR teams lining up from a dozen different agencies and areas as far away as British Columbia. Boats seemed to be everywhere now, crisscrossing the Lower Nine with boatloads of exhausted-looking rescuees. Some looked grateful; some looked angry; all seemed bewildered as to why the rescue efforts were taking so long.

At eleven o'clock the night before, the National Hurricane Center had announced that Hurricane Katrina had been completely absorbed by a frontal boundary in southeastern Canada, with "no discernible circulation" remaining. The news was little comfort to the residents of the Lower Ninth Ward; Katrina's effects were still "discernible" there. It had been almost thirty-six hours since the hurricane had passed through—thirty-six long hours that people had been confined to asphalt griddles or tiny attic ovens that reached 130 degrees in the afternoon sun. Many had perished, and Nick was having no trouble finding their bodies today—because at this temperature, thirty-six hours was more than enough time for the sea to surrender her dead.

Nick and Jerry had already found seven bodies that day, and none of them looked unusual. Many of them were older victims with no other marks on them; they had probably died from heart failure, perhaps in the first few minutes of panic. Others had eventually succumbed to exposure or dehydration due to the suffocating heat. Regardless of the cause of death, the accelerating effects of the water had caused all of them to reach the "early floating" stage of decomposition, bringing them slowly to the surface where Nick could easily find them.

They approached a house where the attic vent had been smashed in—or possibly out, by someone escaping from inside. *In*, Nick thought; below the vent the words "2 bodies" had been spray-painted in red across the siding. Apparently someone had already stopped by for a quick look—maybe a FEMA team doing a primary search.

J.T. pointed to a large white object bobbing in the water like an ice cube. "What's that thing?"

"Looks like a refrigerator," Nick said.

"Refrigerators float?"

"They do when they're full of air."

J.T. suddenly stiffened. "Over there!" he shouted, his hawklike eyes detecting a dark line in an open expanse of water.

"Looks like a log to me," Nick said.

"Nope."

"Maybe it's a gator," Jerry said. "Some of this water backed up from the bayous."

J.T. turned and looked at Nick.

"Don't worry about it," Nick said. "If it's hungry, it'll go for Jerry first."

The boy's eyes were accurate as usual. Nick brought the boat in for a closer look; it was the body of a man, floating facedown.

"How come most of 'em float facedown?" J.T. asked.

"Physics," Nick said. "As the body breaks down, it makes gas—things like methane, hydrogen sulfide, and carbon dioxide. The gas collects in the torso because that's where the natural cavity is. So when the body starts to rise, it tends to float torso-first, with the limbs hanging down like ropes from a weather balloon. That makes the body rotate in the water and come up facedown. See?"

"But we saw one faceup," the boy said.

"That's right—but he wasn't very tall, did you notice that? Short people tend to have shorter arms and legs. Shorter limbs mean lighter limbs, and that means less drag. Short people are more likely to come up face-first." *Kids too*, he began to say—but quickly decided not to.

Nick looked the body over; there was nothing unusual about it. The color and condition of the tissues were consistent with a Katrina postmortem, and there were no indications of blowfly activity that would suggest death prior to the hurricane.

He reached into his equipment bag and took out a palm-sized electronic device. He checked the battery, switched the unit on, then clipped it securely to the clothing of the floating body.

"What's that?" the boy asked.

"It's a transmitter," Nick said, "sort of like my GPS unit—only that one receives, and this one sends. Once every hour it sends out a signal that tells us where it is. We can pick up the signal on a laptop computer and overlay it on a map; that way, we can find the body again even if it floats all the way across town."

"Why not just tie it to something like you did the other day?" Jerry asked.

"That seemed like a good idea at the time," Nick said. "Then I talked to that DEA guy last night. I don't know how long they're planning to leave these bodies out here; another week in this water, and we'll have the problem of—you know."

"What?"

"Disarticulation," he said, hoping that he wouldn't have to spell it out in front of the boy: If he tied one limb to a lamppost, that might be all they would find later on.

They heard the sound of an approaching engine and looked up to see a familiar black rescue boat speeding toward them with Officer LaTourneau at the helm. Nick waved him down, and the Zodiac boat cruised to a stop on the opposite side of the floating corpse.

"You're slacking off!" Nick called out, nodding to the empty boat. "What'd you do, break for lunch?"

"I don't break for lunch," LaTourneau called back. "You need something?"

"Not really—just wanted to say hello."

"I'm kind of in a hurry here. They put a curfew into effect yesterday, in case you hadn't heard. We've only got a few hours of daylight left."

"I met one of your colleagues the other day. He was looting a store about half a mile from here."

LaTourneau glared at him. "What's your point?"

"He was in uniform and everything. I was just wondering: Is that an official NOPD function—shopping coordinator?"

"Yesterday the mayor ordered the entire NOPD to abandon search-and-rescue efforts and help restore order. One of the first priorities is to control the looting."

"Good plan," Nick said. "Steal everything yourself so there won't be anything left to take."

"Some of these looters are carrying automatic weapons," LaTourneau said.

"I noticed that. There was one pointed at my head."

"What were they taking?"

Nick reviewed the list.

"You'd arrest a man for taking home diapers to his kids?"

"Six cases of beer," Nick said. "What was he doing, throwing a baby shower?"

"How many men were there?"

"Your friend had four associates."

"Four—and you say one of them was armed? What's one lone officer supposed to do, walk up to four men and say, 'You're under arrest'? We're on our own out here—you can't call for backup."

"Your officer had his sidearm," Nick said. "Maybe he could have—I don't know—pointed it at somebody? Seems like a good idea to me—the other guy sure thought of it."

"Our instructions are to maintain order, not create more chaos. This may come as a surprise to you, but people are a little frustrated out here. Tempers are short; you better be careful who you go waving a gun at."

"I thought that's the point I was making."

"Look, our people are having to improvise. One of our officers came across five looters in a drugstore the other day—they were trying to break into a glass display case. You know what he did? He smashed the case himself, to keep people from cutting themselves on the glass."

"Tell him to meet me at the bank," Nick said. "I'd like to make a withdrawal."

"We're first responders out here. A guy slashes his wrist, we're the ones who have to take care of him. Ever think about that? Sorry to get your blood pressure up, but if you don't mind me saying so, you look pretty healthy to me. Why don't you fellas stop whining and get back to work?" LaTourneau looked at J.T. "Is that the same boy I saw you with the other day?"

"It's his brother," Nick said. "Well, nice chatting with you. Oh, by the way: We've had a change in job assignment."

"What, you're not chief of police anymore?"

"We're not doing SAR anymore—we're locating bodies now. We're not recovering them yet, just marking locations for later on."

"Sure hate to lose you guys," LaTourneau said. "You've almost rescued an entire family in just two days."

"Have you come across any bodies this morning?"

"Sure, a few."

"Did you take GPS readings?"

"I'm not as high-tech as you guys—try the National Guard. Now, if you don't mind, I'm losing daylight."

He started his engine and roared away. Nick did the same.

Jerry turned and looked at him. "He's right, you know."

"About what?"

"We need to cut people some slack out here."

"I just don't like that guy—I don't know why."

"I do," Jerry said. "He's just like you."

"What does that mean?"

"He likes to work alone, he does things his own way, and he never quits. Plus he's a wise guy—sound familiar? It's like looking in a mirror, and you don't like what you see."

"Please," Nick groaned. "One psychiatrist is enough."

They spent the next hour waving down other boats and inquiring about the whereabouts of any deceased. Some of the SAR teams had taken GPS coordinates for the floaters they encountered, but the rescuees were an even better source of information; they had been on the rooftops, they had heard the cries from neighboring attics—and they knew which voices had stopped. Nick and Jerry took down all the information.

The body that interested Nick most was described by a member of a swift-water rescue team from California. "A real gross-out," he called it, which is what first caught Nick's attention.

"Was the gut bloated and extended—like this?" he asked, thrusting his own midsection forward.

"Not really," the man said. "It was sort of like that all over."

"Was it faceup or facedown?" J.T. asked.

The man ignored him.

"Answer him," Nick said. "It's a good question."

"Faceup," he said. "What difference does it make?"

J.T. had a follow-up question: "Was he a short guy?"

"Not that I noticed. Why?"

J.T. shook his head. "It's complicated."

The man looked at Nick. "Who's the kid?"

"He's a grad student," Nick said. "See you guys later—thanks for the info."

When the boat pulled away and the roar of its engine finally died down, Nick said, "Sounds like a refloat."

"A *refloat*," Jerry said. "What's that?"

"A body floats, it sinks, it floats back up again—that's a *refloat*. If a body's been in the water long enough, it'll release the gas from the gut and sink to the bottom again. Decomposition continues underwater, and the process continues to produce gas—only the gas can't collect in the gut again, because the gut's ruptured. This time the gas is distributed throughout the whole body, so when it finally comes to the surface again, it's more likely to rise faceup. It's a possible indication of advanced decay. We need to check this one out."

"Why?" Jerry asked. "If all we're supposed to do is locate bodies, aren't we finished here? He gave you the GPS coordinates; why do we need to look?"

"We're supposed to look for anomalies, Jerry."

"You've got one: *advanced decay*. Write it down, and let's get out of here."

"Where's your curiosity?"

"That's what killed the cat."

"I hate cats."

Jerry sighed. "I was afraid of that."

16

"Nick, you're insane—you've completely lost your mind." Jerry pulled back the corner of a plastic tarp that covered the bottom of the boat, revealing two black body bags resting side by side.

"Put that back," Nick said. "It'll be dark in another few minutes—then we'll go."

"What if somebody sees us?"

"So what if they do?"

"You heard what LaTourneau said—there's a curfew now."

"What are they going to do, arrest us? We've got identification, Jerry. If anybody stops us, we'll just tell them who we are. We've got nothing to hide."

"What about two dead bodies?"

"We're with DMORT. That's what we do—we collect bodies."

"That's not what we're supposed to do."

"They won't know that. Relax, will you?"

"I don't get you," Jerry said. "Denny told you not to collect bodies; the DEA told you not to collect bodies. What does it take to get through to you?"

"It just doesn't make sense," Nick said. "Denny told me not to collect bodies because it presents the wrong image—that we care more about the dead than we do the living."

"Well, don't you?"

"Give me a break, Jerry. Did you ever read the sign over the door at DMORT? '*Mortui vivis praecipiant,*' it says—'Let the dead teach the living.' How are the dead supposed to teach the living if we won't let them talk?"

"Denny had his reasons," Jerry said.

"And I found out what the reasons were when I talked to the DEA—they're the ones calling the shots here. Denny was just following orders."

"Now there's a concept," Jerry said. "Maybe you should try it some time."

"I am following orders—in a way."

"How do you figure that?"

"The DEA knows that some of these people were murdered; they said that recovering bodies would make their identities public and tip off the people who killed them. Okay, we'll just collect them ourselves; that way, the guilty parties will never know."

"Do you actually expect me to buy that?"

"I was hoping you would. That's the best I've got."

"Tell me the truth: Are you doing this so the bad guys won't know, or so the DEA won't know?"

Nick paused. "I don't trust them, Jerry. It just doesn't make sense."

"Nick, it doesn't have to make sense."

"Look—have you ever seen the way an orb web spider spins a web? It begins with a series of long threads that radiate outward from the center, like the spokes of a wheel. Then the spider sits in the center of the web and keeps each leg on one of those radial threads. When an insect flies into the web, the threads carry the vibration to the spider, and he goes right to it."

"What does that have to do with—"

"Did you ever try throwing a stick or a leaf into a spider's web? Did you notice that the spider didn't move? That's because the spider can tell the difference between an insect and an inanimate object—they send back different vibrations across the web."

"You must have been one sick kid," Jerry said.

"They can sense the difference, Jerry. A leaf or a stick just doesn't feel right to the spider—the spider knows."

Jerry squinted at him. "So we're smuggling bodies at night because your spider-sense is tingling?"

Nick shrugged. "Something like that. I don't trust that Turlock guy from the DEA. I don't buy his explanation. I can't tell you why yet—it just doesn't feel right to me."

"And what are we supposed to do with these bodies?" Jerry asked. "Have you thought about that? You can't take them back to DMORT—they'll send us home for sure. And if you can't take them back to DMORT, what's the point in collecting them? No DPMU, no pathologists, no autopsies—"

"We don't need to do autopsies, Jerry. I'm just trying to cut our losses here; in a few more days this water will destroy all forensic evidence. I'm just trying to salvage what I can."

"What for?"

"I don't know yet. It depends on what I find."

Jerry nodded to the boy, who was sound asleep in the bottom of the boat. He was curled up on two pillows between Nick's feet and the feet of the two cadavers. "What about the boy? We're really bending some rules here, Nick—we have no right to keep involving him."

"You're right," Nick said. "I need to take care of that."

Their boat sat in the water between two houses about fifty yards from the Industrial Canal; directly ahead of them was the two-hundred-foot breach in the concrete floodwall. It was almost completely dark now; the setting sun left only a greenish-blue glow across the western horizon, silhouetting the city beyond.

"We'd better get going while we can still see," Jerry said.

"I was thinking the same thing." Nick started the engine and twisted the throttle, guiding the boat through the breach and out into the Industrial Canal. The canal at that point was a hundred yards across, and in the dark expanse of water Nick felt a sudden chill. He had no idea how deep the water was; there were no comforting rooftops to reassure him that land was just a few feet below. He turned around and looked; with no setting sun behind it, the Lower Nine was already one vast sea of blackness. Nick found himself wondering if this was really such a good idea, but he put the thought behind him; he knew from long experience that things always look less certain in the darkness than they do in the light of day.

J.T. sat up and rubbed his eyes. "Somethin' stinks," he said.

"I noticed that," Nick said. "I think it's Jerry."

"Where are we?"

"Not far from home," Nick said, trying to sound as confident as he could.

J.T. looked at the broken floodwall behind them and knew immediately where he was. "Never been out this far," he said.

That's because you're a smart guy, Nick thought. "I thought you might like a tour of the city."

"Cool."

Nick crossed the canal into the Upper Ninth Ward and followed the flooded streets west across the neighborhoods of Bywater and St. Claude. He tried to keep Claiborne Avenue in sight on his left, remembering from a map that it eventually turned south and followed Interstate 10 into the heart of the downtown.

The trip was less than five miles, but it took them much longer than it would have by car. The boat could only motor along at a few knots, since Nick was hesitant to run the engine at top speed with its earsplitting whine.

"What if we bump into more looters?" Jerry said. "I'd hate to lose the boat at this time of day."

"Let 'em take it," Nick said. "How far do you think they'll go when they find out what we're carrying?"

Nick was astounded at how dark the city became once the sun finally set. He had taken for granted how much ambient light a neighborhood creates: the street signs, the headlights, the soft glow from kitchens and living room windows—even the faint glow of cell phones or the tips of cigarettes. Each tiny point of light was a reminder of life—but there was no light here. There was at least a partial moon, but even its light seemed to be swallowed up by the darkness. Details were impossible to distinguish; rooftops and billboards rose silently from the water and took on ominous forms.

The water never seemed to end—that was the amazing thing. They were able to travel by boat across an entire city, as if they were living in Venice instead of New Orleans. They were approaching the downtown now, and taller buildings began to loom up ahead—but the water surrounded them all. Nick found himself tipping his head from side to side, as if the entire scene might be a gigantic trompe l'oeil that would disappear if viewed from a different angle. Instead of light, there was darkness; instead of asphalt and concrete, there was water; instead of front doors and awnings, there were buildings that appeared to begin at their second floors.

"Wow," J.T. said, and it was the only word spoken for several minutes.

Nick caught a glimpse of the Superdome half a mile ahead; its damaged roof looked like a half-peeled orange in the moonlight. He chose a random street and turned left, following it east toward the Mississippi. He knew that the ground would eventually rise as they approached the river, the result of centuries of annual floods that had built up the banks into natural earthen levees. Sure enough, several blocks later, the roadway emerged from the water.

Nick stopped the engine and rocked the motor into the boat. He let the boat cruise forward until they heard a scraping sound against the hull; then Jerry jumped out into ankle-deep water and dragged the boat up onto the dry pavement.

J.T. turned and looked at Nick. "What are we doin'?"

"You're getting out here," Nick said.

"What? Why?"

"Jerry and I have to work tonight."

"We work together," the boy said.

"Not tonight. We can't take you with us."

"How come?"

"It's for your own good," Jerry said. "It's too dangerous."

"I don't care 'bout that."

"I know you don't," Nick said, "but I do. I'm taking you to an evacuation center—I want you to spend the night there."

"The Superdome?"

"No, not the Superdome—they've already got too many people there. It's the Convention Center—do you know where it is?"

J.T. nodded.

"Well, I talked to a FEMA guy this morning. He told me there are only a couple thousand people at the Convention Center. They should have food and water there, plus a place for you to sleep."

"What about my father?" the boy grumbled. "You promised."

"I haven't forgotten," Nick said. "Who knows? There's a chance he's at the Convention Center—keep an eye out for him while you're there."

"What about tomorrow?"

"I want you to wait for me at the Convention Center. Hey, you might know some people there. Ask around about your dad; find some friends—have fun."

The words sounded stupid and empty, but Nick was trying to leave the boy on an upbeat note. It didn't work; the boy turned without a word and started up the road toward the river.

"Wait a minute," Nick said. "I'll walk with you."

"Don't need no babysitter."

Nick and Jerry watched him until he reached the end of the street and disappeared around the corner.

"You think he'll be okay?" Jerry asked.

"He'll be fine—he's halfway there already."

"I hope the place is decent."

"It was either two thousand at the Convention Center or thirty thousand at the Superdome—it's the best we could do. He'll be okay, Jerry—he's a tough kid."

"Do you plan to go back for him? Or are we just dumping him off?"

Nick rolled his eyes. "What do you want, anyway? You didn't want to bring him along in the first place—you said we were using him. Tonight you said we have no right to keep involving him—and now you're complaining that we're dumping him off."

"You made the kid a promise. You made me a promise too."

"Why does everybody keep reminding me I made a promise?"

"What do you expect, Nick? You don't follow orders; do you keep promises?"

"I keep promises," Nick said. "That's different. I want to help the kid, Jerry; I just don't want to put him in harm's way. And I'll help him—I just don't know when. Now, are we going to talk all night or are we going to do this?"

They shoved off in the boat again and followed Canal Street west; when they were a few blocks inland, Nick took out his GPS receiver and retrieved a set of coordinates stored in memory. Most of the street signs were underwater, and Nick knew almost nothing about the city; the only way to find a specific location was by satellite—especially at night.

A few minutes later, they emerged from an alley and into an open area of water that covered half a city block; in drier times it must have been a parking lot. At the far end of the parking lot stood an old, multistory building. Every window in it was dark.

"That's got to be it," Nick said. "Charity Hospital—the largest public hospital in the city. That giant building across the street—that must be Tulane University Hospital. Charity's the one we want; we'll draw less attention there."

"We're checking in to a hospital?"

"Sort of. Grab your oar—we'd better row from here."

They brought the boat up to the back of the building. The water had completely inundated the first floor and covered part of the second. The glass windows were shattered in several places, either from the pressure of the water forcing its way in or from floating debris inside.

They heard gunshots and looked around.

"What do you suppose that is?" Jerry asked.

"Maybe more looters," Nick said. "Maybe some cops shooting out display cases. Either way, it works to our advantage—nobody will be listening for us."

Nick took out his flashlight and shone the beam through a shattered opening. It was an office; the water came almost to the top of the desk but stopped short, leaving the desktop still neatly arranged.

"Move down to the next one," Nick said.

The next window opened into a small common area, followed by a records room with row after row of color-coded file drawers.

"This is all administrative," Nick said. "Keep going."

Several windows later, their flashlights illuminated a wide-open laboratory area with work-height counters lining the walls and one large table in the center. The window was almost completely missing, with only occasional shards of glass protruding from the top edges; the counters were almost bare.

"Looters," Nick said. "Most of the expensive equipment is missing."

"Maybe the hospital took it upstairs before the flood," Jerry said.

"Look at the glass—it's completely broken out. Somebody didn't want to get cut climbing through the window; he was probably in and out of here several times. At least we should have some privacy; there's nothing much left to take. Grab the top of the window—watch the glass."

They slid the boat through the window and into the room; there was just enough space before the center table. Nick swung his legs over the side of the boat and hopped out into the waist-deep water. He reached back into the boat and dragged the tarp off the two black body bags.

"C'mon," he said to Jerry. "Help me unload."

17

"Find me some containers," Nick said. "Forget the drawers—they're all flooded. Check the cabinets above the counters."

"What kind of containers?" Jerry asked.

"Any kind, the smaller the better—glass, plastic, forget the lids. See if you can find any coffee filters—you might have to go across the hall and see if there's some kind of break room or something. If there's a fridge, open it up—bring me any leftovers you find."

"There's no electricity. It'll all be rotten."

"I need some rubber bands too. And hurry back with that flashlight—we'll need both of them to do this. I'll meet you back here in ten minutes."

While Jerry scrounged for the items in the flooded lab, Nick waded out into the hall. In the doorway he stopped and looked back. The scene was utterly surreal: a medical laboratory half filled with water and a fishing boat floating in the center. Beyond the boat was a window with no glass; outside the window was an endless black lake. Nick shook his head; it was like a still photograph from some bizarre dream.

Even though there were no lights, the room was not completely dark. There was a faint reflection of moonlight that shimmered on the ceiling and walls. But in the windowless hallway there was no light at all except for the narrow beam from Nick's flashlight; it was like wading through a cave—or a sewer.

He found the offices they had passed by in the boat. He pulled out one of the desk drawers and held it up to allow the water to drain out, then dumped its contents onto the desk and found an ink pad. He took a tablet of white paper and two pens, then headed back for the lab again.

While Jerry stood over him with both flashlights, Nick pulled the long zippers on each of the body bags and folded back the flaps.

"What are you going to do?" Jerry asked.

"The same thing DMORT does—find out who they are. Let's see if we can get prints. We'll do him first—he should be the easiest."

The two bodies appeared very different; one was in a much less advanced stage of decay and was largely intact, except for the emaciating effects of a large maggot mass in the abdomen. Nick started with this one; he carefully turned the left hand palm-down and placed the ink pad under the fingertips. He pressed each of them against the spongy black pad, then transferred the prints one at a time to the white paper. When he finished, he took one of the flashlights from Jerry and examined the prints closely.

"No good," he said. "The skin is too wrinkled. Find me a syringe."

Jerry rummaged through the cabinets again. "I don't see any."

"The looters probably took them," Nick said. "There's a Sharpsafe container on the wall—get me a used one. Watch the needles—they're contaminated."

Jerry broke open the red-and-white container and gingerly picked out an intact syringe.

"I don't suppose you noticed any saline," Nick said.

Jerry shook his head.

Nick stuck the syringe into the water at his waist and drew back the plunger; the barrel slowly filled with the dark liquid.

Jerry grimaced. "You're using *that*?"

"Won't matter to him; he's been floating in the stuff."

Nick held up the cadaver's index finger and slid the needle under the skin. He gently pushed the plunger and the wrinkled skin began to plump out again.

"That should do it," he said. "Let's try those prints again."

A few minutes later, they had a complete set of prints. Nick added a physical description of the victim: male, Caucasian, about six-foot-one, short brown hair. He checked for obvious identifying marks: He found a gold crown on one upper incisor and a faded tattoo that circumscribed the left arm just above the bicep.

"Okay, let's get prints from the other guy—if we still can."

The second body was in far worse condition. When Nick lifted the right forearm and tried to twist the hand palm-down, the skin sloughed off like a glove.

"Oops," Jerry said.

"Not a problem. Hold the ink pad, will you?"

Nick took the rubbery tissue and carefully pulled it over his own gloved hand, then rolled each fingertip over the ink pad and pressed it against the paper, just as he would with his own fingers.

"That's nifty," Jerry said.

"I always thought so."

The physical description of this body was limited to height and gender; the skin was too decayed to even show its original color, let alone tattoos or identifying marks.

"That'll have to do," Nick said. "Now for the bugs—grab some containers."

He returned to the first body with his larval forceps and searched through the maggot mass inhabiting the abdominal cavity.

"Same kind as before?" Jerry asked.

"Some are, some aren't. This guy hasn't been dead as long as the one we found the other day."

"How do you know?"

Nick held up a maggot with his forceps. "This is a hairy maggot blowfly—the same kind we found before. The species is both predacious and cannibalistic—that means they'll eat anything they can find, including each other. Given enough time, they'll eliminate all the other species on the body. They're present here, but not in very large numbers; they haven't had time to take over yet."

Nick dropped the maggot into a plastic container and added several more. "We have to keep these separate," he said. "They'll eat the other guys."

He held up another maggot and studied it. It had a pale, cream color.

"That one looks different," Jerry said. "Not as dark."

"It's a *sarcophagid*—a flesh fly. You can tell by the spiracles on the posterior end. Unfortunately, there are 327 species of flesh flies in the U.S., and they're impossible to tell apart while they're still larvae. We won't know for sure until we rear them."

"Rear them?"

"Raise them to adults. What did you think we were collecting them for?"

Jerry shrugged. "I've learned not to ask you a lot of questions."

Nick dropped the maggot into a second container.

"There are *calliphorids* too," he said. "Those are the blowflies. We've probably got green bottles, oriental latrine flies, and secondary screwworms—we'll have to rear a cross section and see what we find."

By the time he finished he had eight containers, each containing a small collection of wriggling larvae about half an inch in length.

He looked at Jerry. "Now—did you find a fridge?"

"Yeah. Man, did that thing stink."

"Worse than yours?"

"Not even close."

"Show me what you found," Nick said.

Jerry slid a pile of plastic bags and crumpled brown sacks across the counter. Nick began to open the sacks and dump the contents onto the counter; he nodded for Jerry to do the same.

"Find me some meat," he said. "Take it off the sandwiches if you have to."

He peeled back the translucent blue lid from a square plastic storage container; inside was a slab of meat loaf dotted with bristling tufts of green and white mold.

"Dinner is served," he said. "Talk about your meals ready to eat."

Jerry sneered at the moldy slab. "That is the grossest thing I've seen all day."

"Some would find that ironic." Nick crumbled the meat loaf into smaller pieces and dropped a chunk into each of the containers.

"They'll eat that stuff?"

"*Sarcophagid* means 'corpse-eating.' I don't think they'll mind a few leftovers."

Now he took a coffee filter and placed it over the top of each container, securing it in place with a rubber band.

"What's that for?" Jerry asked.

"They have to breathe, just like you do."

When the containers were all prepared, Nick turned his attention to the second cadaver. He bent over and examined it carefully, moving down the body from head to foot. He found several smaller maggot infestations along the way.

"He was a refloat, all right," Nick said.

"How do you know?"

"The maggots are all dead. That means the body was on the surface long enough for flies to find it and colonize it, but then the body submerged again. The maggots must have drowned. These are all terrestrial species; they can't live underwater any more than we can. This man's been dead for quite a while."

"You can tell that just by looking at him," Jerry said.

"Yeah. I was hoping we could tell a little more."

Nick began to carefully pull back the creases in the remaining clothing and look inside the folds.

"Bingo," he said. "That's what I was looking for."

"What is it?"

"*Trichoptera*—a caddis fly larva, just like the one we found the other day. Check the body bag—see if you can find any more."

"Why the body bag?"

"Maggots hang on to a body even when it's moved, but aquatic insects tend to let go the minute they sense motion. If there are any more, we'll probably find them in the bag."

Jerry pointed to a tiny tubular object. "Is this one?"

Nick looked. "That's it—find me some more."

"It looks sort of like a pecan roll."

"Leave it to you to think of food."

"What's all that junk stuck on the outside of it?"

"Gravel, sand, wood—anything the caddis fly finds on the bottom."

"The bottom of what?"

"The lake, or stream, or pond. See, the female caddis fly lays her eggs on water; the eggs hatch into larvae and sink to the bottom. The larvae make silk—they have a modified salivary gland that produces it. They use the silk to build a protective case around themselves, and they glue on little bits of whatever they can find to act like armor plating. That's why it looks like a pecan roll—that's its case."

Within minutes they had found a dozen more.

"How does the larva find the body underwater?" Jerry asked.

"It doesn't. It just sinks straight down—or drifts sideways if there's a current. When it finally hits bottom it just grabs on to whatever happens to be there—including a body. It's purely random."

Nick opened his equipment bag again and took out one of the small glass vials of preservative. He opened it and began to drop the caddis-fly larvae in one by one. "There," he said. "That should be enough."

"Want some containers?" Jerry asked.

"Wouldn't do us any good," Nick said. "They're already dead. They're aquatic—they have to be kept in water."

"Too bad."

"It doesn't matter—they wouldn't have told us much anyway. Forensic entomology is based on the life cycles of terrestrial insects—mostly blowflies and flesh flies. We've studied hundreds of species; we've timed each stage of their development—that's why we can use them to determine time of death. All we have to know is the species, the local temperature, and the exact time the maggot develops into an adult fly; from there we can count backward and determine when the eggs were laid on the body—which is usually very close to the time of death."

"That's why you put all those maggots in containers."

"'Maggot motels,' we call them. Once the maggots mature, we'll know what species they are—and we should be able to calculate the victim's time of death. The problem is, very few aquatic insects have been studied; only 3 percent of all insect species are aquatic, and some of them have twenty different stages of development. We just don't know enough about them to use them to determine an accurate postmortem interval."

Nick looked around the lab. "Well, I think that's all we can do for tonight."

"For tonight? You're thinking of coming back here again?"

"Of course—we have to check on the maggots."

"Nick, we can't keep coming back here."

"Why not? This place is perfect: The whole floor is abandoned, all the lights are out—we've got the whole place to ourselves. It's even got a drive-thru window."

"What about the bodies?"

"When we're sure we're done with them, we'll put them back where we found them. Until then, we'll leave them here. It's a hospital, isn't it?"

"Nick—what's the point of all this? Suppose you are able to figure out a time of death for that guy—then what? You can't tell DMORT what you've been doing."

"I don't know yet," Nick said. "All I'm doing is saving forensic evidence before it gets destroyed; I'm not sure what happens next."

"And what about the fingerprints? How are we supposed to process them? DMORT sure won't do it for us."

"I've thought about that one," Nick said, "and I think I might know a way."

18

Beth opened her eyes and looked at the clock. It was 3:00 a.m. For the last hour she had lain perfectly still in her cot, hoping that her body might convince her mind to follow—but it was no use. There were nights when her mind just refused to remain shut down, like a trick birthday candle that constantly reignites. Sometime during the night her dreams gave way to conscious thought, like a bubble rising up from a dark pool. Once that happened, she knew that sleep was over for the night—regardless of the clock.

She sat up in her cot and used her middle fingers to wipe the sleep from the corners of her eyes. She brushed her hair back tight and secured it behind her head with an elastic band—except for the one rebellious strand that always refused to be corralled and hung like a comma over her right eye. She pulled on a pair of powder-blue scrubs, gathered a stack of case files from the floor beside her cot, and tiptoed out of the makeshift dormitory.

She headed for the cafeteria, which was nothing more than a handful of folding tables and chairs—but at least it was quiet and brightly lit. She took a cup of coffee to cement her decision to forgo any further attempt at sleep and turned her attention to the case file folders.

From a psychiatrist's perspective, the psychological problems during a DMORT deployment were fairly predictable and mundane: sleep disorders, stress-related issues, and separation anxieties caused by leaving loved ones on short notice—things that could usually be resolved just by managing medications or lending a listening ear. There were always boundary issues too: the need to help dedicated

DMORT employees maintain a healthy distance from the suffering of those they served—to fulfill their duty without taking on their pain. That line was never easy to draw, but it was an essential one if you wanted to keep your sanity. Compassionate people pay a price for caring, and Beth's job was to make sure the price wasn't more than any individual could afford to pay.

Some of the problems weren't caused by DMORT at all; they were brought to DMORT by the people who volunteered to work there. Those were the most serious problems—and, for Beth, the most interesting problems too.

She slid the stack of file folders in front of her. There were eight or ten folders in the pile, but she knew that only the top one could hold her attention at three o'clock in the morning. The label read: POLCHAK, DR. NICHOLAS. She opened it and had just begun to read when, as if on cue, Nick walked through the doorway and swung his equipment bag onto an empty table.

She shut the file folder and looked up. "Well, hello. Are you just getting in?"

"I needed the overtime," Nick said. "I'm saving up for a bigger boat."

She glanced at her watch.

Nick poured himself a cup of coffee. "I know what time it is, Mother. I told you not to wait up."

"Can you sit down for a minute?"

"Is that an official request?"

"It's a friendly request. Why can't you take it that way?"

"Because it doesn't sound friendly." He hesitated, then pulled up a chair across from her and sat down.

"How are you doing, Nick?"

"Look—if it's a friendly request, then let's have friendly conversation. No psychiatric questions, okay? No compassionate looks, no understanding nods."

"Somebody's in a good mood."

"I haven't had my coffee yet." He took a sip. "There. I love you."

"It's three o'clock in the morning—"

"—and only seriously deranged people are still up. So what's your excuse?"

"I was about to say, 'Are you planning to get any sleep?'"

"There's not much point—I have to be up at six."

"Why did you bother to come back?"

"Three blessed hours of air-conditioning—and the pleasure of your company."

"That's hard to believe."

"I like air-conditioning."

"There was a time when you did enjoy my company—remember?"

Nick didn't reply.

"I thought you wanted friendly conversation."

"Men and women have different concepts of 'friendly.' I was hoping for man-friendly."

"As in cold, detached, and superficial."

"There you go."

"I liked that boy you brought in the other night. He was very bright."

"Because he thought you were pretty?"

"He seems to think highly of you. When I asked him to describe his father, he said, 'He's like Nick.' That's quite a compliment."

"His father could be in prison."

"Stop deflecting everything with humor. Accept the compliment."

"J.T.'s a good kid. Have you found out anything from the Department of Social Services?"

"I think they've shut down along with the rest of the city. I called and left a message; I'm not sure when I'll hear back."

"Let me know, will you? I told the kid I'd help him."

She paused. "Where is he now?"

"I took him to an evacuation center. Why?"

"I thought you might still have him with you; I thought you might try to sneak him into your trailer. It's the sort of thing you'd do."

"That's against the rules."

"When did you start following rules?"

"I'm a big rule-keeper. For example, rule number one: Be careful what you say to a psychiatrist."

"I thought we were speaking as friends."

"Come off it, Beth—we're not friends. A friend doesn't psychoanalyze you; a friend doesn't keep a list of all your neuroses, like the one you've got in that folder there in front of you. May I?"

Before she could protest, he slid the file folder across the table and opened it. He began to scan the neatly typed pages of performance reviews and exit interviews and the numerous handwritten notations that filled the margins.

He glanced up. "Does everybody in DMORT merit such careful scrutiny?"

"You're not like everybody in DMORT."

"'Altruism,'" he read. "Sounds like a good quality to me."

"In your case, it's a form of sublimation—channeling your negative emotions into socially acceptable behaviors. You're driven by principle, but at times you become fixated on that principle. It's all you see; you shut everything else out—friends, coworkers, even other principles."

"That's called *focus*," Nick said.

"There's a fine line between focus and fixation. It's a matter of flexibility."

"I'll have to do more stretching. What's this one—'depersonalization'?"

"It means you've been hurt so many times that you've formed an emotional callus to protect you from contact with the rest of the world. Nobody can hurt you because nobody gets close—you won't let them."

"This one sounds great: 'dissociation.'"

"That means you deal with your differences by telling yourself that you're not like other people. You are different from other people, Nick—you're brilliant, and you're analytical, and you're fascinated by things that most people can't even bear to look at. How do you explain someone who's so unlike other human beings? You do it by telling yourself that you're not human. You think of yourself as a bug."

"I never should have told you that."

"I'm glad you did. It helped me understand a lot about you."

Nick scanned another page. "Now, here's a term even a layman can understand: 'savior complex.' Thanks a lot."

"Don't take it personally," Beth said. "That one's more common than you think, especially around here. It's the belief that everything depends on you—that if you quit, everything will fall apart. You can't afford to stop, so you never do. It's what happens to responsible people when they step across the line."

"What line?"

"Every good thing has a line, Nick; you cross the line and the good thing turns bad. Focus becomes fixation; distance becomes depersonalization; responsibility becomes a savior complex. You think I'm keeping a list of your bad qualities, but I'm not. I think you have some remarkable qualities; I just think you've crossed a few lines."

Nick closed the file and slid it back. "Friends don't write performance reviews that make their friends miss DMORT deployments," he said.

"I did that for your own good."

Nick cocked his head and looked at her. "I was always told that friendship is a two-way street."

"What do you mean?"

"You've got a file on me; I should have a file on you. I could, you know—like you said, I used to 'enjoy your company.'"

She blinked. "And what would my file say?"

"It would contain a lot of technical terms," Nick said.

"Such as?"

"'Anal' comes to mind—I believe that's a good Freudian term."

"Meaning?"

"Meaning your ponytail's too tight. You overanalyze everything; you see *lines* everywhere; you see yourself as a kind of mental health crossing guard, standing on one side of the line and holding everybody else back. You get a feeling of superiority by figuring out how everybody else works."

"Fair enough," she said. "What else?"

"*Neurotic.*"

"Neurotic? I am not."

"I'm sorry, I'm a little new at this 'friendship' thing—perhaps 'phobic' is the more accurate term. One example comes to mind: You're afraid of mice."

"That's a common dislike."

"But with you it's more than a dislike—with you it's a full-blown phobia. Mice, rats, gerbils—anything with a tail. It's the tail that really gets you, isn't it? Let me ask you something: When you got out of bed this morning, when you reached down for your shoes—did you find something stuffed into them? Something you put there the night before? A pair of socks, maybe—and not so the socks would be ready to slip right on, but to keep little rodents from inhabiting your shoes at night."

"Okay," she said. "I get the point."

"You can feel them, can't you? You slide your foot into your shoe—what's this? There's something there—you can feel the fur wriggling against your toes."

"Nick, shut up."

"I've read that rats often use socks for nesting material."

"Nick—*shut up.*"

"There's one more term I'd include in your file," Nick said. "'Snob.'"

"How am I a snob?"

"You think you're better than other people. You think you're too good to struggle with the same ordinary neuroses that everybody else does. You know what really bothers you about your fear of mice? *Girls are afraid of mice*—it's an old stereotype, and you fit right into it. That's the thought that really eats your lunch—you're a *girl.*"

She glared at him. "Now you're just being insulting."

Nick shrugged. "I did it for your own good."

She took the file folder and buried it in the middle of the pile. "You're wrong," she said. "Friends do psychoanalyze each other. Maybe they don't use technical terms, and maybe they don't make written reports, but they look into each other's lives and they try to see if anything's wrong. That's what friends do, Nick—a good friendship is like therapy."

"I don't need therapy," he said. "What I need right now is a *real* friend."

She paused. "What does that mean?"

Nick leaned back to the table behind him and opened his equipment bag; he pulled out a tablet of white paper and handed it to her.

She looked at it. The first two sheets were smeared with black fingerprints and hand-scrawled notations. They looked like something a child had made.

"What is this?"

"Fingerprints and physical descriptions from two bodies I found yesterday."

"Nick."

"Hey, I was only doing what they told me to do."

"That's not what I hear. Denny briefed me after your conversation with the two DEA agents."

Nick stopped. "*Two* DEA agents?"

"Special Agents Turlock and Detwiler. It was just last night—don't tell me you forgot already."

"I spoke with Turlock; I never met any Detwiler."

"Denny says you were supposed to locate bodies, and that's all."

"That's not true. Turlock told me to locate bodies *and see what I could learn*—that's what I did."

"How did you take their fingerprints while they were floating in water?"

"*Focus*," Nick said. "It's one of my better qualities."

"So what do you want from me?"

"A *friend* would run them through the system for me to see if we can get an ID."

"If you're only doing what they told you to do, why can't you do this yourself?"

"A friend wouldn't ask me that—not yet, anyway."

She closed her eyes and shook her head.

"It's no big deal," Nick said. "You work with the Family Assistance Center; this should be right up your alley—you're helping me search for two lost men."

"And where am I supposed to tell them I got these prints?"

"Tell them some woman gave them to you; tell them she's looking for her cousins. Tell them you know the physical descriptions are vague, but that's all she could remember."

"In other words, you want me to lie."

"I want you to try out your seldom-used powers of creativity. C'mon, Beth, let down that ponytail for once. Stick a toe over the line—who knows, you might like it over here with the rest of us."

"You have to promise me something first," she said.

"What's going on? Everybody wants promises."

"You have to promise me that you're not doing anything wrong."

He leaned across the table to her. "Believe me—I'm doing the right thing."

She considered for a long time before answering. "All right, I'll do it—but I want you to recognize something: A psychiatrist would never do this for you; this is something only a friend would do."

"Thank you," Nick said. "And while we're in this spirit of friendship, I have one more favor to ask." He took out the vial of caddis-fly larvae and set it on the table.

She picked it up. "What is this?"

"It would take a lot explaining, and you'd probably ask me more questions and want me to make more promises. This favor is even easier, and there's no risk for you whatsoever—even a psychiatrist would do it. Tomorrow, when your shift is over, I want you to take this to a friend of mine at LSU—it's only fifteen minutes from here. I'll give you the name and the office address."

"What do you want me to do?"

"I'll call ahead and explain everything. All you have to do is show up—with this."

She looked at the vial again. "I don't suppose you'd care to tell me how you got this."

"It's late," he said. "You should get some sleep."

He got up from his chair and swung his equipment bag over one shoulder.

"Nick," she said.

"Yes?"

"Mice don't really use socks for nesting material, do they?"

He winked. "Good night. Sleep tight. Don't let the bedbugs bite."

19

He lay spread-eagled on the bed, staring at the palmetto bug on the ceiling directly above his head. Why didn't it move? Was it dead? He had been watching it for almost an hour now, waiting for one of the bristly legs to budge. He never took his eyes away; he refused to even blink, willing his eyes to remain open even when tears gathered in little pools and burned down the sides of his face.

With the tips of his fingers he could just reach both sides of the king-sized bed. He grabbed the edges and pulled, flexing the mattress slightly. He wondered: If he pulled hard enough, could he wrap it around him? There was only a bottom sheet on the bed, and it hadn't been changed in weeks. It didn't matter; he was the only one who slept on the bed anyway, and he didn't really sleep—that had stopped weeks ago.

He had lost the ability to reach a state of sleep; he was like a man in a dark cellar feeling along the wall for a light switch—some mental mechanism that would turn off all the pain and regret and bring on welcome oblivion. But he could find no switch; the walls were bare. Even when he did occasionally slip into unconsciousness, he would suddenly jerk upright like a dozing man who had slipped beneath the water of a bath. At first he could sleep only a few fitful hours each night; later, it was only an hour or two; now he couldn't even close his eyes. He felt like a starving child standing at the back door of a bakery night after night, hoping that the door would open and some crumb would be thrown to him—but it never happened.

He didn't even undress anymore—there was no point. He knew that sleep was gone forever; he wasn't sure why he came to bed at all. It was a sort of penance—a ritual he had to perform each night to remind himself of what he had become: He was the undead, doomed to lie in darkness while eternally awake.

He rolled his head to the right and looked at the empty closet. He wondered where she was tonight. He wondered if she could sleep. He wondered if she had a new husband now, with a new daughter who was still alive. He wondered if she had forgotten all about her, and the thought made his eyes begin to burn.

He had not forgotten. He would never forget. And he would never rest until he had made things right.

He rolled to his feet and stood on the bed. With the butt of his palm he crushed the palmetto bug against the ceiling, then hopped down onto the floor. For an instant he thought he felt rested—but the feeling quickly passed. He no longer felt rested; he no longer felt tired either. He felt—*electric*, as though he were a machine that could run as long as it remained plugged in. It would run as long as it needed to run. Who knows—it might even run forever.

He crossed the hall and entered a second bedroom—her bedroom. The room felt different the moment he entered it; this room wasn't empty like the other one was. This room was still full—full of *her*. The closets were still lined with dresses and shoes, and the chest of drawers was still stacked with neat little piles of cotton and silk. There were still photographs on the desk, though they now rested in a thick layer of dust; there was even a purple-and-gold LSU pennant that hung above the bed. The room was still full because she never really left; she didn't pack her things and decide to run away like his wife did—she would never have done that. She was gone only because she was *taken* away—taken away from him.

He stretched out on her bed, being careful not to wrinkle the comforter or disturb the throw pillows at the head. He looked up at the ceiling; it was pure and white. He closed his eyes for a moment, but he knew that even here he would not sleep. He didn't want to sleep; he wanted to feel her presence, which was never far away—but here it was so very real.

Speak to me, sweetheart—speak to me.

Silence.

He got up from the bed and carefully smoothed the comforter, erasing any sign of his intrusion. He crossed the hall into the bathroom—her bathroom. He switched on the light and found the medicine cabinet open wide; the shelves were empty, except for one small orange plastic bottle on the center shelf. He took out the bottle and opened it; he shook two pills into the palm of his hand. He tossed the pills into the back of his throat and swallowed quickly because the pills had no coating on them and they were bitter. He bent down and took a drink directly from the tap.

He set the bottle back on the shelf again and closed the cabinet door; when he did, he found a message written in lipstick on the glass. "Daddy," it said at the top, and under that simple greeting was the name and address of a man.

At the bottom of the mirror a closing comment had been added. It read: "He was one of them too."

Thank you, sweetheart. Thank you for speaking to me.

20

Friday, September 2

Nick waded out into the water at the end of St. Claude Avenue. The water came almost to his chest before he reached the old magnolia tree and ducked under its branches. He found the boat where he had left it the night before, still chained to the trunk of the tree. He removed the chain and tossed it into the bottom of the boat; when he did, J.T. sat up and rubbed his eyes.

"Where you been?" he asked.

"J.T.—what are you doing in there?"

"Sleepin'."

"I can see that. How long have you been here?"

He shrugged. "All night."

"I dropped you off at the Convention Center."

"You dropped me on the street."

"You know what I mean—you were supposed to go to the Convention Center and wait for me there."

"Didn't like that place."

Nick looked in the boat; it was empty except for two oars and a couple of old bench pillows. "You like this better?"

"It's okay."

"How did you get here?"

"I walked."

"You walked five miles?"

Nick tried to visualize the route the boy must have taken: He couldn't have backtracked the way they'd come—it was all underwater. He must have followed the levee along the Mississippi River, then headed north when he came to the Industrial Canal. But there were no roads and no lights, and there was no one to help him if he couldn't find the way. The more he thought about it, the angrier he became—but he knew he had to let it go. After all, the boy did make it; no sense yelling at the kid because of his own unrealized fears.

"How did you get out to the boat?"

"I walked."

"The water's over your head. What did you do, use a snorkel?"

"I swam a little too."

Now something else occurred to Nick: If the boy had bypassed the Convention Center, he had also bypassed dinner and breakfast too. He rubbed the boy's head. "You hungry?"

"A little."

"C'mon, let's get you something to eat. Jerry's probably got a couple of MREs stashed away in his equipment bag."

He pulled the boat out from under the branches and guided it back to the boat ramp; Jerry was waiting for them there.

"Look what I found," Nick called out.

"What the—how did you get here?"

"We've been over all that," Nick said. "He's a little hungry—see what you can dig up, will you?"

A few minutes later, they were on their way back into the Lower Nine, with J.T. devouring his MRE directly from the bag.

Nick looked at him. "There's something we need to get straight," he said.

J.T. looked up.

"From now on, you need to follow orders."

"You don't."

"That's one of the benefits of being a grown-up: I don't have to do everything I tell you to do."

"How come?"

"Because I'm big, and you're small, and that's how the universe works.

Stop asking questions and eat. But next time I tell you to go somewhere, you go—understand?"

Beth pulled her car into the parking lot of the Life Sciences Building at LSU, a massive six-story structure in the center of campus that serves as home to five different fields of scientific endeavor—including the Department of Entomology. She took the stairs to the fifth floor, though the building had an elevator—a discipline she maintained to keep her calves looking trim. On the fifth floor she found the Louisiana State Arthropod Museum, which occupied four thousand square feet of collection and laboratory space.

"I'm here to see Dr. Benedetti," she announced to a work-study student serving as receptionist du jour. She handed the student her business card, an impressive-looking piece of vellum with raised lettering; the student rubbed his thumb over the letters as if they were braille.

A minute later a door opened, and an attractive young woman stepped out; she was holding the business card.

"Nice card," she said. "Mine has a *Coleoptera* on it."

Beth paused. "Dr. Benedetti?"

"That's right. Nick told me you'd be stopping by."

The woman looked to be about the same age as Beth, but she wore no makeup—which meant that she was probably five years younger. She was dressed plainly, in an LSU T-shirt and jeans, and she wore an open denim button-up with the sleeves rolled up to her elbows. Beth suddenly felt a bit self-conscious; the woman looked as good as she did, but with half the effort—which was always annoying.

"Nick was right about you," the woman said.

"Right about what?"

"He said you were pretty."

Beth blinked. "Did he say anything else?"

"He said you would ask, 'Did he say anything else?'"

She frowned. "I guess the joke's on me."

"If Nick's around, the joke is always on you. That's Nick for you."

"Yes. That's Nick."

"Your card says 'MD'—you're a doctor?"

"I'm a psychiatrist."

She let out a snort. "Then you should have a field day with Nick."

Beth paused. "It sounds like you know him pretty well."

"You don't have to know Nick very well to know he needs a shrink. Oops, sorry—hope you don't mind the term."

"I've heard it before."

"Did you meet Nick through DMORT?"

"That's right. How about you?"

"A couple of years ago the museum did a project at Great Smoky Mountains National Park in North Carolina. We were documenting beetle diversity in the park. Nick came over from NC State and helped out."

"Sounds like a party."

"A big camping trip is what it was. Ask him about the night my tent collapsed."

"I'll be sure to do that. So you're an entomologist too?"

"I'm a systematist—I identify and classify different species of insects. That's what the museum does: We're the principal repository for insects and related arthropods in Louisiana. We've got five hundred thousand specimens pinned and mounted here, mostly from around the Gulf Coast. If you can catch it, we can tell you what it is. Speaking of which: Nick said you've got something to show me."

She reached into her purse and took out the glass vial.

Dr. Benedetti held it up to the light.

"Nick thinks they might be caddis flies," Beth explained.

"He doesn't need me to tell him that—he's looking for something else."

"What?"

"Let's find out."

Beth followed Benedetti into a laboratory, where she opened the vial and removed several specimens. She carefully mounted each on a glass slide, then placed the first slide under a microscope and adjusted the focus.

"So how long have you known him?" she asked.

"Who?"

"Who do you think?"

"Oh, Nick—about ten years. We've been on several DMORT deployments together."

"Funny, he never mentioned you. How much do you know about caddis flies?"

"I'm a psychiatrist," she grumbled. "Four years of medical school plus three more for a psychiatric residency—at Stanford."

"Well, Doctor, take a look."

Beth stepped up to the microscope and peered through the eyepiece. She saw what looked like a piece of spaghetti rolled in bread crumbs—only they weren't bread crumbs. They were tiny bits of wood and sand and other debris.

"What you're looking at is a kind of protective case," she said. "The larva itself is inside. The female caddis fly lays her eggs on top of the water in a gelatinous blob; when the eggs hatch they sink to the bottom, and the larvae build these little cases to protect themselves. They also serve as ballast to help weight them down."

"I don't understand. Why are these important?"

"That's what Nick wants to know." She stepped in front of the microscope again and replaced the slide with a second specimen. "It's the same thing," she said. "This case is constructed of the same materials as the first one. That means they must have come from the same area; the question is, which area?"

"Can you determine that?"

"If we're lucky. The caddis-fly larva spins silk to make itself sticky; then it picks up anything it finds around it to construct its case—so the case is a sort of sampling of whatever occurs naturally in that area."

She used a probe to begin to pick apart the tiny particles comprising the case. "He's kind of attractive, isn't he?"

"Who?"

She glanced up from the microscope.

"Oh. I suppose he is—in a weird sort of way."

"You could say that about all men. I think it's his eyes—you have to see them without those glasses."

Beth thought for a moment; she had known Nick for ten years and had never seen him without his glasses. He was practically blind without them—his medical reports confirmed that. Beth wanted to ask, "How did you manage to see him without his glasses?" but she didn't—she didn't particularly care to hear the answer.

"This is cypress wood," Benedetti said. "There are slivers of it on each of the larvae."

"What does that mean?"

"Nick said he collected these cases in the city—in the Lower Ninth Ward. That's a densely populated area; I doubt you'd find a lot of cypress trees there."

"Where would you find them?"

"New Orleans is surrounded by cypress swamps. I'd say these cases probably came from there."

"How would they get into the city?"

She looked up. "I'm assuming Nick collected these from a body—I mean, that's what he does, right?"

"I'm sorry, but I'm not free to discuss that."

"Whatever. All Nick told me is that he collected these cases from an 'object' floating in ten feet of water in the Lower Ninth Ward. You can tell Nick that he may have found this 'object' there, but it didn't originate there."

"How do you know?"

"I see some sand particles, but they're the wrong kind; if these cases originated in the city, I should see construction-grade sand—the kind they use for roads and buildings. I see bits of seashell too. And frankly, I don't think all these larvae would have collected on a single object in ten feet of water. It's just too deep; the water would have to have been much shallower."

She studied the specimen again. "Well, what do you know? This may be Nick's lucky day after all."

"What is it?"

"If I'm not mistaken, it's a flake of copper. I can have it tested to make sure."

"What does that tell us?"

"The land around the city of New Orleans is sinking—the city itself is sinking about a third of an inch every year. That may not sound like a lot, but think about it: In a hundred years, that's over thirty inches. The reason it's sinking is because of the levees; for thousands of years the Mississippi used to flood every spring, and when it did it covered the floodplain with silt—that kept the land built up. But when people built the levees to control the flooding, they also caused the land to start sinking. The bayous are constantly rising, and areas that used to be workable land are now underwater—they've been taken over by the bayous. As I recall, there used to be a copper mine somewhere south of the city—I'll have to check with one of our geologists to make sure. If I'm right, we might be able to pin these caddis flies to a very specific area of cypress swamp."

"Then the body was moved," Beth said.

"What body? You mean the 'object.'"

"Oh. Right."

"Tell Nick I'll confirm all this by this afternoon—and tell him he got lucky this time."

"Nick tends to be lucky."

"Except in love—but hey," she said, wiggling her empty ring finger, "who is?"

It was a fifteen-minute drive back to St. Gabriel, following the interstate along the Mississippi. Her mind meandered in and out with the river; she kept thinking about Nick and what he might be up to this time. *This time*—the phrase brought back to mind a dozen past deployments together and a long string of strange and convoluted involvements. Each time, Nick seemed to get himself into trouble—not because of a flagrant violation of any regulation or law, but because of his dogged determination to finish the job no matter what the cost, and the cost was always high—sometimes higher than anyone wanted to pay.

The cost was high for Nick too. Once he had a goal in sight he became relentless, like a machine with no off switch. He stopped sleeping; he stopped eating; he began to exhibit erratic behaviors that bordered on the truly psychotic. She first became concerned when she heard Nick refer to human beings as "*your* species." She wondered if that expression was just a quirky affectation, or whether it was an indication of something deeper—perhaps a fragmentation of his personality due to stress.

He's attractive, isn't he? Dr. Benedetti's words kept buzzing in her face like an annoying gnat. She kept trying to focus on her professional relationship with Nick, but she found it difficult to do. They had never been anything more than colleagues, except for once—their third deployment. She still remembered the day; she remembered preparing her office for his arrival, placing their chairs a little closer together than usual but not admitting to herself why. She remembered sitting across from him, looking into those soft brown eyes floating like chestnuts behind his glasses; and she remembered the exact moment when he began to lean toward her—and then he kissed her, and she was surprised to learn that she was not surprised at all. To this very day, whenever Nick sat across from her or stood a little too close, she found herself tensing slightly—anticipating the moment when he might lean toward her again. Every time she felt that way her face grew hot and she hoped he would never notice—but not much got past Nick.

Their relationship lasted only a few days, and then Nick suddenly changed; he never mentioned their relationship again—as though it never happened. It left her feeling confused and frustrated. Most of the time, she wished it had never happened; sometimes she wished it would happen again. Now it was the elephant in the room, the thing from the past that was never really over, the words left unspoken between them that at times they could almost hear.

"It's his eyes," Benedetti had said. "You have to see them without those glasses." The words made her angry, and that made her angrier still. Just when she thought she was back in control again, something like this happened—and she felt like a stupid schoolgirl about to lose her seat on the bus. *You can have him,* she thought. *I'm done with bugs.*

Why had she ever let herself get involved with a patient? She told herself that they were only colleagues—that's what made it all right. But as a psychiatrist she should have known better. She had interviewed him for hours; she knew about his drivenness, and his authority issues, and his sense of alienation from the whole human race—but she let her heart go anyway. She should have known better, but at least she knew better now—or did she? Then what was she doing in Baton Rouge? Knowing Nick's past—knowing *their* past—why in the world would she even consider helping him now? She didn't have an answer—at least not one she was willing to admit.

At the DPMU she pulled up to the gate and flashed her credentials at the guard, who waved her past. She headed directly for her office and checked her phone messages; she found one from the Department of Social Services in Baton Rouge.

She dialed the number.

21

"I don't smell anything," the nurse said. "Stop complaining—you'd think you're the only patient in the hospital."

"You can't smell it from over there. Come over here, by the window."

The nurse walked to the window and drew a deep breath through her nose. "I don't smell anything," she said again.

But she did.

"I'm telling you, something's dead—and I want outta here."

"Just where do you think you'll go? You know all of Charity's surrounded by water, right up to the second floor. They said they'll come for us—now you just stay put."

"When? When will they come for us?"

"As soon as they can, that's when. You've been asking me that for three days."

"They're not coming, are they? That's what I'm smelling—people are dying."

She stepped closer to his bed. "You lower your voice now—the other patients will hear you. You know what's going on here, Mr. LaFourche; the whole city is flooded, and Charity Hospital is just one little part of it. There are five hundred people here at Charity, and a thousand more at Tulane across the street. They said they'll evacuate all of us, but it takes time."

"I hear gunshots at night."

"Did anybody shoot you?"

He didn't answer.

"Then hold your voice down. We don't have enough doctors, and we don't have enough nurses—we're having to make do. We're doing all right here; you'll be fine. I'll be back to look in on you as soon as I can."

"Somebody's not 'fine,'" he grumbled. "I can smell it."

The nurse worked her way down the impossibly crowded hallway; the corridors were jammed with beds and supplies that had been evacuated from the second floor. In twenty years she had never seen the hospital in this condition. The hospital's main power grid had shut down the night of the storm, automatically switching over to emergency generators—but the generators were only enough to maintain emergency lighting and life-support systems, not to power the enormous air-conditioning system. In the afternoons the temperature in the hospital was well over ninety degrees, adding an enormous burden to the weaker patients. Soon the water also overwhelmed the generators, throwing them into complete darkness—and worse, shutting down respirators and infusion pumps. Three patients had already died, and their bodies had to be deposited in a stairwell for later removal.

City officials had promised that they would be evacuated as soon as was humanly possible, but people were losing hope. It was true, what she told Mr. LaFourche—they were just one building in a whole sea of troubles, and there was no telling when rescuers would get around to them. It was still too dangerous for a full evacuation; just the other day, a nurse had tried to leave the hospital and was held up at gunpoint. No wonder no one was coming to help; in the city of New Orleans, it was just not a good time to get shot.

And even when the streets were safe again, where would Charity fall in the pecking order? Tulane would come first, she was sure of that. They had more people to evacuate—and besides, it was a private hospital. That's the way it always was; in this world, people who can't afford to pay just have to wait their turn.

But people were tired of waiting. They were running out of food, water, and medical supplies; infusion pumps were being operated by hand; patients were helping other patients; the scant handful of doctors and nurses were on their last legs; the oppressive heat was sapping them all.

And then there was the smell. With the windows open, when the wind blew the wrong way—

She passed a room and spotted a doctor making a notation on a patient's chart; she waved him out into the hallway.

"Have you smelled it yet?" she asked.

"Of course I have."

"I think it's coming up from below."

"So do I."

"Patients are starting to panic—they think other patients are dying."

"Tell them it's coming up from the morgue—the morgue's in the basement, and the coolers shut down when the power went off."

"Do you think that could be it?"

"I don't know—I don't think so. The smell's too strong. I thought it might be the bodies in the stairwell at first, but that's a sealed fire exit—that's why we put them there. It seems like it's coming from outside, but I can't see anything from the windows."

"I think it might be coming from the second floor," she said.

"There's nothing on the second floor—it's underwater."

"I'm telling you."

He had no reply.

"It's getting worse all the time," the nurse said. "I can't keep telling people to ignore it; we've got to take a look, and we've got to do it before it gets dark."

"I've got better things to do than track down bad smells," the doctor said. "Tell the patients it's coming up from the morgue; tell them whatever you want, but I've got to get back to work."

She shook her head as she watched him pick a zigzag path down the hall.

She turned and headed for the stairwell—the unoccupied one. She took the stairs down toward the second floor. At the first landing she stopped and looked; halfway down the stairway, the steps disappeared into brackish black liquid.

She shuddered, then waded down into the water.

She twisted the door handle and pulled; the door moved slowly and heavily, pushing a waist-deep wave of water ahead of it. She waded down the hallway, stopping at each doorway to look in and sniff. She found nothing—until she came to a large, empty laboratory with a shattered window.

She cupped her hand over her mouth and stared.

22

"Both bodies are in an advanced stage of decay," the doctor said.

"Yeah. I figured that out."

Special Agent Turlock waded into the empty laboratory and looked around the room. It was late afternoon, and the room was already deep in shadow. He saw a table in the center of the room with two black body bags lying side by side, and a shattered window beyond.

"We sent word as soon as we discovered them," the doctor said. "Our phones are still out; we had to shout a message to some National Guard people passing by in a boat. I know there's a lot going on right now, but we thought somebody ought to know."

"You did the right thing." Turlock stepped to the window and looked out; he could feel the glass crunching under his thick rubber boots. Why didn't the fools mention the window? He could have brought his boat directly around to the room.

"I'm a little surprised they sent the DEA," the doctor said.

"Yeah, well, everybody's pulling double duty right now."

"At first I thought the bodies might have come from our own morgue. I thought maybe somebody found them and put them in here to get them out of the water—but the body bags are made of some kind of mesh. They're not the kind we use here."

"They're for pulling bodies out of water," Turlock said.

"Well, they don't contain the smell very well."

"No, they wouldn't."

Turlock began to draw the long zipper on one of the bags.

"Are you sure you want to do that?"

"I'm sure." He opened the flaps and laid them aside, exposing the entire body. He found both hands covered in brown paper sacks rubber-banded at the wrists.

"What are the bags for?" the doctor asked.

"Beats me," Turlock said—but he knew exactly what they were for: It was a standard crime-scene technique to preserve forensic evidence from the fingers and nails. The sacks were wrinkled and spotted with grease; he looked across the room at a counter and saw a pile of sandwich bags and rotting fruit.

He moved around to the counter to take a closer look. He found a row of plastic containers of differing shapes and sizes; each one had a coffee filter stretched across its mouth. He lifted one container and shook it a little; he saw a handful of milky white maggots wriggling on a chunk of rotting meat. He checked a second container, then a third—they were all the same.

"What is all that?" the doctor asked.

"Nothing," Turlock said. "Just somebody's rotten lunch."

He heard the sound of the metal fire door opening at the end of the hall, followed by a heavy thump and a muttered curse; he turned to see his colleague standing in the doorway, shaking water from his dripping hands.

"There's junk all over the floor," the man said. "Can't see the stuff underwater."

Turlock glanced at the doctor. "Doc, this is an associate of mine—Special Agent John Detwiler of the DEA."

Detwiler ran a hand over his sandy red hair and nodded a quick greeting.

Turlock frowned at his partner. "Took you long enough."

"It's a long way by boat, Frank. I came as soon as you called."

"Called? Are cell phones working again?" the doctor asked.

"Satellite phone," Turlock said.

"Can we get one for the hospital?"

"We got ours in Dallas."

Turlock waited while his colleague made his own quick study of the room. Detwiler followed the same path that Turlock had taken: first the window, then the bodies, then the counter along the wall. Turlock handed his partner one of the plastic containers; Detwiler held it up to the afternoon light and peered inside.

He looked at Turlock and nodded.

"Who would do this?" the doctor asked. "Do you have any idea?"

Turlock took the doctor by the shoulder and turned him toward the door. "I wouldn't worry about it, Doc. The truth is, we've got bodies everywhere right now—on sidewalks, on rooftops, even floating in the streets. People pull them out of the water, maybe throw a blanket over them—they're just trying to help. That's probably what we've got here—just some good Samaritan trying to lend a hand. He saw the open window, and he probably figured, 'Why not? It's a hospital after all.' We'll figure it all out later—right now the important thing is to take these bodies off your hands."

"I'd appreciate that," the doctor said. "We've got patients on the floor above, and some of them are starting to panic."

"Don't worry, we'll take care of it."

He waited until the doctor reached the stairway, then turned and glared at his partner.

"It's Polchak, all right," Detwiler said sheepishly.

"You think so? You were supposed to be following this guy."

"I did—he must have done this after dark."

"So what? We're not working 9 to 5 here, John—we can't afford that right now. You should have followed him anyway."

"How could I, Frank? I have to keep my distance—otherwise he'll spot me."

Turlock ripped the coffee filter off one of the containers and flung the contents across the room.

Detwiler grimaced. "What is all this?"

"They're maggots from the bodies," Turlock said. "Polchak is a forensic entomologist. He knows how to read these things—that's what he does. Here, help me get rid of this stuff—toss it out the window."

He turned back to the body bags. He unzipped the second one and folded back the flaps; the stench was almost unbearable.

"Recognize them?" he asked.

Detwiler pressed one hand over his mouth and nose and squinted. "I can't tell anymore."

Turlock pointed to the faded tattoo that encircled the first man's arm.

"Crap," Detwiler muttered. "How did Polchak manage to find him?"

"That's what he *does*, John—that's what I keep trying to tell you. What about the other one?"

Detwiler looked; the condition of the body was even worse. "I can't tell if it's him or not. Maybe."

"Probably," Turlock said. "If Polchak pulled him out of the water, he must have had a reason."

"C'mon, Frank, you can't even recognize these guys—how much could Polchak really know?"

Turlock pulled the paper sack off one of the hands; he found ink stains on each of the fingertips.

Detwiler let out a groan.

Turlock took a minute to think. "Have you really been following this guy?"

"Every minute of the day—I swear it. I took pictures, too, just like you said."

"Is he working with anybody else?"

"He has a partner—another guy from DMORT. His name is Jerry Kibbee; he's a funeral director from somewhere in Indiana."

"Anybody else?"

"Just a boy."

"What boy?"

"Some black kid, maybe ten or twelve. He rides in the boat with them every day."

"Why?"

"I'm not sure."

"Did you get the boy's name?"

"Not yet."

"Get it."

"Why?"

"Because he's with Polchak every day, that's why. These are the people he talks to—whatever he knows, they might know. What about DMORT?"

"What about it?"

"Who does he associate with there? Who does he talk to? Who does he room with? Find out, John. Somebody's helping Polchak, and we need to know who it is."

"How do you know?"

"He took prints, didn't he? They won't do him any good unless somebody can run them through the system. He can't do it through regular channels; somebody's got to be helping him on the inside."

Detwiler gestured to the bodies. "What do I do with these two?"

"I'll tell you what you're going to do: You're going to bring your boat around to this window, and I'm going to help you load them in. Then you're going to take them and dump them someplace where Polchak won't find them again. After that, you're going to find Polchak—and you're going to put an end to this."

"That won't be easy, Frank. He's working the Lower Nine; there are boats all over the place now."

"He's made it easy for us; he's working nights now. A lot of bad things happen in this city at night."

"But it's almost dark now. I won't be able to find him until morning."

"Get back to St. Gabriel and wait for him there; he has to go back to DMORT eventually. When he does, follow him—and look for an opportunity."

"Kibbee too?"

"Kibbee too. No loose ends."

"What about the boy?"

"Did you hear what I said? *No loose ends.* Now get going."

Detwiler started for the doorway.

"And John," Turlock called after him.

"Yeah?"

"Get it right this time. If he works at night, you work at night. No excuses; get it done. I don't have to tell you what happens if this guy screws things up."

"I'll get the boat."

Turlock looked out the window; the sun was already beginning to set. He shook his head. "I knew this guy was going to be trouble."

23

Beth angled the spotlight up at the trees. The old bald cypresses surrounding the bayou were draped in Spanish moss that hung down over the water like a witch's fingers.

"Keep the light on the water," Nick said. "We're not sightseeing here."

"Sorry," she grumbled, directing the spotlight in front of the boat again.

Nick sat at the boat's tiller, using his GPS receiver to guide the boat down the narrow, winding channel. "Let's try not to run into anything, shall we? I had to put down a month's pay for the security deposit."

Beth looked down at the flimsy wooden hull. "What a bargain."

"Hey, there's a shortage of boats out here. We were lucky to find one at all."

"I thought you already had a boat."

"But no trailer. I couldn't exactly drag it behind your car."

They were several miles southeast of the city now, in a section of the Barataria Basin where civilization ended and solid ground gave way to marshy bogs overgrown with cordgrass, vines, and palmettos. Massive cypress stumps protruded from the water, blackened and chewed-off at the ends, their bulging knee roots spreading out around them like skirts. The water was coffee black but still looked clear—not like the muddy green water that filled the city of New Orleans.

There was a pole-mounted spotlight in the bow of the boat, attached to an old Autolite battery with a pair of alligator clips. Beth swung the spotlight from side to side, illuminating the area just ahead of the boat with an eerie blue-white light. She caught glimpses of snapping turtles silently slipping from logs; she saw something long and black drop from a tree limb into the water with a quiet splash.

"Nick—stay in the middle."

"I will if I can find it. You keep giving us the Woodland Creatures Tour."

A heavy mist lay across the water like strips of cotton batting. Beth shivered. "I'm cold. How can I be cold when it's almost ninety degrees?"

"It's the humidity," Nick said. "It has a chilling effect, like an evaporative cooler."

"I didn't think it would look so—dark."

"It's night. What did you expect?"

"I don't mean that kind of dark. I mean—you know—creepy."

"You thought it would look like *Pirates of the Caribbean*. Sorry, this is a real bayou."

"Why did we have to come out here at night?"

"You didn't give me any choice."

"Me?"

"I didn't get back to DMORT until after dark—that's when you told me what you found out at LSU. This is the first chance I had."

"We could have waited for daylight."

"Some people work during the day. We're not rich psychiatrists."

"Some people never stop working—that's how psychiatrists get rich."

"Stop complaining—you didn't have to come, you know."

"Nick, you *asked* me to come."

"What else could I do? Jerry wouldn't come—he wanted to sleep. I couldn't bring J.T. along—I had to leave him with Jerry. That only left you."

"Thanks," she said. "It's nice to be wanted."

"I can't follow the GPS and steer the boat and point the spotlight all at the same time. Women expect you to do everything." Nick looked at her. "So—why did you come?"

She twisted around and looked at him. "Because I pictured us driving down here in my climate-controlled Lexus and maybe taking a nice walk down some quiet country road."

"I like that Lexus."

She glared at him. "What if we run out of gas? What if this spotlight goes out? What if the batteries go dead in that GPS receiver and we can't find our way back?"

"Are you always so cheery? No wonder you're still single."

She slapped at her neck; the mosquitoes were having a field day with the exposed skin of her neck, wrists, and ankles. "What exactly are we looking for, anyway?"

"The caddis-fly cases contained bits of cypress wood and flakes of copper; there's only one area around New Orleans where you could find both in one place. If we can find that old copper mine, we'll know where that body came from—and probably the body I found the other day as well. It had caddis-fly cases on it, too, but I didn't take samples before I turned the body in. I'm betting both men were originally killed out here, and their bodies were hidden in the shallow water—that's how the caddis-fly larvae were able to collect on them. After the hurricane, somebody dredged them up and dumped them in the Lower Nine."

"Why would they do that?"

"To cover up the real cause of death."

"Who do you think did it?"

"I'm not sure yet. I'll let you know."

"How are we going to find a copper mine at this time of night? You can't see a thing out here."

"We don't have to see it; it's probably underwater anyway. It's a good thing they could give you the GPS coordinates at LSU."

Beth paused. "I met Dr. Benedetti today."

"So you said."

"I didn't know Dr. Benedetti was a woman."

"Really? I could tell the first time I met her."

"She said you met on a camping trip."

"Not at all; it was a legitimate nature study."

"She said her tent fell down."

"That was a nature study too."

She narrowed her eyes at him. "You know, I find it really annoying when you—"

"Be quiet."

"I beg your pardon? I have every right to—"

"Be quiet." Nick shoved a switch on the old outboard motor; it made one last cough before the low, chugging sound sputtered to a stop. Suddenly the bayou seemed deafening, as if every living thing for miles around was closing in on their boat.

"Listen," Nick said. "Do you hear anything?"

"What?"

"I keep thinking I hear another engine."

"Maybe it's just an echo."

"I don't think so. Kill the spotlight."

"What?"

"Turn off the light, Beth."

She twisted one of the clips from the battery terminal and the light went out. Beth blinked wide-eyed in the darkness; they were lost in an infinite sea of black. The boat was drifting with the water; they had no way to know how close they were coming to the shore on either side.

They waited.

"Why did we have to turn off the light?" she whispered.

"The only way someone could follow us is by our spotlight."

"You think someone is following us?"

"I don't know. I was listening for an engine to stop."

"Did you hear anything?"

"I'm not sure," Nick said. "The cicadas and tree frogs are drowning everything out. I can't tell if—"

Suddenly Nick fell silent again.

"What's wrong?"

"I was just thinking."

"What?"

"There's a piece of rope back here. I wonder how you would have reacted if I'd tossed it across your shoulder."

Beth grabbed the spotlight cable and shoved it back onto the battery post; she spun the spotlight around and shone it directly into Nick's eyes.

"Hey! What's the big idea?"

"Do you think this is funny?"

"I did until a second ago—now I'm blind."

"This is not one of your camping trips, Nick, and I'm not the woman in the tent next door. We're in the middle of a bayou at night, and I don't mind telling you *I'm scared*. There are snakes and crocodiles all around us, and you want to play practical jokes?"

"Alligators," Nick said.

"What?"

"This is North America. We have alligators here."

"I don't care! For once in your life, would you please try to have a little compassion? Just because you're comfortable with bugs and death and darkness, that doesn't mean everybody else is! Think about how normal people might feel!"

"You're normal?"

"Compared to you, *everybody* is normal!" She turned the spotlight forward again and left Nick sitting in the darkness. "What am I even doing out here?" she grumbled. "I must have been out of my mind."

"That's not the kind of thing you like to hear your psychiatrist say."

"When have I ever been *your* psychiatrist?"

"You're the only one I see."

"You only see me because you have to—and you never listen."

"I listen. I don't always agree, but I listen."

"Then listen to this: *You only slept three hours last night.*"

"So what? So did you."

"I tried to sleep, but I couldn't—did you even try? I took a nap during my break today—did you? And right now, I'm thinking about how good it would feel to be back in my bed again—even that lousy cot in the DMORT dormitory. What about you, Nick? Are you even thinking about getting some rest tonight? Or will this day just blend in with the next one, and the next one after that? This is how it always starts for you; this is the way you become self-destructive."

"Not this again," Nick groaned.

"Listen to me: A person who's been sleep-deprived for seventy-two hours is as susceptible to hallucinations as someone taking LSD is—any psychiatrist can tell you that. When you start telling me you're hearing engines and we're being followed, I don't know what to think."

"You think I'm hallucinating?"

"I don't know—but I do know you're headed in that direction. Admit it, Nick—there's only one reason we're sitting in the middle of this god-forsaken swamp in the middle of the night: You just couldn't wait to get out here."

"Maybe," Nick said. "But you need to admit something too: You wouldn't be here if you didn't think I was on to something."

"Is that why you think I'm here?"

He paused. "Why else?"

She shook her head and turned away. "I guess you're not as bright as I thought."

Nick allowed a full minute to go by before he said, "Can we go now?"

"What are you waiting for? Get me out of here."

"I'm waiting for my vision to return. I've got this supernova burned on the back of my retinas."

"Serves you right," she said.

It was another twenty minutes before they finally approached the coordinates supplied by the geologist from LSU.

"This should be the place," Nick said, "give or take a few meters."

"I don't see anything here," Beth said.

"Shine the spotlight on the shore. This is your chance to look at all the trees."

As they came around a slow bend, the channel widened slightly; Nick knew that it would undoubtedly widen more as the bayou opened up into the Gulf. On the right, the shore was still crowded with cypress, black gums, and buttonwoods right up to the water's edge—but on the left there was a wide, flat clearing covered only in low marsh grass. Thirty yards back from the water, Nick saw a long tin shack partially hidden behind a stand of water tupelos.

"That's what we're looking for," Nick said.

"How do you know?"

"It's the only thing out here. Let's take a look."

"Wait a minute—you want to get out of the boat?"

"Well, we can't see it from here."

"You never said anything about getting out in the middle of a swamp."

"You never said anything about an impromptu lecture on sleep deprivation, but you managed to come up with one. C'mon, loosen up—we're improvising here."

"I'm staying in the boat."

"Fine. I'll just pull up under these tree limbs. Is that just moss hanging down like that? It's so hard to tell—I could be hallucinating."

Five minutes later they were standing in front of the shed. Beth kept her arms wrapped around her shoulders and she rocked from foot to foot with a soft sucking sound, minimizing the time she spent in contact with the boggy soil.

Nick ran his flashlight over the corrugated metal panels. "It's not very old," he said.

"How can you tell?"

"There's hardly any rust; this galvanizing wouldn't hold up long out here." He raised the flashlight and looked at the joint between the walls and the roof; a two-inch gap had been left for ventilation. Along the edge of the roof he could see long licks of black soot. "There was a fire here."

They walked around to the end of the shack and found the doorway. The door itself was missing; he shone the flashlight at the slatted floor and found the door there. "Looks like there was a forcible entry." He examined the doorframe; it was charred black. He pointed the flashlight inside and ran the light along both walls; he saw the burned remains of overturned wooden benches and a mound of shattered glass and blackened metal pans. "We'd better not go inside," he said. "No telling what's holding this thing up."

He poked his head in the doorway, then drew back. "Whoa."

"What's the matter?"

"Smell this."

Beth cautiously stepped up to the door and sniffed. "Smells like ammonia to me."

"Me too."

Suddenly a spotlight went on, flooding the front of the shed with blinding light; it was coming from the water behind their boat.

"We're federal agents," a voice blared over a megaphone. *"Come out with your hands in the air. Do it now!"*

Beth began to step out from the shadows and into the glaring light, but Nick grabbed her by the arm and jerked her back.

"What's the matter? They're federal agents."

"So are we."

"They don't know that."

"Maybe they do."

"Nick, we should at least identify ourselves."

"They know who we are," Nick said. "They wouldn't be out here if they weren't looking for us."

They heard the crack of a rifle and an even louder *bang* on the corner of the shack near their heads.

"Still think I'm hallucinating?" Nick asked.

"Maybe it was just a warning shot."

"They fire warning shots into the air."

There was a second shot; it struck the shack in exactly the same spot. *"Stay where you are,"* the voice commanded—then they heard the low rumble of an engine.

"Nick—they're coming after us!"

"They have no choice—we're sure not coming out."

"What do we do?"

Nick pointed his flashlight at the marshy area behind the shack; it was a solid wall of vegetation. "C'mon," he said, taking her by the hand.

She pulled her hand away. "We can't go in there."

"Why not?"

"Because we don't know what's in there, that's why."

"Well, we know what's out here. Look, you've got a choice: You can take lions and tigers and bears in *there*, or a sniper with a rifle out *here*—take your pick."

A third shot sounded—but this time the rifle seemed to have a different timbre and the shot came from a different place; it seemed to come from the water, too, but this time farther downstream. Now the beam of the spotlight swung away from the shack and illuminated the bayou instead. Nick and Beth heard a series of three single shots echo from behind the spotlight, followed by a pause . . . and then a reply.

From downstream came an eruption of automatic-weapons fire. The first shot shattered the spotlight and returned the entire bayou to darkness. Nick wondered if the other shots had found their mark; as if in answer, he heard the first boat's engine rev and then begin to slowly fade away upstream.

Nick and Beth stood in the darkness, staring in the direction of the water. They heard the sound of another engine now, low and rumbling and steady; a boat was approaching from the left. When it pulled up even with their position, a flashlight clicked on. Nick and Beth instinctively shielded their eyes.

"You two," a deep voice said. "Get in da boat."

24

Beth huddled beside Nick on a wooden bench that spanned the bow of the boat. They faced backward, staring at the forms of two very large men who shared the bench in the stern. From the upward slant of the boat, it was obvious which couple contributed the bulk of the weight. They motored along slowly, heading deeper into the desolate bayou—precisely where, they didn't know.

The men were concealed by the darkness, but Beth had caught a glimpse of them when she'd first stepped into the boat. Their faces looked similar in shape and proportion, though one was considerably younger than the other. They were unshaven, at least for several days, and they both had dark tousled hair—though the older man's was longer and streaked with gray. They were dressed in well-worn khaki and faded flannel, and their leather boots were black from repeated oiling.

The two men said nothing when Nick and Beth cautiously approached the boat. They didn't stand up; they barely moved; there were no warnings, or threats, or further instructions. "Get in the boat" was clear enough, and their automatic weapon left no room for negotiation. The younger man just pointed at the bench in the bow and waited for Nick and Beth to climb aboard before shoving off. The older man appeared indifferent, almost bored; he slumped motionless on the bench, with the butt of his rifle resting on his thigh and the barrel pointing into the sky. The younger man held a flashlight at shoulder level and moved it back and forth from Nick to Beth, observing their faces.

"Thanks for helping us out back there," Nick offered.

Neither man replied.

The younger man glanced over at his companion. "Police?"

The old man made a huffing sound. *"La femme? Non."*

Beth was shivering even harder now that adrenaline had flooded her bloodstream. She kept her arms folded tightly across her chest, but it didn't seem to help. She found herself wishing that Nick would put his arm around her shoulders, but she knew she might as well wish that their little boat ride would turn into a dinner cruise. She couldn't help wondering what it might turn into instead; the thought made a knot in the pit of her stomach.

She could feel a thick blanket or rug in the bottom of the boat; she could feel the warm fur against her exposed ankles, and she wriggled her feet in as deeply as she could. She wanted to reach down and pull the rug up around her shoulders, but she knew she didn't dare.

"Excuse me," Nick said unexpectedly. "I couldn't help noticing your ring."

Beth turned and looked at Nick. The two men dressed like rejects from an L.L. Bean outlet store, and Nick was commenting on their accessories? What was he doing?

The younger man slowly extended his left hand and held the flashlight out to illuminate it. His ring was silver with deep black engraving, with a black onyx stone shaped like a football in the center. The stone was outlined by two lines of gems that looked like diamonds, and the words NATIONAL and CHAMPIONS surrounded them both. The ring was enormous; on his thick, stubby fingers it looked almost the size of a golf ball.

"LSU Class of 2004," Nick read. "Go Tigers."

"Whomped da Sooners in da Sugar Bowl," the man said.

"Congratulations," Nick said. "What position did you play?"

"Guard. Defense, mostly."

"I didn't figure you for a running back. What did you study?"

"At LSU?" The letters blended together when they rolled off his tongue—it sounded like *elleshyew*.

"Yeah, at LSU."

"Wildlife management."

"Is that what you do out here, you and your friend?"

"Him? Dat's my *nonk*—my uncle. I call him Tonton; he calls me Boo—dat's Cajun."

"I thought so," Nick said. "You guys look like hunters."

"Hunters, sometimes—trappers most of da time."

"What do you trap out here? I guess it depends on the season."

"Not in da bayou. We trap what we want."

Nick nodded.

"Boo," the old man said.

"Ain?"

"Axe 'em—*Que voulez-vous?*"

"My uncle, he wants ta know what you want out here."

Nick paused. "We were trying to get away from some federal agents."

Beth waited, but Nick said nothing more. She opened her mouth to offer further explanation, but Nick put his hand on her thigh and squeezed.

The old man considered Nick's words, then nodded; it seemed to be enough for him.

"Thought you might be gang wardens," Boo said.

"Gang wardens?"

"Wildlife agents."

"Don't worry, we're not with Fish and Wildlife."

"Figured. Not dressed for it. The woman, she dressed for a *fais dodo*."

"A what?"

"A party. You two ain't from da bayou."

"Does it show?"

Suddenly, the boat ran aground and lurched to a stop. Beth felt herself jerk backward; if Nick hadn't been holding her thigh, she would have fallen off the bench. The uncle shoved the tiller to the side and gunned the engine briefly, swinging the stern of the boat into shore. Without a word, he took the flashlight from his nephew's hand and stepped out of the boat with a splash. He waded into the marsh grass and headed inland, leaving the three of them sitting together in total darkness.

"It's a small world," Nick said.

"Ain?"

"You went to LSU; I'm a college professor."

"Where?"

"NC State, in Raleigh."

"Wolfpack," Boo said. "ACC football sucks."

"Won't argue with you there."

Thank you, Beth thought.

"I've been to LSU several times. My friend here—she was there just this morning."

Beth instinctively smiled, though she wasn't sure why; there was no way the man could see her face in the darkness.

Just then they heard a single shot from the automatic rifle; Nick and Beth turned and looked in the direction of the sound. A minute later they heard the marsh grass whisking apart again; the old man planted one foot in the shallow water and the next one in the boat, pushing off from the shore. He held the rifle in his left hand and the flashlight in his right; but there was something else in his right hand too—something large and heavy.

Boo took the flashlight and pointed it at his uncle's hand. The man was holding a large, brown, furry creature with a tail like a rat.

"*Très bon*," Boo said. "Good fur."

To Beth's horror, the old man swung the creature by its foot-long tail and plopped it into the bottom of the boat near her feet; it landed in the darkness with a sickening *whump*. Her mouth dropped open; she drew in a sharp breath but didn't let it out.

"May I?" Nick said, pointing to the flashlight.

Boo shrugged and tossed it over to him.

Nick held the flashlight over his head to illuminate the entire floor. It was covered with dozens of the lifeless creatures. They had blunt, rounded snouts with coarse white whiskers that angled down and back, and two enormous front incisors that were a sickly yellow-orange. Their ears looked like little black seashells pasted to the sides of their heads, and their meaty haunches curved up over hairless black feet.

They stared up at Beth with glistening eyes.

Beth jerked her feet up onto the bench. "What is *that*?"

"Beats me," Nick said. "I'm not into mammals."

"Nutria," Boo said. "Swamp rats, some say."

"Rats?"

"Nutria," Nick said. "I've never heard of them before. They're awfully big—how much do they weigh?"

"Eighteen, twenty pounds—seen 'em up to twenty-five."

Beth was panting like a spent mare. The lack of oxygen was causing her head to spin; she imagined herself passing out and falling forward, landing face-first in a pit of yellow teeth and wriggling tails. In a panic, she threw both arms around Nick's neck and began to scramble up onto his lap.

"Ouch," Nick said. "Watch the heels."

The uncle turned to his nephew. *"Quel est le problème?"*

The nephew just shrugged.

"Sorry," Nick said. "My friend is muriphobic—she's afraid of mice. She has a hard time with the little ones; I'm afraid twenty-pounders are over her limit."

"Dat's no mouse," Boo said. "Dat's a nutria." He hoisted one by the tail and stroked its fur, as if to reassure her.

Beth squeezed her eyes tight and climbed even higher, wrapping her arms around Nick's head like a python. Nick twisted his neck from side to side and straightened his glasses as if he were pushing his head through a turtleneck sweater.

"Better put it down," Nick said. "She'll be up on my head in a minute, and I don't have the neck strength for that."

Whump.

Beth could feel the dead rodents coming to life all around her, poking their blunt snouts into the air and sniffing; they could sense her presence, they could taste her flesh—their whiskers were almost tickling her feet. She jerked her head up and measured the distance to the shore.

"Don't even think about it," Nick said.

Beth told herself again and again that her fears were irrational. Only minutes ago she had welcomed the soft warm fur around her ankles—she wanted to pull it up over her shoulders like an afghan on a chilly night. It was no different now, she told herself, nothing had changed. The fur was exactly the same; the only difference was that this time the fur was attached to a body—the bulbous body of a hideous, twenty-pound *rat*.

It was no use—no matter what mental hallway she started down, there was always the same demon in the closet at the end. She felt a wave of nausea rising over her; she tightened her grip on Nick's neck to force it back down. She began to tremble like a leaf. She tried every relaxation method and breathing technique she could remember, all the ones she so glibly recommended to her own patients. None of them worked; she wondered if they ever did.

"Nick," she whispered. "I'm begging you."

Nick looked across at Boo. "Mind if I ask where you're taking us?"

"Our place."

"Is it much farther? I hate to complain, but she's squeezing all the blood out of my head."

"Five minutes. Hungry?"

"Starving."

"Stay for supper den."

"Glad to. What are we having?"

He nodded to the floor.

"Thanks," Nick said. "Maybe just a salad for her."

25

The boat veered around to the left and pulled up in front of a rickety old dock. The nephew threw a loop of rope around the closest pier and pulled the boat in; when he did, the dock leaned so far toward them that Nick thought it might collapse.

"Hurricane wrecked it," Boo said. "Not much good before—even worse now. We go one at a time, or we go swimmin'."

"The woman first," Nick said. He lifted Beth in his arms and set her on the dock; it shifted even more under her weight. She still had her arms wrapped tightly around Nick's neck; he gently pried them away and said, "Walk to the shore. Take it slow. I'll be right behind you."

She struggled to her feet and started forward, picking up speed as she went, as though the nutria might be right behind her. When she safely reached land, Nick crawled out onto the dock and followed.

Thirty yards from the dock was a rectangular cabin made of peeled cypress logs chinked with mortar in between. The roof was made of corrugated tin, just like the shack upriver, only this one was covered with cancerous splotches of brownish-orange. The design was basic, and the structure was undoubtedly handmade, with a simple slab door in the center surrounded by a window on either side. The entire cabin sat three feet above the ground on short, stubby stilts made of hand-hewn cypress posts. The cabin windows were dark; there were no signs of activity inside.

The uncle headed directly for the cabin, hauling two nutria by their ropelike tails. The door had a simple lift-latch and bore no lock. The nephew went around behind the cabin; a few seconds later came the low, rattling sound of a generator starting, and the two cabin windows slowly glowed with a warm yellow light.

Nick and Beth stood together in a bare dirt area in front of the cabin, watching this scene and wondering what they were supposed to do next. The nephew appeared again from behind the cabin and started for the door. He turned to them and said, "Supper in a few minutes." He stepped inside and closed the door.

Beth looked at Nick. "They're just going to leave us here?"

"They might as well," Nick said. "There's sure no place to go."

"Nick—we've been kidnapped."

"Don't be silly. They're fixing us supper—we're guests."

"You don't invite dinner guests at gunpoint."

"You haven't tasted my cooking."

"Nick, I'm serious—they could kill us both, and no one would ever know. We're in the middle of nowhere—we could be a hundred miles from the nearest town."

"Look," he said, pointing to a pickup truck parked just a few yards beyond the cabin. "There's obviously road access out here. We're not that far away from things, we just don't know where we are. They're not killers, Beth, they're poachers—that's why they asked if we were 'gang wardens.' Remember? It was just before your psychotic episode."

She glared at him. "It was not a 'psychotic episode.' I happen to have a common phobia, that's all."

"You should see a psychiatrist—that's what I do with all my problems."

She looked at the narrow dirt road behind the pickup. "They're not looking—maybe we should run."

"Now you are being psychotic. Where would we go? Besides, we haven't had supper yet."

"Supper? Are you actually hungry?"

"Man does not live by MREs alone. Some of these Cajuns can really cook."

"I am not setting foot in that cabin. The old man was carrying two of those . . . *things*." The word came out with a shudder.

"They were dead."

"I don't care. I'm staying right here."

"I hate to point out the obvious, but they shot one of those *things* just a few minutes from here. Are they carnivorous? Do they hunt in packs? They have to eat supper, too, you know."

"Nick, shut up."

"Sorry. I hate to take advantage of your irrational fears."

"You *love* to take advantage of my irrational fears."

"Actually, I do, but I'm not just jerking your chain here—I need you inside."

"Why?"

"Because a woman can have a civilizing influence in a situation like this. These guys probably haven't seen a woman in weeks—maybe months."

"I'd rather not remind them of that."

"Would you rather we talked *with* you, or *about* you? You know what I say to your face; there's no telling what I might say behind your back."

He took her by the arm and coaxed her toward the door.

"Sometimes I could strangle you with my bare hands," she said through clenched teeth.

"I know. That's *my* irrational fear."

The aroma that met them in the doorway was mouthwatering—at least Nick thought so. The old man stood with a black iron skillet in front of a simple propane cookstove, with a sizzling column of steam rising into the open rafters above. Boo cleared off a rough wooden table made from an old cable spool; it still had the words *EXXON MOBIL* stenciled in black across the top.

Neither man bothered to look up when Nick and Beth entered. Beth went directly to a chair in the corner of the cabin; she checked under it before sitting down, then crossed her arms and pressed her back against the wall.

Nick walked over to the nephew. "We appreciate the hospitality," he said.

"No problem."

"I didn't get to introduce myself. My name is Nick Polchak; my friend there is Beth Woodbridge." He extended his hand, and the young man took it. He had a grip like a hydraulic press. "How did you guys fare in the hurricane?"

"Not bad. Lot o' rain."

"Your cabin looks dry. Didn't it flood here?"

"Water came up, but not dis high."

"Why not?"

"Da bayou—soaks up da storm surge like a sponge. Da city's what floods—it's da levees. Supposed to keep water out; now dey keep water in."

"Your uncle—does he speak English?"

"Sure. He don' want to."

"Why not?"

"He's Cajun. Old Cajuns, dey like da old ways. Dey still speak French mostly—Cajun French, anyways."

"And you?"

"I speak it when I want to—mostly to him. But I'm a college boy, remember?" He made a fist and held up his ring again. "I'm capable of speaking perfect English whenever I wish," he said, articulating each word crisply and clearly.

Nick smiled. "I wouldn't expect to find a 'college boy' out here."

"I'm Cajun too; Cajuns are born and bred on the bayou—it's hard to get it out of our system. *It's in da blood,*" he said, assuming his accent again.

"Do many Cajuns make it to college?"

"No money, no interest—you don't need a degree to run a shrimp boat. I was lucky; I weighed twelve pounds at birth. I got a football scholarship."

Nick's stomach growled a reminder; he glanced over at the uncle. "What's Tonton cooking? It smells terrific."

"Mudbugs."

"Excuse me?"

"That's what we call crawfish. He's making crawfish étouffée: You start with a good roux, then add peppers, onion, garlic, and a little cayenne. Restaurants always use butter, but it won't keep out here—we use the crawfish fat. You'll find étouffée everywhere in New Orleans, but only Cajuns know how to make it right. *Da woman, I figger she don' go for nutria.*"

"Good figuring," Nick said. "The nutria—do you trap them for the fur?"

"We used to. Nutria make good coats—it's a midgrade fur, not as nice as mink or even muskrat, but it's a lot cheaper." From a wooden wall peg he lifted a quilt-sized fur, hand-stitched together from individual pelts. He folded it back on itself and ruffled the fur. "See that? Three sets of hairs—very soft."

Boo turned and offered the fur to Beth. "Still cold? This'll help."

She eyed the fur warily.

Nick leaned out from behind the nephew and mouthed the words, *Take it*.

"Thank you," she said, taking the fur as if it were radioactive.

"They sell most of 'em overseas—South America, Europe—used to sell plenty in the old Soviet Union. Nutria, that was Russian mink; every middle-class babushka could afford a nutria coat. 'Course, that was forty years ago. My uncle, he was around back then—says he used to get twenty bucks a pelt."

"And now?"

"A buck—can you believe it? A man can't make a living that way. When the Soviet Union collapsed, the whole fur market crashed. Can't afford to trap nutria for the fur anymore; these days we only trap 'em to save the bayou."

"The bayou?"

"The government pays us to kill 'em off—four bucks apiece."

"Why would the government care?"

"'Cause nutria destroy the wetlands. They eat everything in sight, right down to the roots, then they dig up the roots and eat those too.

When the plants go, the wetlands go—there's nothing left to hold the soil in place. And nutria breed like crazy—they're fertile at six months, and they can have two litters a year. They're a real nuisance down here—some folks are claiming the nutria made the hurricane worse than it was."

"How's that?"

"The wetlands soak up the storm surge—they hold the water, they keep it from moving on. That's why Fish and Wildlife is paying a premium now: four bucks each—after the hurricane, it might go up to five. All we've got to do is collect the tails and turn them in."

Nick paused. "No offense, but you didn't seem eager to bump into Fish and Wildlife back there."

Boo shrugged. "A man can't feed himself on a buck a tail; it's hard to get by even on four. You've got to bend the rules a little to make a living out here—especially after the hurricane. There's a season for trapping nutria—end of November through March. But the hurricane killed off a lot of 'em , and we lost a lot of traps. We have to start a little early this year, and we have to ignore a few regulations to make up for lost time. The folks in Baton Rouge, they don't like that. No love lost; we don't care much for them either."

"I take it you're not too fond of the law."

"We're Cajun—the bayou belongs to us. You leave us alone, we leave you alone—that's the way we live."

"You fired on federal agents tonight—doesn't that worry you?"

"He was bluffing—there was only one."

Nick stopped. "Are you sure about that?"

"Got a real good look."

"Okay, so you fired on one federal agent—doesn't *that* worry you?"

"He fired on *you*; it seems to me you're the one who ought to be worried."

"Good point," Nick said.

"My uncle took the shot—he doesn't miss. We weren't trying to hit him, just run him off. I got the feeling he was trying to hit you."

"Yeah," Nick said. "I got that feeling too."

"*Mangeons*," the uncle called. Nick turned to find the old man already seated at the table, with four steaming plates of étouffée around him.

Nick motioned to Beth.

"I'm not hungry," she said.

He bent closer. "It's suppertime. They're offering—we're accepting."

"I can't eat a rat."

"We're not having *rat*. It's a shrimp dish they made just for you—apparently it's served in all the finer restaurants."

"What's it called?"

"I'll tell you later. C'mon, they're waiting."

The two men sat side by side in the only chairs in the cabin; the uncle rested his rifle against the table between them. Nick and Beth pulled up an old footlocker from the end of a bed and used it as a bench. Beth tried to smile and make eye contact with each of the men, but her eyes kept going to the gun barrel poking up above the table like a requiem candle.

"Tonton," the nephew whispered. "*Le fusiller.*"

The old man sighed and laid the gun across his lap.

"Nice rifle," Nick said to the old man. "It's an AK-47, isn't it?"

"*Oui.*" The uncle crossed himself and dug into his meal.

"They're hard to come by these days. Mind if I ask where you got it?"

The old man glanced at his nephew, who said, "Russia—the good ol' days."

"Direct from the factory," Nick said. "I hear you can buy a tank these days if you know where to shop."

The old man let out a snort. He scooped up another mouthful of étouffée and glanced at Beth. "*Très jolie*," he said.

"Thank you," Beth replied.

"You two speak French?" Boo asked.

"Not me," Nick said, "but she knows 'pretty' in eight languages."

She kicked him under the table.

Nick rubbed his shin and looked at Boo. "That shack where you found us tonight—can you tell me anything about it?"

"Like what?"

"Like: Who owns it? What's it there for?"

"Don't know who owns it."

"Ever see anybody there?"

"Once or twice. Two men."

"When was the last time you saw them?"

"Couple weeks ago maybe—not since before the storm."

"Ever talk to them?"

"Why would I?"

"They're you're closest neighbors, aren't they?"

"Neighbors keep their distance out here. They don't bother us, we don't bother them."

"Any idea what they do—for a living, I mean?"

"None of my business. Trappers, I figure, just like us."

"Why?"

"Not much else to do out here."

"*Les renards*," the old man said without looking up from his plate.

"My uncle thinks they trap fox."

"Fox? What makes him think that?"

"Ever smell a fox?"

"Can't say I have."

"Nothing stinks like a fox—it's their urine. We can smell it when we pass by sometimes."

Nick nodded. "It looked like there had been a fire—the place was burned out."

"Could be. We saw smoke."

"When was that?"

"Couple weeks back."

"Didn't you check it out?"

Boo looked at him.

"Got it," Nick said. "You don't bother them, they don't bother you."

The meal ended as abruptly as it had begun. The old man swept his plate from the table and stepped to a plastic utility sink mounted on the wall. In one continuous motion he dipped it into a wash basin, wiped it with the palm of his hand, set it upright on a vinyl dish rack, and wiped the fronts and backs of his hands on his flannel shirt.

Beth looked down at her plate; she had barely begun her meal.

"I can drive you into town if you want," Boo said.

Beth's eyes widened. "You mean—we can go?"

Boo looked confused.

"Sorry," Nick said. "Somehow she got the crazy idea that you were kidnapping us."

Boo looked at her and frowned.

"But—you had a gun," Beth said.

"Ma'am, we didn't fire at you—we never even pointed it at you."

"You told us to 'get in the boat.'"

"What were you going to do, stay out there all night? That little dinghy of yours didn't look like it could hold two people."

Beth just sat there, blinking.

"Thanks again for the hospitality," Nick said. "Speaking of which: Can I ask one more favor? We left our little boat back there; it might not look like much, but it was a rental. The next time you're by there, could you tow it back with you? I'll find a time to come by and take it off your hands."

"No problem."

The uncle walked past the table with a dead nutria in each hand. "Boo," he called back, *"venez avec moi."*

"He wants us to come with him," Boo said.

They followed the old man to the rickety dock. As they walked along the bare dirt path, Nick looked over at the nephew. "You didn't ask me why that federal agent was trying to kill us."

"I figured you'd tell me if you wanted to."

"Thanks for trusting us."

"I don't trust you; it's just none of my business."

At the dock, the old man stood waiting with one of the nutria in his extended left hand. He positioned a knife at the base of its haunches, and with one quick *slit* removed the tail and dropped the carcass to the ground. He bent down and took it by the fur, then turned and slung it into the water by the dock. The instant it struck the surface, the water erupted in a tangle of twisting limbs and flashing teeth.

Beth gasped and stumbled back into Nick.

"Alligators," Nick said. "Now aren't you glad you didn't swim for shore?"

"We feed them to draw them in," the nephew said. "Sort of a home security system."

"I'm sure it's effective," Nick said. "Thanks for the heads-up."

"They won't bother you as long as you don't bother us—that's all you need to remember. I think my uncle is trying to send you a little message."

Nick watched the gators as they sank back into the water until only the armored black domes of their skulls protruded; in the dim light of the cabin, their eyes shone bloodred.

"What do you know," Nick said. "I speak French after all."

26

Beth settled back in the plush leather passenger seat, resisting the almost overwhelming urge to drift off into sleep. She had reclined the seat almost halfway, and that only made it worse; she longed to lay her exhausted body flat and surrender to oblivion, but she felt an obligation to stay awake and help Nick drive.

It was after 5:00 a.m., and they were almost back to St. Gabriel now. The nephew had driven them back to the car and refused to accept payment for the service. The Cajuns' cabin was apparently not as remote as she had thought, but it was definitely isolated: The road back was nothing but dirt and shell and gravel, and at times was nothing but a single lane.

It felt so good to slip back into her Lexus again, to fire up the seat warmers and set the air-conditioning to a soothing 72 and let it blot the clinging humidity from the air. Now they were on Interstate 10 and it felt even better; the road was wide and the ride was smooth, and the bayou with its alligators and swamp rats seemed a universe away. Even the dashboard seemed to comfort her, with its little glowing lights that welcomed her like a town at Christmastime.

She rolled her head to the left and looked at Nick. He sat erect and still, staring straight ahead out the windshield. He didn't slump or lean, and his head didn't droop or bob. She couldn't tell if he was even blinking; he was like an extension of the car, a part of the machine. He showed no sign of fatigue at all, and Beth knew why: His mind was engaged—he had a problem to solve—and his body would not rest until his mind could do the same.

"Are you okay?" she asked.

He didn't answer.

"Nick."

"What?"

"I was talking to you."

"Oh. Did I miss anything?"

"I just asked if you're okay."

"Why don't you lower that seat back and get some sleep?"

"That's just your way of saying you don't want to talk to me."

"I have no problem saying, 'I don't want to talk to you.' It doesn't work, but I have no problem saying it."

"I was thinking about tonight. Do you think the man who tried to shoot us was really a federal agent?"

"He wanted us to think he was. It might have just been a way to get us to step out into the open. People respond to authority."

"You don't."

"I have authority issues—my psychiatrist told me so."

"If you hadn't pulled me back, he might have killed me."

"What else could I do? You had the car keys."

"Thank you for saving my life."

"Any time."

"On the other hand, I wouldn't have been in danger if it wasn't for you."

"Boy, talk about fickle."

"I don't know whether to thank you or shoot you."

"That pretty much sums up my whole relationship with women."

"I think you owe me an apology."

"What for?"

She shuddered. "For those swamp rats."

"They're called nutria," Nick said. "They're harmless herbivores. What is this thing you have about rodents anyway? It doesn't make sense."

"It's not supposed to make sense, Nick—that's why they call it an *irrational* fear. Take it from me: Nothing is harder to comprehend than someone else's neurosis." She looked out the window. "I felt like such a weakling."

"Why? You faced your worst nightmare and came through it—the Mickey Mouse Club from Hell. How many people can say that? You should be proud of yourself."

"I don't feel proud. I climbed up in your lap—I had my arms around your neck."

"It wasn't the first time."

She looked at him. "I didn't think you remembered."

He shrugged. "What do you know about methamphetamine?"

"What?"

"Methamphetamine: speed, meth, crank."

"I know what it is, Nick."

"What do you know about it?"

"I'm familiar with the psychopathology of addiction, if that's what you mean. I've treated lots of addictive personalities in the past. In my level of practice, I mostly get cocaine users; heroin addicts usually can't afford me."

"I forgot what a high-class shrink you are. What about meth?"

"Different drugs attract different kinds of users. Methamphetamine isn't like cocaine; people don't take it just for the euphoria, they take it because they have the need for speed—the need to stay awake or focus for extended periods of time. It's traditionally been a white, blue-collar drug—truck drivers, people like that. But young professionals are getting into it now. Computer programmers seem to go for it; so do college students—you can get a lot of studying done when you can stay awake for two weeks straight. It's a pretty bad way to make the dean's list, though; it can lead to psychosis. Eventually you just burn up—you die from heart failure, or brain damage, or stroke."

"Sounds like you've dealt with a meth user before."

"I thought so."

"You *thought* so?"

"Yes. You."

Nick turned and looked at her. "I don't do drugs, Beth. I never did."

"I know that now. I wasn't sure then."

"Thanks a lot."

"Face it, Nick, when you get focused you manifest some of the classic symptoms of meth addiction: insomnia, suspiciousness, hyperactive behavior. I had to watch you very closely at first. It took a long time before I realized that you got your neurosis the old-fashioned way: You earned it."

"So how did you know I was clean?"

"You lacked some of the other classic symptoms: confusion, tremors, pupil dilation, impaired speech. You've never had trouble talking—you just don't make any sense. Why are you asking about this?"

"That shack we found in the bayou tonight—I think it was a clandestine meth lab."

"How do you know?"

"The smell. Remember?"

"Yes—it smelled like ammonia."

"The Cajuns thought the guys who owned that shack were trappers—they thought they must have been trapping foxes because the place smelled like urine. That's a dead giveaway that somebody's been cooking meth: anhydrous ammonia. It's used in the manufacturing process."

"How do you know all this? Maybe I was wrong about you."

"I've worked with the DEA before—it's part of what forensic entomologists do. Sometimes when they make a major drug bust they call me—they want to know where the shipment came from. I go through the stuff and look for insect parts; if I'm lucky, I can pin the point of origin to a specific location. I've learned a few things about the drug industry; I've learned a few things about the DEA too. Tough business, tough people. You don't want to mess with the DEA."

"Is that what you think we're doing?"

"I don't know yet."

"The shack was burned out. What do you think happened?"

"Hard to say—might've been the ammonia. Pure ammonia is dangerous stuff, and it's hard to come by. You can find it on any cotton farm; sometimes meth producers steal the stuff but store it in improper containers, like propane tanks. But the tanks weren't designed to hold ammonia, so they blow up. Meth labs blow up all the time—that's another dead giveaway. Maybe that's what happened to this one; maybe that's why the smell was so strong."

"The man who tried to shoot us—he did it when we were looking at the shack. Do you think it was just a convenient place to try—just the first place we happened to stop? Or do you think he fired at us because we found the shack?"

"You're full of good questions," Nick said. He glanced over at her. "So you thought I might be a drug addict."

"That was a long time ago."

"Was it? You thought I was hallucinating tonight."

"I never said you were hallucinating. I said you could have been."

"The point is, I wasn't."

"No. The point is, you could have been. People depend on you, Nick—that's what I was trying to tell you. My life was in your hands tonight."

"And things turned out just fine."

"Yes, because you were thinking clearly—because you made good judgments. But what if you weren't thinking clearly? What if you had let me try to swim to shore?"

"In other words, what if I was hallucinating when you were out of your mind?"

"Yes, if you want to put it that way. The point I'm trying to make is, *people depend on you*. You throw yourself in harm's way without thinking twice about it—but you forget sometimes that there are other people with you."

"You're talking about Jerry."

"Jerry's a big boy. Jerry's known you as long as I have; he knows what he's getting into. I was thinking about J.T."

"What about him?"

"You take him out in that boat with you every day. I was in a boat with you for one night, and look what happened to me."

"Nothing happened to you."

"Are you sure it's a good idea, Nick—taking J.T. out there with you every day? He's a boy—he'll throw himself off a cliff if you dare him to. Can he count on you to make good judgments for him?"

"He's safer with me than he would be anyplace else," Nick said.

"Even after tonight?"

"What does that mean?"

"You didn't answer my question earlier."

"Which one? There were so many."

"The man who tried to kill us—do you think he really was a federal agent?"

Nick paused. "I don't know. I don't believe we just happened to bump into him out there, especially in the middle of the night—and I can't believe it was a coincidence that it happened at an abandoned meth lab. Whoever he was, he must have followed us. I think he waited to see if I'd find that lab before he tried to kill me."

"You mean us."

"No, I mean me. Bringing you along was a last-minute decision; I think he was only looking for me."

"But he would have shot me too."

"Yes, he would have—just to cover his tracks."

"And what about J.T.? This man, whoever he is—he's still out there. If he decides to come looking for you again, will J.T. be with you?"

Nick didn't reply.

She watched his face carefully when she spoke her next words: "By the way, I spoke with the Department of Social Services yesterday."

"Did you get the name of his social worker? What did you find out?"

She paused. "Can I ask you something first?"

"I'm sure there's no way to stop you."

"I've never seen you form an attachment with a child before. What's different about this one?"

"What do you mean? I've always liked kids."

"Come on, Nick, this is me you're talking to. There's never been room in your world for a child. You're a scientist and a professor. If I asked you to list the ten things you love most, bugs would be nine of them—and children wouldn't make the list. What's different this time?"

Nick shook his head. "I took him to the New Orleans Convention Center the other night; I wanted him to have a safe place to sleep and something to eat. Do you know what he did? He hiked five miles across town in the dark and slept in a boat by himself."

"Who does that sound like?"

"He's quite a kid."

"You sound proud."

"Well, you've got to appreciate that kind of initiative."

"Some people would call that rebellion. What did you say to him?"

"I told him he needed to follow orders next time."

"You were angry with him?"

"Sure, a little."

"Good. That means you were afraid."

He frowned. "You know, you really are annoying sometimes."

"Fear can be a healthy thing, Nick. It means you know what might have happened; it means you know what could happen still. Fear is like our headlights: It illuminates things, it lets you anticipate what might be coming down the road."

"Headlights also *project*," Nick said. "That's the problem with fear: You can never tell when you're just imagining things—like our 'kidnappers' tonight."

"Okay, I was wrong about them. They turned out to be nice fellows—a little rough around the edges, but nice."

"I think the uncle likes you," Nick said. "You know, if you play your cards right, you could get a fur coat out of this."

"Just think about what I said, okay?"

"Don't I always?"

"I seriously doubt it."

"Now, what about Health and Human Services? What did you find out about the boy?"

She stopped and looked him over; she wasn't sure whether to tell him or not. He had a right to know—but something inside her told her to wait. There was something different about Nick—something about the way he was connecting with this boy. Nick Polchak had always thought of himself as an insect, but somewhere deep inside he seemed to be feeling the first stirrings of pride and anger and fear for another human being—and the therapist in her wanted those feelings to continue. In her heart she still wasn't certain whether Nick was good for the boy, but one thing she felt sure of: This boy was good for Nick.

"Nothing yet," she said. "I'll let you know when I find out anything."

They arrived at the gate of the DPMU. Nick stopped at the guardhouse and handed their credentials to the guard.

"I suppose you'll head back to the city," Beth said.

"I have to," Nick said.

"No, you don't—you want to. Take responsibility for your choices, Nick."

"Okay, I want to. It won't be long before daybreak—I need to wake up Jerry and J.T. so we can catch a ride."

"J.T. slept in your trailer last night? You know that's against regulations. I could report you, you know."

"You won't."

"How do you know?"

Nick leaned closer. "When have I ever invited you to 'take a nice walk down some quiet country road'?"

"What are you talking about?"

"I asked you why you came along tonight, and that's what you told me. Who are you kidding? You knew what you were getting yourself into."

"You think I *wanted* to sit in a boat full of dead rats?"

"I think you wanted to get out of that stuffy little office before all your arteries hardened. I think you wanted to get out of people's heads and into the real world for a change. I think you wanted what the rest of us want—to feel like you're alive while you still can."

"I think you're nuts."

"Take responsibility for your choices, Beth—that's what I always do."

"Get out of the car," she said angrily.

Nick got out and closed the door—then he leaned in the window and smiled. "You broke the rules," he said. "You were out all night. You defied the orders of a federal agent. You broke curfew. You broke the law. You're a bad girl now, Dr. Woodbridge—welcome to the club."

27

Saturday, September 3

"Somebody *shot* at you? Are you sure?"

"Gee, let me think," Nick said. "I heard a gun fire, and then a bullet whizzed by my head—yeah, I'm pretty sure. Give me a break, Jerry, I know when somebody's shooting at me."

"Did you get a look at him?"

"It was pitch black. Some guy followed Beth and me out into the bayous last night. He identified himself as a federal agent and ordered us to come out; when we refused, he opened fire."

"You were with Beth? Are you sure she didn't shoot at you?"

"Very funny, Jerry."

"What were you two doing out in the bayous?"

"Long story. The point is, somebody took a shot at me, and I wanted you to know."

"This is bad," Jerry said. "You're usually on the job at least a week before somebody wants to kill you. Do you think the guy was really a fed?"

"That's not their usual way of doing business," Nick said. "I made somebody mad, that's for sure."

"You make everybody mad, but they don't usually try to shoot you for it. Are you planning to report this to somebody?"

"Yeah, how about that LaTourneau guy? I'll ask him to check it out in his spare time. Half the cops in the city are off-duty and the other half are working overtime; there's nobody to report it to. Besides, who's going to pay any attention to one random shooting? There are guns all over the city right now."

"At least tell Denny. He should know."

Nick didn't reply.

Jerry rolled his eyes. "You weren't supposed to be out there, were you?"

"Let's just say that, given the current status of my relationship with Denny, it might be best not to mention it right now."

"So what are you going to do?"

"I'm going to keep looking at bodies, that's what. Somebody's upset with me, and it's not because I'm helping out with the rescue efforts. I've been told three times now not to recover bodies, and somebody just let me know they're serious about it. I want to know who they are—and I want to know why." He looked at Jerry. "All kidding aside—we're working together, so I thought you should know. I don't expect anybody to try anything out here in broad daylight, but let's keep our eyes out; keep that head down on that enormous body of yours."

"Yeah, thanks."

Suddenly J.T. stamped his foot on the center bench and pointed across the water. "Over there!" he shouted. "Down the end of this street and go left."

Nick squinted but as usual saw nothing. He called up to Jerry: "Do you see anything?"

"I never do," Jerry said. "Trust the kid—he's never wrong."

Nick took the boat down a long row of houses and swung around into a wide-open area, where they found a collection of coffins of various shapes and colors tightly roped together and floating half-submerged like a raft of logs.

"The kid's amazing," Jerry said. "He can spot bodies inside coffins."

"What're they doin' here?" J.T. asked.

"They came up out of the graveyards," Nick said. "There's air inside the coffins—that's what makes them float."

"Like the refrigerators."

"That's right—like the refrigerators. Looks like somebody's collecting the coffins and storing them here until the water goes down. I guess they'll eventually have to figure out who they are and where they came from and bury them all over again."

"What a headache," Jerry said.

"Yeah, the fun never stops around here."

They heard the sound of another engine now; Nick spotted the boat and waved it down. This time it was a FEMA Urban Search and Rescue Team.

"Afternoon!" Nick shouted over the engine. "We're with DMORT up in St. Gabriel. We're looking for—"

"—my father," J.T. called out. "Have you seen him?"

The crew looked at the boy, then at one another.

"The boy's searching for his dad," Nick explained. "They got separated in the storm. We've been looking for him ever since."

"Have you tried the Superdome yet?"

"Not yet."

"That's where I'd look—that's where most everybody went after the storm. I hear they finally got buses through; they're lined up to take people to the Astrodome in Houston. They hauled five thousand off on Thursday; they say the whole place could be empty in a day or two. If you're gonna look there, you'd better do it soon."

"Thanks. By the way, we're looking for bodies. Spread the word, will you? When you pass other boats, tell them the guy with the glasses is the man to call."

"How do they contact you?"

"Any word on when cell phones might be working again?"

"Sorry, haven't heard a thing."

"Well, I'm out here every day; just tell them to wave me down."

"Will do. You fellas have a good day; be careful out here."

"Yeah, you too."

They watched as the powerful FEMA boat roared away.

Nick looked at his watch. "It's about one o'clock, and we don't have any bodies to look at right now. I suppose we could keep cruising around and hope that old Hawkeye here finds us some more, but I think this might be a good time to visit the Superdome." He looked at J.T. and smiled. "What do you say?"

The boy just shrugged. Nick was a little surprised at his lack of enthusiasm. Maybe he knew that their chance of finding one man among thousands was slim; maybe he was afraid that Nick was trying to dump him off again. It didn't matter; if there was a chance of finding the boy's father at the Superdome, Nick wanted to try. He kept remembering Beth's words from the night before: *People depend on you.* Yesterday he was in no hurry to be rid of the kid, but that was yesterday; last night someone had tried to kill him, and he knew he owed it to the boy to get him back to his father and out of harm's way.

"We're not planning to leave you there," Nick told him. "We're looking for your dad, that's all. If we find him, you go with him; if we don't find him, you stay with me—fair enough?"

J.T. grinned and nodded.

Nick looked at Jerry. "I'm just trying to keep my promise here. If his dad gets on a bus for Houston, there's no telling when we'll be able to find him. Are you okay with this?"

"Might as well try," Jerry said. "Like the man said, it's now or never. So how do we get to the Superdome?"

"The same way we got to Charity Hospital—they're just a few blocks apart. That's the quickest way I know."

Nick turned the boat around and headed back for the break in the Industrial Canal. From half a mile away they could already feel the heavy beating of helicopter blades. Lumbering Chinook helicopters formed a dotted line in the sky overhead, hoisting three-thousand-pound sandbags and dropping them into the breach one by one. The Army Corps of Engineers had been at this seemingly futile task for days now; at first, the bags had just disappeared into the water without a trace. But persistence was paying off, and the massive white sacks now protruded from the water like garbage bags at a landfill; the breach was slowly beginning to close from south to north.

"They're making progress here," Nick said. "We may not be able to pass this way much longer." He guided the boat through the remaining opening and out into the Industrial Canal.

They followed the same route they had before, through the Upper Ninth Ward and across the neighborhoods of Bywater, St. Claude, and St. Roch. Nick found that his memory was a poor guide; everything looked different in the light of day. At night the entire city blended together into a vast black landscape; now he could make out individual buildings and rooftops. The shingles looked newer here; gables had been repainted. This neighborhood looked better than the Lower Nine—but, then, they all did.

They could see the Superdome from blocks away; the sun, just past its zenith, reflected brightly off the mustard-yellow surface of its damaged roof. They stopped their boat a few blocks back and surveyed the area; the sidewalk surrounding the stadium was a teeming mass of lawn chairs, mattresses, garbage, and people.

They sat silently and watched.

"So how do we do this?" Jerry asked.

"Good question," Nick replied. "We can't just sail up to the front door—that's a good way to lose a boat. Some of these people have been here for almost a week." He searched the area and discovered a narrow alley just two blocks from the stadium. It was concealed by shadow from the afternoon sun, and Nick saw a way that he could approach the alley unseen. "We'll hide the boat in that alley," he said. "We'll wade in from there."

"Wade? In the water?"

"That's where most wading is done, Jerry."

Jerry looked at the water and frowned. "Isn't there some other way?"

"We could use you as a raft and row ashore, but either way you'd get wet. Have you got any other ideas?"

He didn't.

Ten minutes later, the boat was chained securely to an alley downspout and the two men lowered themselves into the sickly green water. Nick's elbows just touched the surface.

"It's filthy," Jerry complained. "It's hot too."

"Let's not do any snorkeling then," Nick said. "J.T., climb onto my back. You're a little short on clothing right now—let's keep you as dry as we can." The boy leaned out of the boat and wrapped both arms tightly around Nick's neck. Nick hunched over, dragging J.T. out of the boat and onto his back. The boy was heavier than Nick had anticipated, and the sudden weight made him stumble forward.

"You got me?" J.T. asked.

"No problem," Nick said. "Beth helped me train for this."

They slowly waded down the alley and out into the street toward the stadium, carefully shuffling forward like men testing thin ice, keeping their center of gravity back in case they encountered underwater debris. The going was hard at first, but it got easier as they went; the water gradually grew shallower until they arrived dripping wet on the hopelessly congested sidewalk.

Nick half-expected the crowd to fall silent and part down the middle when they emerged from the water—after all, it was a pretty good entrance. It didn't happen; he had to push his way through the crowd, stepping over blankets and water bottles and shoving aside piles of garbage with the sides of his legs. He was wading through a sea of humanity and their refuse; compared to this, the water had been easy.

People were everywhere—thousands of them. Some sat calmly in lawn chairs, watching the chaos around them as if it were a passing parade. Others lay on mattresses peacefully asleep, as if some prankster had transported them here from a nearby hotel. The heat was oppressive in the heart of the crowd; no air could move between the people. Women fanned themselves; men stood shirtless and cussing; children wandered in their diapers or in nothing at all. People seemed to rotate from the center to the perimeter like bees in a hive, releasing the heat and taking their turn for the relief of a passing breeze.

Debris covered everything. Evacuees had come to the Superdome six days ago hauling whatever precious possessions they could carry, spreading them out around them and establishing little settlements. There were laundry baskets, boxes, pillows, houseplants, televisions—even framed paintings and upholstered chairs. None of it looked precious now; it was all in ruins, just part of the burden of staying alive.

The stench was almost overwhelming. Disposable diapers had been dropped everywhere, some not even folded; men and boys urinated in the street or against the stadium walls; the air reeked of sweat, and feces, and rotting food. The stench was nauseating, but somehow people seemed oblivious to it. Nick found it astonishing how quickly the human species grows dull—especially to itself.

The noise was nearly deafening, and the buses only made it worse. There were shouting and panic as families tried to stay together, calling out family names and searching frantically for wayward children. People gathered up remnants of their household possessions only to be turned back at the bus doors; there was room for people, but almost nothing else. Many ignored the buses altogether, either waiting for some better option or just paralyzed by the stupor that hopelessness can bring.

Nick leaned back and let J.T. slip off onto the sidewalk. "You've got legs," he said. "Time to use them."

They pushed forward until they reached the stadium and went inside, eventually finding their way onto the playing field itself. They looked up; the arena looked like a half-empty salad bowl. The same debris that covered every square foot of pavement outside was scattered across every section of the stands.

"Look at this place," Jerry said. "Who's in charge here?"

"Don't expect anybody to raise their hand," Nick said. "C'mon—over there."

Two National Guardsmen in full combat gear stood near the goalposts in the Saints' end zone. They were armed to the teeth, with formidable-looking M16s slung from shoulder straps and angled at the ground. Nick almost laughed; he knew it was just a show of force, a vague reminder to troublemakers that law and order still existed in some parts of America and might even return to New Orleans one day. *It won't be today*, Nick thought; if this crowd got nasty, they could overwhelm two soldiers in seconds.

Nick pulled out his credentials and held them up as he approached the first Guardsman—a healthy thing to do when approaching an armed man in a crowd.

"Afternoon," he said. "Aren't you guys hot in all that gear?"

The Guardsman studied his credentials before responding. "We're dying. What can I do for you gentlemen?"

"You can help us find somebody."

The Guardsman rolled his eyes. "He'd better be twenty feet tall, or you'll never find him around here. Who you looking for?"

"This boy's dad."

"Good luck. There's no power, so there's no public-address system. The JumboTron is down; so are the scoreboards. There's no way to get a message out around here; you'll just have to look for him."

"Anybody got a megaphone?"

"Our people do; we're using them to organize food distribution and get people to the buses. There's no way they'll let you use one just to look for somebody—half the people here would want to use one."

"I'm with a federal agency," Nick said. "Maybe I could pull rank."

The Guardsman grinned. "Friend—you've got no rank around here. And if you don't mind a suggestion: I wouldn't tell anybody I'm with a federal agency right about now."

Nick pointed to the binoculars hanging around the Guardsman's neck. "Mind if we borrow those? You're not using them standing here."

"I suppose not," he said, lifting the leather strap from around his neck and looping it over the boy's. "You know how to use these, son?"

"Sure," J.T. said, beaming.

"He's a smart guy," Nick said. "He knows everything."

J.T. immediately turned and ran toward a stairway that headed up into the stands.

"Whoa!" Nick called after him. "Where you going?"

"Up top," the boy said, pointing to the bleachers. "Can't see from down here."

Nick shook his head. "I'd better go after him—I'd hate to get separated here. That's all I need right now: *two* lost people." He turned to Jerry. "Do me a favor, will you? The father's name is Bastien Walker. Make a loop around the sidewalk and yell his name—see if you get any takers. Try the main concourse and mezzanine too."

"You think he'll hear me over all this noise?"

"It's the best we've got, Jerry. You're a good baritone; breathe from the diaphragm—project. The kid's got the eyes, but you've got the voice; if anybody can do it, you can."

"What about you?"

"I'll stick with J.T. We'll go up top and look for faces in the crowd. We'll meet you back here in one hour, okay?"

"What do you think the odds are of us finding this guy?"

Nick looked at the Guardsman. "How many people do you have here?"

"About thirty thousand, last count."

"There you go," Nick said. "One in thirty thousand—about the same odds as your getting married."

"Thanks. I'm a bundle of hope."

Nick started for the stairs. "One hour, Jerry—right here."

Outside the Superdome, another man waded ashore. He bent down and picked up a discarded black ball cap with the logo of the New Orleans Saints.

28

"Bastien Walker!" Jerry shouted. "I'm looking for Bastien Walker!"

He waited, but again heard no response. He looked from side to side, searching for any pair of eyes attempting to make eye contact, but there were none. He was starting to feel a little silly; what was the point? In a normal setting, the very fact that he was shouting would have turned at least a few heads, but not here. He heard a dozen other voices shouting someone else's name with even more volume and more urgency, and no one was paying any attention to them either. These people were immune; they had lived with the roar of the crowd for so long that a single voice no longer stood out—even a shouting voice. What were the chances of finding the boy's father this way? He'd almost have to stumble over the man, and what were the odds of that?

Still, he'd promised Nick he would try.

Jerry finished his search of the sidewalk without success and decided to try inside instead. That's where he would be if he were the man—even without air-conditioning it was better than standing in the brutal Louisiana sun. He headed into the main concourse and was just about to call out the man's name again when someone poked him on the shoulder from behind.

He turned to see a man about his own height in a black cap with a gold fleur-de-lis logo.

"Are you with the government?" the man demanded.

"Well . . . sort of," Jerry said.

"I want to know who's responsible for this."

"For what, exactly?"

"For what? For all *this*. I been here since Sunday night—that's a week ago tomorrow. 'Head for the Superdome,' they told me, 'they got everything there.' Only there was no food and almost no water—they forgot to mention that. 'You'll be safe there,' they said—except the hurricane ripped the roof right off the place and rain came pouring in. Then the power went out—no electricity. Then the johns overflowed—no bathrooms. Still no food, still no water, and every day they tell us, 'Trucks are on the way! Buses any minute to take you all out of here!' I saw my first truck day before yesterday—it took four days to get here, and it didn't have but a handful of supplies!"

The man kept moving closer to Jerry; he was becoming more and more agitated.

"Sir, please keep your voice down," Jerry said.

"Don't tell me to keep my voice down! People are dyin' here, man, don't you know that? We got old people, sick people; we got women and children. I want to know what you people are going to do about it."

"Sir, I'm not in charge here."

"You're with the government, aren't you?"

"Yes, but—"

"You can do something, can't you? We got people who need medicine. We got bodies pilin' up in the hallways."

Jerry blinked. "What bodies?"

"Are you kidding? Don't you people know nothin'? We've had murders here, mister—we've had old folks dyin' in their sleep. The bodies started to stink—we had to haul them off to a back room just to keep people from getting sick."

"Are you sure about that?"

"Am I sure? I helped haul them there myself."

"How many bodies are we talking about?"

"Who knows? Twenty, maybe thirty—we had to stack 'em up."

Jerry looked at his watch; he still had a few minutes. "This back room you mentioned—can you take me there?"

"Sure, if you want. Follow me."

The man led Jerry down a service corridor that grew darker as it went; there were doorways on either side that opened into pitch-black rooms. The man stopped at each doorway and poked his head inside, though Jerry couldn't imagine what he could see. Maybe he wasn't trying to see; maybe he was sniffing the air. Jerry did the same.

Finally, the man stepped aside and gestured to one of the rooms. "In here," he said. "Watch your step."

Jerry stepped past the man and into the darkness.

Suddenly, he felt a hand grip his chin and jerk his head back violently. He felt a body press up against his and a searing pain in his right side just below the rib cage—and then, strangely, all the lights went on. The light was brilliant, almost blinding—

And then it slowly faded into nothing.

29

Nick looked at his watch. It was almost 6:30—if they left right now, they would just have time to make it back before dark.

"Where's Jerry?" J.T. asked.

"I told you, I don't know."

Nick and J.T. waited at the edge of the sidewalk where they had first waded ashore. It had been almost four hours since the two men had parted company, and there was no sign of Jerry anywhere. Nick kept reviewing their departure in his head: He was supposed to follow J.T. into the stands, and Jerry was supposed to circle the stadium to call out the father's name. "We'll meet you back here in one hour," he told him—those were his exact words. "One hour—right here"; there was no room for confusion or doubt.

Jerry was now three hours overdue, and Nick had a very bad feeling.

Nick and J.T. had spent their hour searching the stands for any familiar face. J.T. had taken up position on the fifty-yard line in the final row of seats, planting his elbows on his knees to hold the binoculars steady while he scanned the crowd. He was delighted with his new toy; he spent as much time looking at the binoculars as through them, and Nick had to keep reminding him of the task at hand. At first they looked only for his father; then Nick suggested that they widen their search to include neighbors, friends, anyone who looked at all familiar who might have knowledge of the boy's dad. They found no one; after an hour of futile searching, they returned to the playing field to see if Jerry had had any better luck.

But Jerry wasn't there.

Nick told himself that the trip around the stadium could have taken longer than he estimated, especially considering the crowded conditions. And if conditions in the main concourse and mezzanine were no better, even more time might be necessary—another hour, maybe more. But that explanation didn't satisfy him; there was no reason that Jerry wouldn't at least check in to let Nick know his need for more time.

Nick considered every possible explanation he could think of: Jerry forgot, Jerry was detained—or maybe Jerry was spotted by FEMA officials and called away on some emergency duty. But that was too fantastic, and Nick knew in his heart that there be could only one reason that Jerry didn't come back.

Jerry couldn't come back.

They had waited two additional hours with the National Guardsmen. After that, they made their own circle of the sidewalk and still found no trace of Jerry. Nick thought about searching the concourse and mezzanine, but by then the knot in his gut was beginning to tighten, warning him away. He didn't want to risk taking the boy back into the building again, and he couldn't leave him behind. The safest place to be was outside, in plain view of everyone. They returned to the spot where they first came ashore, hoping against hope that Jerry might meet them there.

It didn't happen, and it was getting dark.

"What do I do with these?" J.T. asked, holding up the binoculars.

"They're yours," Nick said.

"I can keep 'em?"

"Courtesy of your Uncle Sam. He wants you to have the best."

Nick looked all around; he had no idea what to do next. He thought about reporting Jerry's absence, but who would he report it to? There were no authorities here, there was no chain of command. He could at least tell the two National Guardsmen, but what would they do? They wouldn't help search for him; they wouldn't be allowed to leave their post.

People depend on you, Nick thought.

He looked down at J.T. and knew what he had to do: He had to get the boy out of here. He looked at the alley where the boat was hidden, growing darker by the minute; someone could be waiting for them there. He thought about the long trip back across all those flooded neighborhoods; he thought about how exposed they would be crossing the Industrial Canal. There could be danger almost anywhere, but Nick knew one thing was certain: If anything did happen to Jerry, it had happened to him here—they had to go.

He looked at the alley again. *The sooner the better*, he thought. *If anybody's waiting in that alley, better to face him while there's still some light to see.*

"Come on," he said to J.T. "We're getting out of here."

"What about Jerry?"

"Don't worry about Jerry," he said. "Jerry's a big boy—he can take care of himself."

He hoped to God it was true.

30

Detwiler punched Memory 1 on the satellite phone and waited for the signal to connect.

"Special Agent Turlock," said the voice on the other end.

"It's me, Frank."

"Where are you? I've been waiting."

"I've been busy," Detwiler said. "I'm in the boat. I'm downtown, not far from the Superdome."

"The Superdome? Why?"

"I followed Polchak and Kibbee there."

"And?"

"I took care of Kibbee," he said. "Polchak and the boy got away."

There was silence on the other end.

"You still there?"

"I'm here. Did Polchak see you?"

"No—and they won't find Kibbee for days. As far as Polchak knows, his friend just disappeared."

"I told you to take care of this in the Lower Nine."

"It's impossible—there are boats everywhere now. I was following them just like we agreed; they headed across the canal again. This time I went after them, but I had to keep my distance 'cause it's still daylight—I'd be even easier to spot than before."

"You're making this too complicated, John. Pull up beside them, take out your gun, and finish the job."

"It's not that easy, Frank. Gunshots carry for miles over water—what if somebody saw me? We'd be in big trouble then."

"We're in big trouble now," Turlock said. "That's what I can't seem to get through that thick head of yours."

"Look, I tracked 'em as far as the Superdome. They must have stashed their boat somewhere nearby; by the time I got there they were already wading in—Polchak, Kibbee, and the boy. I don't know what they were doing there."

"I do. Polchak is helping the boy find his father—that's why the boy's been with them every day. He must have decided to check out the evacuation centers."

"How do you know that?"

"Dr. Woodbridge's phone log; she did a background check on the boy with Health and Human Services. Remember Dr. Woodbridge? There's another little detail we've let slip."

"That wasn't my fault," Detwiler said. "I was under fire out there in the bayou—I couldn't get a clear shot. Some guy had an assault rifle—where'd he get that?"

"Welcome to Louisiana."

"Well—at least we know who's helping Polchak on the inside."

"And now we've got another loose end to take care of. What went wrong at the Superdome?"

"I don't know. I followed 'em in. The place was a madhouse. People everywhere—it stinks like a pigsty. There's a lot of angry people there; I figured, a couple of FEMA workers turn up dead—who wouldn't believe that? And the boy, I figured I'd just haul him off by himself—nobody'd make the connection. It was perfect."

"Then what went wrong?"

"I couldn't get them all in one place. I spotted Kibbee first—he was easy enough—but when I finally found Polchak and the boy, they were standing with a couple of National Guardsmen. They must have stayed there for two hours; I thought maybe they were on to me, so I finally left. I went back out to my boat and waited for them to leave—figured I'd let 'em come to me instead."

"And?"

"They just disappeared. I figured they'd go back the same way they came, so I picked a good spot to do the job and waited for them there—but they never showed up. I can't understand it—where did they go?"

"Never mind," Turlock said. "What we need to decide is what to do next—and we'd better think of something fast. Why do you think Polchak was in that bayou last night? He went straight to that lab; somehow he found out about it. He's making the connections, John—how long before he connects it all to us?"

"What do you want me to do now?"

"The same thing you were supposed to do last night and today: Find Polchak and the boy and finish the job."

"And the woman?"

"That could get complicated," he said. "Better leave that to me."

"Right. I'll be in touch."

"And John."

"Yeah?"

"No more excuses—we need results."

31

"How come we're rowin'?" J.T. asked. "We outta gas?"

"I thought you could use the exercise," Nick said. "Keep going—it's not much farther."

The boat glided silently through the flooded streets. Nick kept close to the buildings even though the sky was dark; he didn't want to risk being silhouetted by a glint of moonlight reflecting off the water. He needed time to think; he needed time to sort things out.

Where was Jerry? Why hadn't he come back?

Nick knew there were plausible explanations for Jerry's disappearance; the problem was, there was no way to evaluate the likelihood of any of them. Something utterly unforeseen and unpredictable could have called Jerry away. It was possible; it's what he wanted to believe—but he didn't. Someone had tried to kill Nick and Beth just the night before—someone who was still out there, and that fact alone changed everything. He had done the right thing, he had told Jerry about the attempt on his life, but now he wondered if he should have done more. Maybe they should have stayed out of the Lower Nine for a day or two to let things cool off. Maybe they should have split up.

People depend on you, Nick. Beth's words kept coming back to him. *You throw yourself in harm's way without thinking twice—you forget that there are other people with you.*

What happened to Jerry? His gut told him the answer, but he tried not to let his mind go there. He needed to think, he needed to focus on the situation at hand, but his mind kept leapfrogging back to Jerry—just a farm boy from central Indiana, that's all he was. Just a guy with cold hands and a big heart who never quite found the woman who could appreciate both. Nothing to prove, nothing to lose—that was Jerry, the sort of guy who would give you the shirt off his back if you asked him to.

The sort of guy who would die for you.

Nick felt his stomach twist into a knot.

You don't know what happened to Jerry, he kept telling himself. *No matter what you might suspect, you have no way to know.* He kept repeating the words to himself over and over again until he almost believed them—almost.

He pulled off his glasses and wiped his eyes.

"How come you stopped?" J.T. asked.

"Just keep rowing," Nick said.

He clenched his fists until his fingernails dug into the palms of his hands and almost drew blood. He needed to think; he needed to act; he had to decide what to do next. No matter what happened to Jerry, there was still the boy to think of.

People depend on you, Nick.

If Jerry's disappearance wasn't accidental, if someone really was out there, the attacker could be anywhere at all: back at the Superdome, searching for them; climbing into a boat, coming after them; or somewhere up ahead, lying in wait. Nick felt like a man who had just stumbled into a spider's web and wondered where the spider was now. He knew that he had to anticipate every possible point of attack—and that's when he realized that they couldn't go back the way they'd come.

"How much farther?" the boy asked.

"Keep rowing. Don't wimp out on me now."

Nick did most of the pulling in the stern; the boy knelt in the bow and paddled with far more enthusiasm than skill. That was good; Nick wanted to keep the boy occupied. It would keep his mind off their missing friend and burn off energy too.

"Hold it here," Nick commanded, back-paddling until the boat came to a complete stop. Directly ahead of them was an open area of water where they would be easy to spot; just beyond the area was the flooded second floor of Charity Hospital. Nick looked all around; he waited and listened but heard nothing.

"See that building up ahead?" he said to J.T.

"Can't miss it."

"See the big broken window? The water goes right up to it."

"I see it."

"When I say 'Go,' I want you to row straight for it—don't stop until we pass right through."

"Into the building?"

"That's the idea. You ready?"

J.T. nodded.

"Then let's go—and no more talking until we get inside."

Three minutes later, they slipped through the broken window and into the darkness of the abandoned lab. They were both panting; their breathing sounded thin and raspy in the cavelike room. Nick held his breath and listened for the sound of any approaching boats; there were none.

"Where are we?" J.T. asked.

"Charity Hospital."

"What're we doin' here?"

"I left some things here," Nick said. "I need to check on them. We won't be long." He fished through his equipment bag for a flashlight; he aimed it at the table in the center of the room.

The bodies were gone.

"What the—"

He shone the flashlight around the room. Everything was gone: both body bags, the specimens, the containers with their coffee-filter lids—all of it. Someone had cleaned the place out.

"There's nothin' here," J.T. said.

"Be quiet—I'm trying to think."

If the bodies alone were missing, anyone could have been responsible—anyone detecting the odor or making a search of the floor. But at a glance the specimen containers would have looked like nothing more than garbage, and the entire floor was covered with debris. No one would bother to do cleanup in the middle of a disaster; no one would have taken the specimens unless they knew what they were.

Nick tried to refocus his thoughts. He knew he was beginning to see shadows now, imagining bogeymen where they might not really exist. He didn't know what happened to Jerry, no matter what his gut told him—he didn't *know*. And there was a simple and reasonable explanation for the removal of the specimens, the same reason for the removal of the bodies: the stench. The developing maggots had been left to feed on decaying meat, which produced the same gut-wrenching odor as the bodies themselves—not as overpowering, maybe, but just as bad as any six-month-old leftovers found hidden in the back of a fridge. After removing the bodies, someone might have detected the lingering stench of decay and discovered the specimens too. It was a logical explanation; it was simple, and it was reasonable. But was it true?

He had to know.

"Come on," he said to J.T. He crawled out of the boat and onto the table where the bodies had lain, then lowered himself into the waist-deep water. He steadied the boat while J.T. climbed out after him; the water came halfway up the boy's chest.

"Where we goin'?"

"Upstairs."

"How come?"

"I lost something, and I need to know who found it."

They headed out into the hallway; it was utterly dark except for faint white rectangles of moonlight glittering through open doorways. Nick turned left and started down the corridor, hoping to find a stairway at the end. He felt his way along the walls as he went; he caught his foot on something sodden and heavy and stumbled forward. He turned and looked back at J.T., who was holding his precious binoculars above his head to keep them out of the water.

"Watch your step," Nick said. "Take it slow."

Three minutes later, they stood dripping on the concrete landing of the hospital's third floor. Nick found the door and tried the knob; it was locked. He wondered if the hospital's exit doors were routinely locked; he wondered if the purpose was to keep looters out or to hold patients in. He knocked politely, but there was no answer—so he pounded with his fist until he heard a woman's voice on the other side shout, "Who's out there?"

"My name is Nick Polchak!" he shouted back. J.T. covered his ears; in the hollow stairwell the echoing shout was deafening.

"What's your business?" the woman demanded.

"I'm with DMORT," Nick said. "They told me you've got a couple of bodies to pick up."

Nick heard the click of a dead bolt and felt the door slowly open toward him. "Hold your voice down," the woman scolded. "We can't have talk of dead bodies around the patients. What's wrong with you?"

"Sorry," Nick said.

A flashlight clicked on, directed at Nick's face. In the pitch blackness of the stairwell the light was blinding; Nick grimaced and squeezed his eyes shut. He heard the woman gasp; the light reflecting off his huge lenses must have taken her by surprise.

"Took you people long enough," she grumbled, stepping aside. She pointed the flashlight at J.T., who shielded his eyes and turned away. "Who's this boy?"

"My assistant," Nick said. "Who's in charge around here?"

She turned the flashlight and illuminated her own face; she wore nurse's scrubs and a stethoscope around her neck. The flashlight cast dramatic shadows across her face, making her look like a camper in front of a fire—or a demon. Based on Nick's past experience with nurses, it was probably the latter.

"Can you take me to the you-know-whats?" Nick asked.

"Follow me."

"Then they're still here?"

She frowned at him. "Where do you think they'd go?"

Nick felt a wave of relief.

She led them down the long corridor to the opposite stairway. The entire hallway was in darkness, except for the glow of an occasional candle and the flashlights blinking off and on like fireflies, illuminated for seconds at a time to conserve dwindling batteries. Nick glanced in the rooms as they passed. He could see the silhouettes of patients tossing fitfully in the sweltering heat; he heard moans and calls for assistance from everywhere.

"How are you holding up?" Nick asked.

"Better than they are."

"How long have you been without power?"

"Since the day after the storm. We had emergency generators for a day or so, then they went under too. Been dark ever since."

"How can you run the medical equipment?"

"We can't. Why do you think you're here?"

The opposite doorway bore a hand-scrawled sign that read: "KEEP OUT—HOSPITAL PERSONNEL ONLY." The nurse unlocked the dead bolt and glanced back down the hallway before opening the door. The stairwell was black; she switched on the flashlight and started up the stairs.

"This way," she said. "We keep them upstairs to hold down the smell."

On the fifth-floor landing five bodies were laid out side by side, covered only in white hospital linens.

Nick blinked. "There are five of them."

"I hope you can take them all."

He took the flashlight from the nurse's hand and knelt down beside the shrouded forms. He pulled the sheets back one by one and examined each body; they were fresh, dead less than a week, still dressed in hospital gowns.

He looked up at the nurse. "These aren't the bodies I'm looking for."

"What?"

"They told me there were only two."

"Well, they told you wrong. We lost three of them the first day when the ventilators went off. We ambu-bagged them as long as we could, but you just can't do the work of a ventilator. We lost the other two to the heat."

"These are hospital patients. I was sent to pick up two bodies that were found downstairs on the second floor."

"Oh, those. Somebody beat you to it."

"Who? When?"

"Your people, I suppose. Just yesterday."

"Did they say they were from DMORT? Did they show you any identification?"

"They were willing to take the bodies away, that's all we cared about. Those two were stinking to high heaven—they were scaring all the patients. Who were those poor souls, anyway? How did they manage to end up on the second floor?"

Just then they heard the sound of the stairway door open below them. A moment later, a flashlight beam flickered up the shaft between the stairs.

"Who's up there?" a man's voice called out. "This stairwell is off-limits."

"It's me, Doctor," the nurse called down. "They finally sent somebody to take these bodies away. Come on up—he's got a question for you."

Nick could hear the scratchy echo of leather-soled shoes as the doctor climbed the two flights of stairs. As the doctor approached, Nick extended his hand. "Dr. Nick Polchak," he said. "Disaster Mortuary Operational Response Team."

"Well, it's about time," the doctor said.

"There seems to be some confusion here. I was sent to recover two bodies that were discovered on the second floor, but your nurse tells me they were already taken away."

"That's right. Two men came by yesterday."

"Two men. Did you see them?"

"Yes, I met with them briefly."

"Did they identify themselves?"

"I didn't catch their names. They said they were with the DEA."

Nick paused. "You're sure about that?"

"That's what they told me. I thought it was a little strange, but they said everybody's pulling double duty right now."

"That's true," Nick said. "Tell me, did any of your hospital staff help with the cleanup?"

"What cleanup?"

"I was expecting to find two bodies downstairs, but it looked like the whole room had been cleaned out."

"You'd have to ask them—they handled the whole thing."

Nick slowly nodded.

"How do you plan to remove these?" the doctor asked, pointing to the bodies.

"What?"

"I'd appreciate it if you'd take them downstairs and out through the second floor. I don't want you carrying them through the occupied floors—the patients would freak out."

"I'm not taking them," Nick said.

"What?"

"I was sent to collect two specific bodies. I'm not equipped to take five."

The doctor looked at J.T. for the first time, then turned to the nurse. "Would you excuse us for a minute? I'd like to talk to Dr. Polchak alone."

The nurse shrugged and started back down the stairs.

The doctor waited until he heard the click of the door before speaking again. "Do you mind telling me what's going on here?"

"What do you mean?"

"I'm not a moron, Dr. Polchak. Two bodies show up mysteriously on the second floor, but they have no wristbands—they weren't hospital patients. We pass the word, and the same day two DEA agents show up to collect the bodies—*the same day*. They can't get us the food, water, or medical supplies we need—they can't even medevac our critical patients out unless we boat them across the street to Tulane first—but they can come to remove two dead guys? Now you show up claiming to be with DMORT, and I give you five cadavers—but you're not interested in any of them. You only want the ones the DEA took away. Who were those two, anyway? What did they do?"

"I don't know," Nick said.

"You mean you won't tell me."

"If I did know, I probably wouldn't tell you—but the truth is, I don't know."

"Who's the boy?"

"A kid I rescued from a rooftop in the Lower Ninth Ward. I'm trying to figure out what to do with him."

"I'm looking for my father," J.T. said.

The doctor looked straight at Nick. "You thought you'd carry two bodies away with no one to help you but him? Who are you kidding? You didn't come here to take away any bodies at all. Why are you here? What is it you want?"

"I can't tell you," Nick said, "and if I did it wouldn't help you anyway."

"Then you're wasting my time," the doctor said. "I've got work to do, and you don't belong here. You need to go—now." He stepped aside and motioned for Nick and J.T. to go first.

Back on the third floor, the doctor brushed past Nick and into a patient's room. Nick spotted a flashlight flickering a few doors down and headed for it; he poked his head into the doorway and found the nurse.

"Can I talk to you for a minute?" he said. "I need a favor."

The nurse glared at him. "You need a *favor*?"

"I need to leave the boy with you."

J.T. looked at Nick. "No *way*. I ain't sick!"

"Let me get this straight," the nurse said. "I've got five stinking you-know-whats in my stairwell, but they're not the ones you're looking for, so you're leaving them here. And not only that, you want to leave me one more mouth to feed."

"That's about the size of it," Nick said. "No wonder they call you 'ladies of mercy.'"

"I ain't stayin' in no hospital," J.T. said. "I'm coming with you, Nick."

"No, you're not," Nick said, taking him by the shoulders and pulling him aside. "Remember that talk we had about following orders?"

"So?"

"So I need you to do it now. I'm leaving you here, and I want you to stay."

"No way!"

"Listen to me. I think something bad happened to Jerry—do you understand? I think somebody tried to hurt him, and he might be trying to hurt us too."

"I ain't afraid."

"I know you're not—but I am. I can't keep you with me, J.T. I know I told you I would, but things have changed. I need to leave you someplace where I know you'll be safe—someplace where there are lots of people around, where you'll have food and water and someplace to sleep. I can't take you back to the Superdome; it's not safe there, and by now the Convention Center might not be any better. You'll be safe here. The nurse will watch out for you."

"I'm stayin' with you, Nick."

"You can't stay with me."

"I'm lookin' for my father."

"That will have to wait."

"You promised!"

Nick straightened up and looked at him. This wasn't about keeping promises anymore; this was about keeping the boy alive, and Nick wished he knew a way to do it without breaking the boy's heart—but he didn't.

"I don't want you around anymore," Nick said.

"What?"

"You're no good to me. You get in the way."

"I got good eyes. I can see things."

"I can't have you in the boat with me. It's against the rules."

"You don't follow no rules."

"You're staying. That's final. Get used to it."

Nick turned and started down the hall.

"Liar!" J.T. shouted after him. "You promised! You lied! *Liar!*"

Nick didn't look back. *This isn't about promises*, he told himself. *This is about life and death.* But when the door closed behind him, he still felt sick to his stomach.

He waded back to the second-floor lab and climbed into the john-boat again. He put the palms of his hands against the ceiling and turned the boat back toward the open window. He stopped and stared out into the darkness, considering his next move—but he couldn't seem to focus his thoughts.

Jerry is dead, a voice inside him said. *You know it's true—and it's all your fault. You got him into this. He trusted you, and you let him down. People depend on you, Nick. People depend on you, and you let them down.*

He shook his head. The DEA had removed those bodies, and they had probably destroyed his maggots too. By now Turlock knew what Nick was up to—that he was disobeying orders and removing bodies from the water to preserve forensic evidence, evidence from victims the DEA didn't want identified.

Jerry was dead, he felt sure of it. But he couldn't go to the authorities—he was disobeying the authorities. Besides, he had no body to point to, and no one would bother to search for one until it was too late.

Someone was using the hurricane to cover up a series of murders, but Nick had no way to prove it. There were no bodies; there were no maggots; there was no physical evidence. Without evidence, he had no way to justify his actions to the DEA. Without evidence, his accusations would sound like nothing but paranoid delusions—which, Beth would probably point out, fit very neatly within his psychological profile.

He looked out the window again. He had to get back to the Lower Ninth Ward—not by the way he had come, but working his way block by block down flooded side streets and alleys so that no one could spot him or lie in wait. He would hide in the Lower Nine, under the magnolia tree where he kept the boat chained up each night; he would wait until daylight, when the boat ramp would be swarming with SAR teams putting in for the day; he would mingle in among them and head out into the neighborhood again, staying close to other boats while searching for any evidence that might still remain. It wouldn't be easy, but it was the only way. There was safety in numbers; Jerry had died alone.

Jerry.

Nick felt something like a warm blanket sliding up his back and around his shoulders. He felt his mind misting over, as if a thick bayou fog were settling in, confusing his thoughts and clouding his logic. It was something he had felt many times before—something Beth tried to warn him about—but he never listened, and he couldn't listen now. Nick needed to find evidence, evidence that was being destroyed with every passing hour.

He had to find it—and he couldn't stop until he did.

32

Sunday, September 4

Nick awoke at the first sound of an approaching vehicle. It had taken most of the night to work his way back from Charity Hospital to the Lower Nine, hiding in the shadows of buildings and houses, rowing most of the way to avoid running his engine. He'd arrived at the old magnolia tree less than an hour ago and stretched out facedown in the bottom of the boat. He was unconscious in seconds—a dreamless, deathlike sleep that satisfied nothing but his body's basic requirement to survive.

He lifted his head; his neck and shoulders ached from the rowing. He touched the left side of his face and felt a deep crevice running from his chin to his cheekbone, impressed into his flesh by the seam in the bottom of the boat. The left side of his face was as cold as a cadaver and numb, drained of life by the aluminum hull; the right side of his face was still soft and warm. That's how he felt right now: half dead and half alive. He would have killed for a cup of coffee—black, light, espresso, cappuccino, even the sweet fluffy crap from Starbucks—anything to help bring the rest of him back from the dead.

He pushed himself onto his knees and reached into his equipment bag, feeling around for the slick Mylar MRE bags. He pulled one out and looked at the label, but it was barely daylight, and in the shadow of the magnolia it was too dark to read. Breakfast, lunch, dinner, it didn't matter; it was food, and that's what he needed right now—fuel for his sputtering engine. He tore through the bag with his teeth and began to eat.

He lifted the lower branch of the old magnolia tree and peered out at the growing line of boats and vehicles awaiting put-in on the St. Claude Avenue "boat ramp" fifty yards away. A FEMA Urban Search and Rescue

Team was first in line; their rubber inflatable was already in the water and just about to shove off. A Wildlife and Fisheries trailer was just behind them, backing toward the water with two khaki-clad men guiding the way. He counted seven trucks and boat trailers waiting their turn, and more were coming across the bridge. There were men everywhere—hauling fuel cans, hoisting coolers, checking equipment bags, and loading rescue gear. Nick's plan was to wait until several boats had put in, then slip out from under the magnolia's branches and tag along close behind—but then he saw him, walking down the center of St. Claude Avenue between the boat trailers and the 4x4s, with his hands stuffed deep in his pockets and his head hung low.

J.T.

Nick muttered a curse and slid the boat out from under the tree. Halfway to the avenue he vaulted over the side and into the water, dragging the johnboat up onto the pavement.

"You're out early," one of the FEMA crew called out.

"The early fly gets the cadaver," Nick said.

"What?"

"Watch my boat—I'll be right back."

He met J.T. coming down the road; the boy looked up at him without saying a word. There was no anger in his eyes—no look of defiance or contempt—just a simple matter-of-fact expression that said, "So what did you expect?"

Nick opened his mouth to speak, but nothing came out. He just stood there looking at J.T., imagining what it must have taken for the boy to make his way here once again. It was a hard enough trip from the Convention Center, but that was all dry ground; Charity Hospital was completely surrounded by water. He must have jumped from a third-floor window, or at least found his way back to the second floor and then out through the broken lab window. The boy had to swim to dry ground, possibly several blocks—and then once again make his way through the looters and the armed gangs wandering the downtown streets.

That's when Nick noticed that the boy had a black eye—and that his binoculars were missing. He felt as if he had been punched in the stomach.

"I didn't expect to see you this morning," Nick said.

"I'm looking for my father."

"So I've heard. You don't give up easy."

The boy just shrugged.

"What happened to your binoculars?"

"Lost 'em."

"Did you get that black eye in the process?"

He shrugged again.

"I'll get you another pair," Nick said. "We'll need them to find your dad."

Now he knew that the boy had to stay with him—there was no place in New Orleans where his safety could be guaranteed. He couldn't leave him at DMORT—the facility was strictly off-limits to civilians. All they would do would be to transport the boy to one of the evacuation centers—the Superdome or the Convention Center. But the evacuation centers had become places of violence. The hospitals were overcrowded and understaffed, working without power or supplies, and the streets weren't safe either—the boy had been lucky to get away with a black eye. There was only one place where J.T. had a chance of being safe—with someone who cared about him. And in all the city of New Orleans—maybe in all the world—Nick might have been the only one who did.

"Okay," he said. "Let's get the boat and get going. I'm going to need those eyes of yours today."

They sat in the boat and allowed several other teams to go before them. When Nick finally spotted an armed National Guard unit preparing to put in, he called out, "Mind if I tag along today? I'm a little shorthanded. I'm with DMORT. I'm looking for bodies. You guys can handle the living, and I'll take care of the dead—how does that sound?"

"Sounds good to us," one of the Guardsmen called back.

Nick followed the National Guard boat deep into the Lower Nine. The

Guard boat was much larger and heavier than the johnboat; it had a deeper draft and left a much bigger wake. Nick stayed close behind and kept to the middle of the wake; it was like sailing down the center of a ditch. J.T. no longer took a standing position on the center bench—Nick told him to sit in the bow. He told him that without Jerry he needed the boy's weight in front to balance the boat, but that was a lie; seated in the bow the boy was a much smaller target.

Nick wasn't sure what was supposed to happen next. Was he just supposed to wait until the Guardsmen stumbled across a body, then examine it for anomalies? How long would that take? The Guardsmen had their eyes peeled for the living, not the dead. And what if they came across a body with no living rescuees in sight? Would the Guardsmen wait for them? Nick knew he couldn't just head off by himself—he needed the protection of the Guardsmen's rifles.

He needed evidence, but he needed safety. He motored along silently, lost in thought, considering how to satisfy those two seemingly irreconcilable goals—when a thought suddenly occurred to him.

They knew we'd be at the Superdome.

Their decision to go to the Superdome had been made last-minute, on the boat, just among the three of them: Nick, Jerry, and J.T. No one could have been waiting for them at the Superdome; no one could have known they'd be there.

We must have been followed.

Nick twisted around and looked behind him. A hundred yards away he saw another boat following at a steady pace—a gray-green fiberglass boat not much larger than his own. He turned forward again. *Of course there's a boat behind us*, he thought. *There are boats everywhere in the Lower Nine. That doesn't necessarily mean the boat is following us.*

But it might.

When the National Guard boat finally rounded a corner and took a different street, Nick turned and watched again, measuring the distance to the intersection behind him. *Twenty-five yards, fifty, seventy-five*—right on cue, the second boat rounded the same corner and followed.

Once could be a coincidence, Nick thought. *The next time I'll know for sure.*

He twisted the throttle and accelerated, lurching over the Guard boat's wake and pulling up along its starboard side. "Hey!" he shouted over the engines. "Take a left at the next big intersection—I want to check something out!"

The National Guard pilot nodded and complied; at the next intersection he slowly veered to port. Nick dropped back and followed, once again watching and measuring the distance behind. Sure enough, a hundred yards back the other boat rounded the same corner and followed.

Bingo.

Nick looked at the surrounding area; the neighborhood was congested, with tightly packed houses separated by narrow alleys. He accelerated and pulled up alongside the National Guard boat again.

"Find what you're looking for?" the pilot shouted over.

"I think so," Nick called back. "Stop at the next intersection."

Fifty yards ahead both boats slowed to a stop. Nick knew that the boat shadowing him would do the same, keeping a discreet distance.

"I spotted something back there," Nick said to the pilot. "I need to check it out. The alleys are really narrow here—I don't think you guys can follow me. Can you wait here for me? It'll only take a minute."

The pilot nodded. Nick waved a thank-you and slowly pulled forward, proceeding at a snail's pace until he was sure his shadow had begun to follow again.

Come on, you moron. Take it nice and slow, just like me.

He eased to the right around the next corner at the same trolling speed. When he was sure he was out of sight, he opened the throttle and accelerated to full speed. The propeller dug deep, churning the water into froth; the stern sank low and the bow tipped back, throwing J.T. backward off the bench and into the bottom of the boat.

"Hey!" he bellowed. "What's the big idea?"

"Open up that equipment bag," Nick shouted. "Get me one of those GPS units. Not the receiver, the little transmitters—the ones we used to tag the floaters, remember?"

The boy fished out one of the fist-sized units and held it up.

"That's the one," Nick said. "Toss it here."

The boy lobbed it to him; Nick caught it in his left hand and flipped the power switch with his thumb. With his right hand he kept the throttle wide open, passing three houses before veering right again, rounding a corner at full speed. The boat leaned hard to the right, sending out a wake on the port side that washed a feral cat off a toolshed roof.

They were now traveling parallel to the street they were originally on, moving fast in the opposite direction. Nick stared straight ahead, visualizing the scenario in his mind like a satellite photo: He saw the position of the Guard boat; the position of the boat shadowing him and its rate of speed; the position of his own boat and its greater acceleration. He made a quick mental calculation, then jerked the tiller toward him and veered right again, steering into a narrow alley between two houses.

He shouted up to the boy. "Did you swim from Charity Hospital?"

"What?"

"Can you swim?"

"Are we goin' swimmin'?"

"Somebody is. Hang on tight. Grab ahold of the bench—keep your fingers away from the edge of the boat."

Thirty yards. Twenty. Nick rechecked his mental calculations. *Ten yards. Five.* With his left hand he grabbed the port-side gunnel and braced himself.

As if on cue, the gray-green boat appeared from the left just as Nick emerged from the alley. Nick's boat smashed into the fiberglass hull at full speed, throwing the astonished pilot over the edge and into the water. Nick caught a glimpse of the man as he tumbled over: red hair cut in a flattop, dressed a little too nicely for search-and-rescue work—like a man who didn't expect to get his hands dirty out here.

Nick released the throttle and pulled on the tiller, swinging his stern in alongside; he reached across and grabbed the empty boat, steadying it—and lifted the lid on the bait well.

The pilot came up sputtering. "You son of a—"

"Didn't see you there!" Nick said. "A week ago you couldn't find another boat out here—now we're having traffic jams! Go figure!"

He grabbed the man's equipment bag and upended it, dumping its contents onto the bottom of the fiberglass boat. He found a small leather folder and opened it; the identification card read:

Special Agent John Detwiler
Drug Enforcement Administration
New Orleans Field Division

From the right, the National Guard boat slowly approached. "What happened here?"

"Had a little fender bender," Nick said. "My bad."

"These streets are narrow," a Guardsman said. "You came out of that alley pretty fast; better slow it down a little. We don't need to be rescuing our own people."

"That's good advice," Nick said, bracing the fiberglass boat while the dripping DEA agent hoisted himself over the opposite side. "My name is Nick Polchak—I don't believe I caught yours."

The man ignored him, wringing the water from his shirtfront and letting it fall in rivulets into the bottom of the boat.

"I'm with DMORT," Nick said. "What about you?"

"Fish and Wildlife," the man muttered, avoiding eye contact.

"No kidding," Nick said. "I thought you guys wore uniforms."

"This is volunteer duty," he said.

"Yeah, I suppose it is. Hey, I know a guy in Fish and Wildlife. Johnny Zubek—you know him?"

"I doubt I'd know anybody that you'd know."

"How about Jerry Kibbee?" Nick watched the man's face as he said the name, but the man never flinched.

Nick held up the business card. "Your name is John Detwiler," he said. "You work for the DEA, and you undoubtedly know a man named Frank Turlock."

Detwiler glared at him. "So?"

"Why is the DEA following me, Mr. Detwiler? I thought we had an agreement."

"So did we—until we got word from Charity Hospital that somebody stowed a couple of stiffs on their second floor. What was that all about, Polchak? You were supposed to locate bodies, not bring them back."

"Nobody said I couldn't bring them back halfway."

"Is that supposed to be funny?"

"I thought so."

"You're a regular comedian, Polchak—that's why I'm following you. Agent Turlock sent me out here to make sure you stick to our agreement—to make sure you leave the bodies where you find them."

"How long have you been following me?" Nick asked.

"Not long enough," Detwiler said. "No more bodies, Polchak. You got that?"

Nick said nothing.

Just then the National Guard pilot revved his engine and brought his boat up alongside. "Love to let you two chat," he said, "but we've got work to do. If you still want to tag along, Mr. Polchak, you need to come now."

"You'll have to excuse my friends," Nick said to Detwiler, keeping his eyes fixed on him. "You know how soldiers are—they get cranky when they have to carry rifles all day. I'd love to stay and talk, but you probably have to go too—you can't sit around in wet undies all day, now can you? If I were you, I'd head for the nearest Red Cross station. E. coli, Norovirus, coliform bacteria—there's no telling what you might have picked up from that nasty water."

Nick pushed away from the fiberglass boat and started his engine. "Nice to meet you, Detwiler," he said. "Now that I know who you are, I'll keep an eye out for you."

33

"That was way cool!" J.T. said, grinning from ear to ear.

"I thought you'd like that," Nick said.

"Bam! Just like a torpedo!"

"Yeah—too bad we didn't sink him."

Nick and J.T. sat cross-legged on the St. Claude Avenue boat ramp, digging into their lunchtime MREs. J.T. had decided on the beef ravioli and tore into it with gusto. Nick had selected one at random and began to eat mechanically, oblivious to the taste of the food; his mind was somewhere else.

The sun was directly overhead now. The temperature wouldn't peak for another few hours, but it was already over ninety degrees and humid, keeping the insects low.

J.T. slapped at the back of his neck.

"That only makes it worse," Nick said.

"How come?"

"A mosquito has a nose like a needle. When she lands on your neck—"

"How do you know it's a girl?"

"The girls are the ones that suck your blood—that's a good life lesson for you. They need protein from your blood to help develop their eggs. When she sticks in the needle, she squirts in a little anticoagulant first—stuff that keeps the blood from clotting. That's the stuff that makes you itch. As she feeds, she sucks most of it out again. If you wait until she's done eating, it won't itch so bad later."

"Just let 'em drink your blood?"

"Everybody has to eat," Nick said. "Even bugs."

Nick had followed the National Guard boat for another three hours, constantly checking behind him to see if Detwiler was still following. Nick felt confident that he no longer was; he enlisted the boy's unerring eyes to make sure. Apparently Detwiler had heeded Nick's suggestion and returned to shore for a change of wardrobe and a dose of antibiotics.

To err on the side of caution, Nick stuck close to the National Guard. But it was an error—it was a waste of time. The Guard were interested only in rescuing the living, and it didn't take long to find some; then Nick had no choice but to follow along patiently while they made the long trip to drop the rescuees at the levee and then head back for more. Most of the morning was spent this way, shuttling survivors back and forth; Nick had no chance at all to search for evidence, and time was ticking away. He knew he couldn't stay with the National Guard; he needed a new strategy, one that would give him more flexibility.

"How come you crashed into that guy?" J.T. asked.

"Just for fun."

"Nah, c'mon."

Nick wasn't sure how much to tell him. "Because he was following us, J.T."

"How come?"

"I'm not sure yet. Did you get a good look at him? Did you see his boat? Would you recognize it if you saw it again?"

"Sure, no problem."

"Well, let me know if you do."

"You think he'll try to follow us again?"

"Could be. If he does, next time we'll see him coming."

Nick heard the sound of an approaching engine and looked up. He saw the black Zodiac boat approaching at three-quarter speed, loaded as usual with a half dozen exhausted-looking evacuees. LaTourneau was at the helm again, working alone as always. He lined up with the ramp and accelerated a little, driving the flat-bottomed inflatable up onto the pavement. He was in uniform, as he seemed to be every day.

And he was wearing a sidearm.

Nick grabbed a couple of MREs and started toward him.

"Afternoon," he called out as he approached. "Remember me?"

"Polchak," LaTourneau said. "How could I forget? You're the wise guy."

"How about some lunch? I've got Meals Ready to Eat right here, sometimes affectionately referred to as 'Meals Rejected by Ethiopians' and 'Meals Refusing to Excrete.' Name your poison: You can have Barbecue Pork Rib or Chicken à la King."

"No time," LaTourneau said. "I've got work to do."

"You can't run a boat on an empty fuel tank," Nick said.

"I'm not a boat."

"You've got me there." Nick stepped a little closer. "Mind if I ask you a question?"

"What is it?"

"Have you stopped working since the city went under? Have you eaten one entire meal sitting down? Have you slept more than three hours in a row?"

"What are you, my mother?"

"No. I'm a compulsive workaholic just like you. I'm too dumb or too pigheaded to know when to quit. I keep driving myself until the problem's solved or until I drop, whichever comes first. Sound familiar? I'm just like you, LaTourneau—and I'm looking for a partner."

LaTourneau glanced at him. "You had a partner. What happened to him?"

"Long story. The point is, I need a new one—and so do you."

LaTourneau shook his head. "I'm doing fine by myself."

"No, you're not—I can see it on your face. You're not moving as fast as you used to; your concentration's slipping; you shake yourself and can't remember where you've been for the last three minutes."

"You don't know me, Polchak."

"No, but I know me. We were both out here the very first morning. You and me, LaTourneau—the only two boats on the Lower Nine.

We've been doing the same work, and we've been working the same hours. I figure we're in about the same place—and we could both use a little help."

"I don't need any help."

"Don't you? Face it, the job is changing. You're finding fewer and fewer healthy survivors, people who can climb into your boat under their own power. All that's left now are the crippled, the sick, and the dead—can you lift them all by yourself? I won't slow you down, I promise. I can work just as long and hard as you can. Give it a try—just for this afternoon. Think of it as a free trial offer—no obligation and no purchase necessary. What do you say?"

LaTourneau stopped and considered; it was the longest Nick had ever seen him stand still. "Okay," he said. "Just for this afternoon."

"Thanks. Oh, there's one more thing: See the boy over there? He comes with us."

"Not a chance. This isn't a tour boat, Polchak."

"He's not a tourist. This is his neighborhood—he knows the place, and he puts in a full day's work."

"He's a civilian—this is a job for professionals."

"C'mon, the place is crawling with civilian volunteers—every Bayou Billy and his fishing buddy are out in a bass boat trying to lend a hand."

"He's a kid."

Nick lowered his voice a little. "Look, the kid is searching for his father—I told him I'd help him out. I promised."

"Well, I didn't."

"It's a big boat. He's a little kid. He's got eyes like a hawk—he can spot a body floating facedown a quarter mile away. You look like you're about my age—how's your distance vision these days?"

LaTourneau looked at the boy and reconsidered. "One afternoon," he said. "If the kid starts whining, he's off the boat. If he gets hurt, it's your responsibility."

"Fair enough," Nick said. "Let me grab my gear."

"You've got three minutes."

Nick turned and found J.T. standing right behind him, ready to go. "Good news," Nick said. "We finally got a bigger boat."

From a Chevy Suburban parked inconspicuously on the St. Claude Avenue Bridge, Detwiler kept his binoculars trained on Nick Polchak. He watched as Nick waded into the water and slid his aluminum john-boat under the concealing branches of a nearby magnolia; he watched as Nick returned a moment later with a canvas duffel slung across his shoulders; he watched as Nick and J.T. climbed into the black Zodiac inflatable and roared away.

He picked up his satellite phone and dialed.

"Turlock," the voice on the other end said.

"It's Detwiler," he said. "You're not gonna believe this."

34

By 6:30 the sun was low on the horizon, sitting like an orange fireball on the western rim of the Lower Nine, setting off the rooftops in silhouette and filling in the streets and alleys with creeping shadow. The Zodiac was cruising west now, headed for the Surekote levee and ferrying three evacuees—one of them an elderly woman strapped to an orange backboard staring blankly into the sky. They'd found her on the second floor of a run-down "retirement community" deep in the Lower Nine, where she had been sitting in a wheelchair for almost six days in water to the knees.

She was too awkward to lift in the wheelchair and too big to fit through the window; their only alternative was to transfer her to a backboard and carry her out lying down. The skin of her legs looked like ground meat and white as a cadaver; in another day or two that's what she would have been. *She was lucky*, Nick thought, *she lived on the second floor—some of her friends were still downstairs*. Nick took a GPS reading and made a note.

When he had told LaTourneau back at the boat ramp that healthy evacuees would soon be hard to find, it was mostly a bluff—just a way to convince LaTourneau of his need for a partner. But Nick's prediction turned out to be more accurate than he knew. Most of the able-bodied survivors had been spotted by now and ferried to safety; what remained were the wounded and the infirm, and each rescue required far more effort than the one before.

Bodies, on the other hand, were becoming easier to find. Houses all over the Lower Nine now bore search markings left behind by FEMA Search and Rescue Teams beginning to go door-to-door. A fluorescent orange *X* was spray-painted near each point of entry. The left quadrant contained the team identifier and indicated the date and time they had entered the house; the top quadrant indicated the time they left; the right quadrant warned of any dangerous hazards or chemicals inside. The bottom quadrant was the portion that interested Nick; a simple *D* preceded by a number told him how many bodies he could expect to find inside.

And after six days of bloating in the tepid water, cadavers in the "fresh-floating" stage of decomposition were conveniently popping to the surface for easy examination. Nick briefly inspected each one but so far had discovered no further anomalies; the blowfly activity and general condition of each of the bodies indicated probable hurricane-related deaths. Nick wondered if there were any more anomalies left to find; just because he had been lucky enough to stumble onto a few didn't mean there were more.

Nick looked down at his feet; J.T. was curled up unconscious in the bow. The boy had been a real trouper all afternoon, working alongside Nick and LaTourneau without complaint—but he was still just a boy, and an hour ago he'd sunk down without a word and surrendered to sleep. Nick turned and looked at LaTourneau in the stern; he wondered if his new partner was as exhausted as he was. He knew there was no way to ask; Nick had promised to work as long and as hard as LaTourneau did, and LaTourneau would have to be the one to call it quits. All afternoon they had worked without a break, hurrying from one task to another. There seemed to be a kind of perverse competition between them. Nick had told LaTourneau that they could help each other, that they could reduce the load between them, but he wondered if just the opposite was happening; he wondered if they were egging each other on, refusing to take rest or refreshment when they might have done so alone. Nick wasn't sure how long he could keep it up, but it really didn't matter—he knew he couldn't quit, and LaTourneau probably couldn't either.

At the levee they unloaded their passengers and pointed those who could still walk toward the evacuation centers in the distance; they released the old woman to an EMS crew waiting on Surekote Road. Nick sat down on the embankment and took his time refastening the backboard straps, hoping that LaTourneau might follow suit. He did, sinking down on the ground beside Nick.

"Long day," Nick said.

"They're all long," LaTourneau replied.

Nick started to ask, "How are you holding up?" but the question seemed too personal. He looked at his new partner; up close, Nick could see that his face was pale and drawn and the blood had pooled below his eyes in gray half-moons. He wondered if he looked just as bad.

"The kid's pretty tough," LaTourneau said.

"Told you so."

"Not like most kids his age."

"Not like any I ever met."

They sat in silence for a few minutes, watching the sun shrink to a brilliant crimson arc. Nick glanced at LaTourneau again; his body seemed rigid, awkward, like a puppet slumping over on a stage. The man could sit, but he couldn't seem to relax; Nick wondered if his exhaustion was more severe than he knew.

"I'm so tired," LaTourneau said unexpectedly. Nick was shocked by the admission.

"I don't blame you. You've been out here longer than anyone else—even me."

"There's so much left to do."

"You don't have to do it all yourself," Nick said. "You can't save everybody."

"I can try. I have to try."

Nick could feel the hair standing up on his neck; it was like talking to himself.

"The people," LaTourneau said. "There are so many."

"Too many," Nick replied. "Somebody's got a lot of explaining to do."

"You keep looking at the dead bodies. Why?"

"That's my job. I'm a forensic entomologist."

"What is that?"

"I study the insects that feed on bodies when they die."

"That's disgusting."

"Funny thing," Nick said. "Everybody loves a caterpillar—but that's just the larval form of a butterfly. That's all a maggot is—a larva. Except when it pupates, a fly comes out instead."

"I can't stand maggots," LaTourneau said in almost a whisper.

"They're an acquired taste."

"I can't stand them," he said again. "Maggots get under your skin; they crawl all over you. You can feel them, especially at night when you try to sleep."

Nick gave his partner a puzzled look. He had worked with maggots for years, collecting them in every possible environment from corpses in every imaginable stage of decomposition. Yes, maggots could get on your skin—and yes, they could crawl on your skin—but *under* your skin? He wondered what LaTourneau was talking about; he wondered if his exhausted partner was in a state of twilight sleep, where dream images begin to mingle with the real world.

Just then they heard the sound of another boat approaching from the south and both men looked up. It was a FEMA Search and Rescue Team; they pulled up alongside the earthen levee and shut down their engine.

"Aren't you that bug man fella?" one of them called out.

"That would be me," Nick called back.

"I thought so. Remember us? You stopped us a couple of days ago—told us to pass the word if we found any unusual bodies."

"Yeah, I remember you guys. What did you find?"

"We didn't find it—somebody else did. A National Guard team passed the word to us; somebody else told them. Said they found a strange one in an attic somewhere—the kind you said you're looking for."

"What's strange about it?"

"They didn't say—they just said to pass it along if we saw you. Spotted the two of you sitting here; thought we'd stop and let you know."

"I appreciate that. Have you got coordinates for me?"

The FEMA crewman read them off and Nick took them down. The

man started his engine again and began to pull away. "Is this all you guys do—sit around?" he shouted. "Cushy job."

The two men watched as the boat roared away.

"*Cushy job*," Nick said. "I hope we find his body sometime." He looked down at the coordinates. "A strange one," the man called it, an anomaly—this could be just the break Nick was looking for. Nick knew he needed to check it out soon, before the body had a chance to decompose any further. He looked over at LaTourneau, thinking of suggesting one more trip back to the Lower Nine—but one look at the man's haggard face convinced him not to.

"Can I make a suggestion?" Nick said.

"Go ahead."

"Try to get some sleep. It's almost dark; there's not much you can do before sunup anyway."

"I can't sleep."

"I know," Nick said, "but give it a shot anyway—you get points just for trying."

"What about you?" LaTourneau asked.

"I have to check out that body."

"Leave it 'til morning, Polchak."

"Can't do that—time is critical. It's complicated."

"You can't do any good at night," LaTourneau said. "Leave it for the day."

"I can't."

"A man can't see at night—you can't find your way."

"I'll have to do my best."

"Then be careful," LaTourneau said. "This is a great town, but everything changes at night."

"It's the same everywhere," Nick said.

"I mean it, Polchak—everything changes at night."

"I'll keep it in mind. See you in the morning, partner."

Nick got up and stretched. He looked down the levee to his right. North Claiborne Avenue and its old lift bridge were just a quarter mile away; half a mile beyond it were St. Claude Avenue and his johnboat hidden under the old magnolia tree. They could walk it in fifteen minutes—in their current condition, maybe closer to thirty. By then it would be pitch black, and Nick would have to follow the coordinates in the dark. It wouldn't be easy, but he couldn't wait; he had to take a look. Besides, the darkness provided cover; it would allow him to investigate without fear of prying eyes and without the need for an armed escort. He knew he had to seize the opportunity while he could.

He went to the Zodiac and leaned across the bow, shaking the boy awake. "Let's take a little walk," he said. "We need some exercise."

Speak to me, sweetheart—speak to me.

He listened for his daughter's voice but heard nothing.

Tell me what to do. Tell me where they are. Tell me who the bad ones are and where to find them. I'll make things right, I swear I will. I'll keep my promise—I'll never rest until I do.

He rolled his head to the left and looked at the clock: Two more hours had passed. He lay on top of the bed, not in it, as if he were lying on a bed of nails; he could feel the prick of each nail point pressing against his skin. He stared at the glowing red LCD and waited for the minute to change; it seemed to take forever. He stiffened, anticipating the exact moment of transformation; when it finally occurred, he jumped and felt a bolt of electricity surge through his pulsing nerves.

Liar, he said to himself. *You told her you'd never rest, but here you are in bed. She knows when you're lying—she can see everything. Get up. Get to work. This isn't where she speaks to you—not here.*

He rolled to his feet and headed directly for the bathroom, where he found the medicine cabinet open and waiting for him. He pried open the familiar orange pill container and found it full again; he took two of the bitter pills and washed them down. He waited a few seconds but felt nothing. He took two more.

Speak to me, sweetheart. Talk to your daddy.

He held his breath and closed the cabinet door; he felt a shock of recognition travel through his body like an electromagnetic pulse. There was a message written on the mirror in lipstick—a street address followed by eight simple words:

In the attic, Daddy. Look in the attic.

35

Nick began to think he had made a big mistake. It was an almost moonless night, and the ink-black water and the forms that protruded from it all merged together into a seamless curtain of black. Again and again he started down alleys only to discover that they had no egress; once he drove directly into a rooftop that he couldn't even see; twice he fouled his propeller by running across underbrush that he would have easily spotted in the light of day.

His goal was to examine this body as soon as possible, before the accelerating effects of the environment destroyed any evidence that might remain—but what was the point if it took all night to get there? Maybe LaTourneau was right, maybe he should have waited for morning—maybe he couldn't find his way through the Lower Nine at night, especially without any help from J.T. fast asleep in the bow. Nick needed the boy's eyes now more than ever, but he couldn't bring himself to wake him again. It was one thing to drive himself to utter exhaustion—he had no right to make the same demands of a boy.

He switched on his flashlight again and checked the coordinates on the GPS receiver, adjusting his course slightly to the east. The GPS unit had its own LED backlight for viewing at night, but Nick used the flashlight instead to conserve the unit's batteries. He was forced to check the coordinates constantly, and he had no idea how much power remained. If the batteries failed he would be completely blind with no way to move forward or back; his only alternative would be to curl up in the bottom of the boat with the boy and wait until morning—and that would waste the entire night.

Finally, the coordinates on the GPS receiver indicated that he was near. Nick switched on the flashlight again and squinted into the darkness. Straight ahead of him were two single-story homes, their low-pitched rooftops protruding from the water like books left facedown on a table. The GPS was accurate only to within a few yards; either house might be the one that held the body. He slowly motored around the first one, checking for FEMA search markings or signs of forced entry. He found none.

But on the second house he found an attic vent completely caved in, leaving a gaping black triangle at the peak of the roof. He shut down his engine and approached by oar, shining his flashlight through the broken roof vent and into the darkness inside. He pulled up alongside the house and looked in; as impossible as it seemed, the attic was even darker than it was outside. It was perfect darkness, the kind you find only in cellars and caves, and Nick's flashlight beam could barely penetrate it—but it was enough to reveal a human form lying faceup halfway across the room. The attic floor was covered with water, and the body seemed to float on top of it like a bar of pink soap.

Nick checked the side of the house for a place to tie up the boat. He found nothing—but there was no current to the water, either, and the boy's weight should have added enough ballast to keep the boat from drifting in the wind. Assuring himself that his transportation would still be there when he returned, Nick swung one leg through the opening and felt around for solid footing inside. When he pulled his other leg through, he inadvertently pushed off slightly from the boat, sending it drifting slowly away. He looked at the boat and muttered a curse; he was hoping for a dry return, and now a short swim might be necessary. Just what he needed to top off a delightful evening—a midnight dip in a pool of toxic waste.

He stood on the narrow edge of the first floor joist and pointed the flashlight at the water. He knew the joists should have been constructed on standard sixteen-inch centers; he reached out with his left foot and tested the water at the appropriate spot—there it was, right where it should have been. He tiptoed forward and repeated the process, working his way toward the body like a tightrope walker, picking up speed and gaining confidence in his footing—until his left foot disappeared into the water and he plunged in up to his hip, landing with his gut across one joist and his collarbone on another.

The impact knocked his wind out completely. He lay there motionless, waiting to take his next breath, feeling around in the water with his dangling left leg to find the reason for his mishap. There it was—a folding ladder. Nick had reached out his foot for the next expected joist but stepped instead into the attic doorway leading to the house below.

The man shut off his engine and rocked it forward, lifting the propeller from the water. He was close now, and he didn't want to take a chance on being heard. He used the electric trolling motor instead, cruising silently forward toward the darkened house.

This was the place—this was the address she'd left him—but there seemed to be no one there. Maybe she was wrong this time; maybe she had made a mistake. But she had always been right before, when she left the messages on the bathroom mirror and the bitter little pills that helped him understand—the pills that helped him think the way she did. She left the pills for him too. The bottle was never empty; no matter how many he took, there were always more waiting for him the next night.

In the attic, she said—*look in the attic.*

In his peripheral vision he caught a faint flash of light at the left side of the house. He motored around to that side and found the open attic vent; the flicker of a flashlight inside told him that the house was not empty after all. He was in there, just as she had said.

Forgive me, sweetheart—forgive me for ever doubting you. I keep forgetting that you can see everything now. How could you ever be wrong?

He pulled the thin metal tiller and steered the boat slowly around to the opposite end of the house where the attic vent was still intact. He peered through the narrow slats and saw the beam of the flashlight clearly now. It was pointed at the floor, illuminating the body of a man lying in the water. Someone was bending over the body, examining it.

He leaned back and looked at the slats of the attic vent, then at the house itself. There was something familiar about the place—something familiar about the body inside—but he couldn't remember what it was. No matter; the man inside had to be the one he was looking for. She told him he would find him there, and she was never wrong.

He was one of them—one of the ones who made the pills that killed you.

Now it's his turn to die.

He twisted the fuel line from the boat's gas tank and attached a length of rubber hose to the tank instead; he quietly fed the other end through the attic vent's slats until the hose dangled just above the surface of the water inside. Now he began to pump a metal handle on the fuel tank up and down; it made a low, sucking sound, drawing gasoline up into the hose and pumping it through, pouring it silently onto the water of the attic floor.

Nick knelt over the body and studied it; he held the flashlight as close as possible, illuminating every detail, examining it from head to foot. Where was the anomaly the men had mentioned? There was nothing unusual about this body; there was no advanced stage of decomposition, there were no unusual wounds. In fact, there seemed to be no wounds at all—the cause of death was not immediately apparent. What was it about this body that had caused them to find it "strange"?

Then he saw it—something he would have spotted immediately in the balanced light of day but now was disguised by the bluish beam of the halogen flashlight. It wasn't the condition of the skin that made the body strange, it was the *color*—it should have been turning a bluish-green by now, but instead it was a bright pink.

Nick sniffed at the air and wrinkled his nose; the stench of petroleum was strong here. There was no telling what the polluted water in this part of the Lower Nine might contain; the floodwaters had inundated gas stations and even entire refineries. He looked down at his dripping clothing and wondered what his skin might be absorbing even now. He held the flashlight low to the water and looked; sure enough, he could see the rainbow reflection of an oil film undulating across the surface.

Nick held his own arm up against the cadaver and made a color comparison. There was no doubt about it: Either Nick had recently died or the body was definitely pink—and that could mean only one thing. He looked around the room for some explanation but saw nothing.

When Nick's flashlight swept past the roof vent at the opposite end of the house, something caught his eye, causing him to look back—something out of context, something that seemed out of place. He looked again; he saw a black rubber tube protruding from between two vent slats and hanging down over the water. Some kind of fluid seemed to be gushing from the end.

It suddenly stopped.

Nick stood up.

He saw a flash of light from outside the roof vent—not the steady glow of a flashlight's beam, but the quick flaring glare of a match. He dropped his own flashlight into the water and took a deep breath.

He turned and dived headfirst through the attic doorway into the house below.

36

Nick's feet had barely disappeared beneath the water before the attic above him exploded in brilliant orange fire.

The impact of his dive ripped the glasses from his face; he twisted in the water and felt around frantically for them, but it was useless. The lukewarm water was choked with particulate matter swirling around him like leaves on a windy day; he clutched at the largest pieces and felt nothing but clumps of soggy cardboard and waterlogged wood. He needed those glasses—without them he was blind—but right now there was something he needed even more.

He needed air.

He felt a wave of panic coming over him; a thousand thoughts rushed, screaming at him like madmen in a crowd.

Go back! Better to burn than to drown!

Get out! Swim hard, swim fast, try to find a way out!

Give in! It's no use, you can't see, there isn't time!

He felt adrenaline pulsing through his system, accelerating his heart rate and robbing him of precious oxygen—oxygen that he couldn't spare. In less than a minute his lungs would begin to feel that aching burn; his mind would grow numb and his thoughts confused; he would begin to lose muscular control; his motions would become desperate and spasmodic. Then his limbs would go limp as his body gently settled to the bottom, where the bacteria in his gut would rage and devour, bloating his abdomen with methane and CO_2 until he slowly floated to the surface again.

Go back!

Get out!

Give in!

You're going to die, Nick—this time you're going to die.

He squeezed his eyes tight and shut out all of the voices—except for one. It was a woman's voice, and it spoke to him quietly and clearly.

People depend on you, Nick. People depend on you.

He forced his body to hang limp in the water like a fetus in a womb, reining in his racing heart and forcing himself to *think*. His biggest enemies were fear and panic causing him to make stupid choices—flailing around in the water, using up his air, hurrying death along. *Think*, he told himself. Nick had made a living using his mind, and if he had to die, he wanted to die the same way.

He couldn't go up again—the attic was in flames. Even if he broke through the fire and drew in a breath, the superheated air could sear his lungs and cause instant death.

He had to go out—but which direction? What if he swam into a closet or a bathroom with no way of escape? He'd better get it right the first time; he'd only have time to try once.

He opened his eyes and looked around the room. The attic was still blazing above him, casting a shaft of yellow light down through the attic doorway and faintly illuminating the room. If only he had his glasses! All he could make out were dark geometric blurs, but what did they represent? The room was like a circus funhouse—everything was inverted or out of place. He saw a big vertical rectangle on one of the walls—a doorway? But the corners looked rounded and the edges seemed to curve—a sofa, maybe, standing on end? He saw a smaller square shape along another wall, the size of a dresser or a coffee table, but it was up against the ceiling—what was it? He couldn't be sure—and he didn't have time to guess.

Then he spotted it—a large, horizontal rectangle near the center of one wall—a window, the quickest way out of the room and up to the surface above. He twisted off his shoes and swam toward the rectangle, wondering if he would have to smash through the glass—but what he bumped into was solid and hard. He felt along the edge; it wasn't a window at all—it was a picture frame hanging on the wall.

He felt a dull ache starting in the pit of his lungs.

Big mistake, ace—you won't have time for another one.

He didn't have time to swim back across the room and try a different direction. He had committed himself, and, right or wrong, he had to keep going. He leaned back from the wall and looked again; beside the picture frame was a tall vertical rectangle. He reached out to touch it and his hand went right through—a doorway. It didn't matter where it went—at least it led out of this room. He grabbed the edge of the doorway with both hands and pulled himself through.

The next room, whatever it was, was as black as a tomb—no light from the burning attic found its way inside. *Now I'm really blind,* Nick thought, and then he stopped. *I'm blind—I'm just like any other blind man who has to find his way out of a strange room. What would a blind man do?*

He closed his eyes again. He knew what a blind man would *not* do: dart back and forth across the room, ricocheting off random objects without gaining any understanding of the space around him. He turned to his immediate right and began to feel along the wall. His head bumped into something projecting from the wall. He felt it; it seemed to be some kind of cabinet. He felt around below the cabinet and found a flat, smooth surface—a Formica counter. He was in a kitchen.

The ache was growing in his chest; he felt his diaphragm contract reflexively, trying to draw breath into his starving lungs.

He grabbed the edge of the counter and pulled himself forward, feeling along the top of the counter as he went, leaving his legs hanging limp to conserve energy and reduce oxygen consumption. He found a twin-basin sink and wondered if he would come to a corner soon. He did, just as expected; he turned left and continued, constructing a mental image of the room as he went.

The counter abruptly ended and he felt metal instead. He reached up and patted the top; he felt the spiraling coils of heating elements—an oven. Beyond the oven should be the refrigerator—but when he got to the appropriate place, the space was empty. Why?

It didn't matter. He had his mental picture, or at least a portion of it: counter, sink, corner; oven, refrigerator—and then what? Every kitchen had an exit door. Where would it be? There were only two walls left to choose from. He consulted his fragmentary mental image again and made a logical deduction—then pushed off and swam to the next wall.

More counters! Was he wrong? Was it the other wall? He felt above the counters and felt glass—a window! But it was a fixed-pane window, too hard to break and too small to pull himself through.

His lungs were on fire now. He couldn't hold back the panic anymore—his mind felt like a wobbling wheel about to spin off into space. He started to feel along the wall, but which way—right or left? He had only seconds of consciousness left. One way meant death, the other life. But there was no way to know—it was a pure guess.

Think!

But Nick could barely hear the word above the dull buzz rising in his head. *Sounds like bees,* he thought—*like angry honeybees. Order Hymenoptera, family Apidae, genus Apis . . . Why are the bees so angry? I like bees—I've always liked bees . . .*

Right! Go right!

He felt furiously along the wall to the right—and found a door.

His chest was heaving, sucking like a dry pump. He let his adrenaline go now, hoping it would buy him an extra few seconds. He twisted the knob and pulled, but the door moved through the water slowly, heavily, like a spoon through jelly. He couldn't wait for it to fully open; he wedged his body into the opening and squeezed through.

He was outdoors now, the air was just above his head—just a few more inches to go. He pushed off with his half-dead legs, launching himself upward, his lungs about to implode.

His head hit the ceiling.

The impact was crushing, but it was the despair that almost killed him. He reached up with his hands and numbly felt along the surface. The ceiling wasn't smooth—it had ridges and grooves.

Paneling. Back porch.

The sound in his head was a rising shrill note now. He was conscious but had no discernible thoughts. He was operating on instinct; it was all he had left. He pulled his knees up and crawled along the ceiling like a spider until his head bounced against something springy and flat.

Screen.

He pushed against it and it slowly gave way, drifting off as if it were in space. He reached around the edge and felt the gutter.

He pulled with everything he had left.

37

"You look terrible," Beth said, "the worst I've ever seen you—and that really says something."

"Thanks," Nick said. "You look terrific—but then, everything does right now. I suppose that's what happens when you thought you'd be dead."

"Dead? What happened?"

"It's a long story."

"I haven't seen you or heard from you in two days. Where have you been? What's going on?"

Nick looked over at J.T., who was wolfing down a Belgian waffle smothered in strawberry syrup topped with whipped cream. "I've seen a lot of disgusting things lately, but I'd put that near the top of the list. You doing okay?"

"Okay," the boy said, never missing a beat.

"We had quite a night, huh, partner?"

"You left me in the boat," J.T. said, frowning.

"I had to—otherwise who would have pulled me out of the water?"

"Spotted you when you popped up," he said.

"It's a good thing you did—I sure couldn't see you."

They sat in a booth at a Waffle House in Gonzales, just off Interstate 10 a few miles from the town of St. Gabriel. It was almost 4:00 a.m. when Beth got the call from Nick to meet him here, waking her from a fitful sleep. A FEMA trailer truck had dropped them off, he said—could she meet him right away? He needed food and coffee, and he had no money to buy them with. More important, he needed a change of clothing and his extra set of glasses—and he said he didn't want to have to answer questions from nosy DMORT personnel about his appearance. She wondered what he meant.

Now she knew. She was astonished when she first saw him; his clothes were in ruins and his face was sallow and pale. He was barefoot, and his hair was plastered to the sides of his head as if he had shampooed it but never rinsed. And most startling of all, his glasses were missing. Beth had never seen Nick without his glasses before; he was functionally blind without them—he would have to be led around by the hand. That was exactly how she found him: shuffling toward her car in the Waffle House parking lot with J.T. hanging on to his arm.

"Where is Jerry?" Beth asked.

Nick turned and looked at the boy again; he had just finished off his waffle and was leaning back against the window now, beginning to doze off. "I tell you what," Nick said. "Beth's car is parked right outside—why don't you stretch out in the backseat and get some sleep?"

"Don't need no sleep," he said.

"Are you working with me tomorrow or not?"

"Sure I am."

"Then get some rest. I can't have you falling asleep on me in the middle of a job. What if we need to blow up another house?" He stood up and let the boy slide out of the booth. "Lock the doors," Nick called after him. "I'll be right here if you need me." He sat down again and watched through the window until he saw the boy climb into the car and slide down into the backseat.

He motioned to the waitress and pointed to his empty coffee cup. "Okay," he said. "We can talk now."

"Nick, what happened? Where's Jerry?"

"Have you heard from Jerry in the last thirty-six hours—at the DPMU, at the Family Assistance Center? Has anybody seen him or mentioned him?"

"No. What's wrong? What happened?"

"Jerry is—missing."

She didn't respond. She could tell that Nick was guarding something, either to prepare her or to protect himself.

"We went to the Superdome," he said. "We were looking for J.T.'s dad. We got separated—I stayed with the boy, Jerry went off on his own. Jerry never came back. I waited all afternoon. I haven't seen him since."

Her heart sank. "Oh, Nick."

"It's my fault," he said. "I was responsible; I should have anticipated; if anything happened to Jerry, it's all my fault."

"No," she said, "it's mine."

He looked at her. "What do you mean?"

"The other night, when we were driving back from the bayou—you asked me if I had heard anything from J.T.'s social worker yet. I lied. I did hear back from his social worker, Nick—she told me that J.T. has no father. He did, once, a long time ago—but his father left the family when J.T. was only four. He hasn't been heard from since. The boy has no mother either; he's been passed from family to family in the Lower Ninth Ward, raised by a loose-knit assembly of 'cousins' and neighbors who took turns taking him in."

"Why didn't you tell me this before?"

"I should have—I know that now—but I saw the connection you were making with the boy and I wanted it to continue. If I'd told you J.T. had no father, you might have sent him away. The more you're around him, the more human you seem to become, Nick; I didn't want that to stop. He's the best thing that's happened to you in a long time."

"You had no right to make that judgment."

"I did it for you."

"That's a load of crap—you did it for yourself. Do I really need to be 'more human,' Dr. Woodbridge, or do you just like me better that way?"

"That's not fair."

"Tell it to Jerry—if you can find him. If you had told me this when you first found out, Jerry and I never would have gone to the Superdome."

"I know," she said, "and it's eating a hole through my stomach right now. If something has happened to Jerry, it's my fault, not yours—how do you think that makes me feel?"

They both sat in silence, staring at the table.

"I've got about a thousand questions," Nick said.

"So do I."

"Me first: If the kid has no father, then what does he want from me?"

"He told you, Nick—he's looking for a father."

"Make sense, will you?"

"He has no father, so he's looking for one—and I think he's found one."

"Who?"

"You, of course."

"Me? You must be kidding."

"For an intelligent man, you can be really thick sometimes. When I first asked J.T. to describe his father, do you remember what he said? 'Tall; smart; with glasses.' '*Like Nick*,' he said. Odd, isn't it, that his father just happens to closely resemble you? And haven't you ever wondered why J.T. doesn't seem to be in any particular hurry to find his father? He seems perfectly content to follow you around day after day."

"I just thought . . . I figured that—"

"Like I said, Nick: He's looking for a father, and he's found one."

Nick shook his head. "Some father. I almost got him killed tonight."

"What happened?"

"I was set up."

"What do you mean?"

"Somebody passed me a message about a strange body. I heard about it from a FEMA crew; they got it from the National Guard; somebody purposely fed the information to them because they knew the word would get to me. Whoever it was knew I'd go and check it out right away; when I did, somebody was waiting for me there. I was in the attic—J.T. was asleep outside in the boat. Someone approached from the opposite side—they fed a hose through the roof vent and pumped gasoline into the attic—then they dropped a match and the whole thing went off like a bomb."

"How in the world did you get out?"

"I dived down into the house and swam out."

"You *what*?"

He shrugged.

"Is that how you lost your glasses?"

He nodded.

"Then how did you ever find your way out? How could you see? Wasn't it dark?"

"The point is, J.T. was outside in the boat—what if that guy had spotted him? He would have killed him for sure. Some father I am—he should have picked somebody else. I don't want him to get hurt, but I'm not sure I can protect him."

She patted his arm. "You're talking like a father already."

"So what do I do with him now, send him away somewhere? He has no family—where would I send him?"

"Maybe he'd be better off in Houston, with the people they're relocating to the Astrodome."

"They went after Jerry in the Superdome," Nick said. "What makes you think J.T. would be safe there?"

"Do you think he's any safer with you?"

"At least I know I'll look out for him. Who would look out for him in Houston? I can't protect him if he's someplace else. No, I'm keeping him with me—but I can't keep putting him in danger."

"What are you going to do?"

"I'm going to expose the guy who tried to kill me tonight—it's the only way to get rid of him. I'm betting it was the same guy who fired on us in the bayou—the same guy who killed Jerry. I know who it was, Beth."

"Who?"

"His name is John Detwiler. He works for the DEA."

"Detwiler? Was he one of the agents you met in Denny's office? The ones who told you not to recover any more bodies?"

"I never saw Detwiler. I only met his partner, Frank Turlock. I think that's why he had Detwiler follow me—he knew I wouldn't recognize him."

"You think the DEA is trying to kill you?"

"I don't think, I know."

"But why?"

"I'm not quite clear on that one yet."

"They wouldn't try to kill you just to keep you from recovering bodies—that would be insane."

"That depends."

"On what?"

"On *why* they don't want me to recover bodies. They told me it would interfere with a major investigation—but maybe that's not the real reason. Maybe they don't want me to recover bodies because they put them there."

"Nick, if that's true, we need to go to the authorities."

"I plan to, the minute I have proof—and I should have it in just a few minutes."

"What proof?"

"Did you bring my laptop?"

She opened her briefcase and took it out. "I can't believe you. If I went through what you did tonight, I'd be curled up in a fetal position."

"It's hard to type that way." He opened the laptop and turned it so they both could see. When the desktop opened, he double-clicked on an icon with the letters *GPS* beneath.

"What are you doing?"

"I tagged the guy's boat."

"You what?"

"Somebody must have followed Jerry and me to the Superdome, Beth—that's the only way they could have known we were there. I think the same guy has been following me around the Lower Nine—I spotted him yesterday."

"What did you do?"

"I circled around and rammed him—knocked him right out of his boat and into the water. It was beautiful, you should have seen it. Then, when he wasn't looking, I planted a GPS transmitter in his boat."

"Why?"

"Because I wanted to keep track of him, that's why. Are cell phones working up here yet?"

"They work pretty much everywhere except in New Orleans."

"Good." Nick made a cellular connection to the Internet and switched over to the GPS program. He entered the zip code 70112 and a map of the city of New Orleans appeared; he repositioned the map and zoomed in closer, focusing on the Lower Ninth Ward. Now he hit Download Data, and a series of multicolored dots began to appear like pushpins all over the map—some red, some green, some yellow, each color connected by a thin black line.

"What are those dots?" Beth asked.

"The present location of every floater I've tagged since I got here. The bodies drift in the current—this is how we keep track of them. The GPS units are battery-powered; once every hour they send out a signal that a satellite picks up—sort of like the EPIRB units the Coast Guard uses for marine rescue."

"EPIRB?"

"Emergency Position-Indicating Radio Beacon. Didn't they teach you anything useful in medical school? Each unit sends a different signal, displayed here as a different color of dot; each dot indicates the exact position of the unit every hour. See there? Beside every dot there's a date, a time, and a set of GPS coordinates. When DMORT finally gets around to recovering bodies, this program will lead us right to them."

Nick traced his finger across the screen. "This is where I was a few hours ago; that's the approximate location of the house that went up in flames. These green dots—they represent the signal from Detwiler's boat." He leaned closer and studied the screen. "Wait a minute."

"What's the matter?"

"They don't match. The green dots—the ones from the GPS unit in

Detwiler's boat—they don't even come close to where I was tonight."

"Nick, I'm not following you."

"Don't you get it? If Detwiler was the one who tried to kill me tonight, there should be a green dot near that house, but look—he never even came close." He put his finger on the screen and traced the series of green dots. "Here's the first dot—see it? That would be the place where I first dropped the GPS unit into his boat. From that point he went—here," he said, following the black line to the second dot. "This is where he was one hour later—that's the levee. Maybe he left his car there—he probably stopped to change clothes. Now look—he headed back into the Lower Nine again. It wouldn't have taken him an hour to get to the next location; he must have stopped along the way—or maybe he was doing something once he got there. There's the third dot, then the fourth and the fifth; looks like he zigzagged back and forth across the Lower Nine. He must have spent the whole afternoon there, until he finally headed—here. Look—he crossed the Industrial Canal and headed downtown."

"Back to the Superdome again?"

"No—look at the dot. That's not where the Superdome is; it's a few blocks west of there—he stopped somewhere else. Then he backtracked again, but he didn't go back across the Industrial Canal—he headed northwest this time, up into this neighborhood here. That's a residential area; I wonder what he wanted up there?"

"Maybe he lives there. We could check the phone book."

"Good idea. Check the Yellow Pages under 'People Who Arrest Drug Dealers.'"

"You don't have to be sarcastic."

"Look—when he left, he headed back across the Industrial Canal and ended up here—at the levee, near the same place he stopped before."

The last green dot was actually a series of dots overlapping one another like the petals of a flower. "He must have docked there," Nick said. "The dots don't move. The boat must have stayed put all night, sending out a signal every hour from the same location." Nick shook his head in frustration. "I was *sure* it was him."

"Are you sure it wasn't?"

"What do you mean?"

"What time did he dock?"

Nick checked the text display beside the final set of dots. "Eight o'clock," he said. "Just after dark."

"Would that still give him time to get to the house?"

"You mean in a different boat."

"Exactly."

"It's possible; but the point is, I have no way to *know*—I can't prove anything. Maybe I was wrong—the guy who tried to kill me tonight could have been anybody: Detwiler, someone else from the DEA—Turlock, maybe—or someone else entirely. Maybe Detwiler was telling the truth—he told me he was only following me to make sure I followed orders. I could be completely off track here."

Nick slumped back against the booth and looked up at the ceiling. "I could use a break down here," he said.

"I didn't know you were a praying man," Beth said.

"I'm a father now—I guess it comes with the territory." He stopped for a moment to consider his options. "If it's a total stranger who's trying to kill me, there's nothing I can do about it but wait until he tries again—but I can't just sit here; I have to do something. I know about Detwiler; I know the DEA is following me; and, like you said, Detwiler isn't off the hook yet—he still had time to get to the house if he used a different boat. Detwiler's the only lead I've got right now; I've got a computer printout of the places he visited yesterday, hour-by-hour. I'm going to retrace his steps, and I'm going to find out where he went and why. Maybe there's something Turlock and Detwiler haven't told me yet."

She watched him as he spoke; she could almost see the gears turning in his head. She couldn't imagine what he must have been through tonight—not just physically, but emotionally; psychologically. The experience would have devastated most men, and yet here he was—contemplating his next move.

"What was it like?" she asked gently.

"What was what like?"

"The house—the fire—diving down into that filthy water and finding your way out in the dark, all alone."

"I don't want to talk about it."

"I would have drowned for sure—I think I would have gone insane. What went through your mind, Nick? What did you feel?"

Nick rolled his eyes. "See, this is why things didn't work out between us."

"What do you mean?"

"You always want inside my head. You're always asking me how I feel. Do you know the difference between a criminal and a husband? A criminal has the right to remain silent."

"Okay," she said. "I just want you to know I'm here. I know you can't go back there right now—I know you've got to focus—but you have to go back sometime. Trust me, Nick, experiences like the one you had tonight don't just go away—please remember that. Either you deal with it, or it will deal with you. If you ever want to talk about it, I'm here."

Nick nodded. He looked out the window at the car. "Do you think J.T. knows?"

"Knows what?"

"That he has no father."

"You mean, is he deluding himself?"

"I mean, how does this end? I can't just keep pretending that I'm looking for his father. Sooner or later I'll have to confront him—I'll have to tell him that I know. How will he respond to that? What happens then?"

"I don't know, Nick. I don't know."

She looked at Nick's face; he looked utterly exhausted, but there was no loss of resolve in his voice—somehow he kept pressing on. How did he keep going, she wondered—and how long could he keep it up?

"You're not an insect," she said.

"What?"

"Just a friendly reminder from your psychiatrist: Even insects have to sleep."

"Ants don't."

"Shut up and listen to me. If you run an engine too long, the engine burns up—it's as simple as that. You have to stop, Nick; you have to rest; you need sleep. I want you to come back with me to the DPMU. Bring J.T. along—sneak him into your trailer if you have to—but promise me you'll get a few hours' sleep."

"It'll be dawn in a couple of hours. I slept in the truck on the way up—I can sleep again on the way back."

"That's only an hour each way. That won't do it, Nick."

"It'll have to—this can't wait."

"Things can never wait with you."

"Look—whoever tried to roast me tonight thinks I'm dead. That means they won't be following me and they won't be trying to kill me again. I'm invisible right now; I need to do whatever I can before they find out I'm still alive. I'll get some sleep tomorrow night—I promise."

"You promise?"

"I promise."

"Are you lying?"

"Probably."

She shook her head in disgust. "I give up on you."

"Now who's lying?" he said.

38

Monday, September 5

"You sure this is the right place?" J.T. asked.

"I wish you'd stop saying that." Nick rechecked the coordinates on the GPS receiver and looked around—but there was nothing there. They were floating in a nondescript section of the Lower Nine, surrounded by nothing but the usual rooftops, half trees, and floating debris. According to his laptop, this was one of the places where Detwiler had stopped his boat just the day before. He passed this point at precisely five o'clock central standard time, when the GPS transmitter hidden in his bait well sent out a split-second signal to a satellite above. Detwiler had been here—but why?

"This looks just like the other places," the boy said.

"I know. Don't remind me."

It was already late afternoon. The day had begun much later than Nick had hoped. After two frustrating hours spent attempting to hitch a ride back to the city, he was forced to call Beth from the Waffle House again and ask her to let him borrow her Lexus. She consented, but only on the condition that Nick would return with it to the DPMU that evening—and that he would sleep when he got there. Nick had no choice; he reluctantly agreed.

By the time he reached the boat ramp on St. Claude Avenue, the sun was climbing overhead and the roadway was crowded with SAR teams putting in. It was exactly what Nick had hoped to avoid; his plan had been to arrive before anyone else and slip out unseen to avoid revealing his presence. If anyone was still watching for him it would be at the boat ramp, the one place he was sure to return to every day. But he was late;

now there were eyes everywhere; now his only choice was to wait until everyone else had put in and then follow behind.

It took hours. It seemed to Nick as though everybody and his brother were mounting a last-minute rescue effort in the Lower Nine. *Where were these people a week ago?* he wondered. *Why did they have to wait until now?* By the time Nick and J.T. finally put in it was almost noon, and precious daylight was slipping away.

They headed directly for the spot where Nick had first rammed Detwiler and slipped the transmitter into his boat. From there they retraced Detwiler's route dot by dot, following the coordinates with their GPS receiver, searching for clues as to why he had taken this path instead of another.

They found nothing. Nick traveled slowly from point to point, realizing that Detwiler could have stopped at any point along the way. But every place looked the same—nothing but flooded neighborhoods. He checked the houses along both sides of the path; he found no FEMA search markings, no signs of forced entry, no telltale odor of decomposing flesh. Detwiler had spent an entire afternoon zigzagging back and forth across the Lower Nine for no apparent reason.

"You sure we got the right spots?" J.T. asked.

"I'm sure."

"There's nothin' here."

Nothing above the water, Nick thought. *No telling what you might find below.* Two bodies had disappeared from Charity Hospital, removed by the DEA—where did they go? If the DEA didn't want the bodies identified, Nick knew exactly where they had gone: back in the water, where the toxic gumbo would finish the job. Maybe that's why Detwiler had come here—to make sure no embarrassing revelations came floating up again.

"Might as well move on," Nick said.

"Where next?"

He checked the laptop screen: They had retraced every dot in the Lower Nine. Their next stop was at the earthen levee along the Industrial

Canal, then across the canal and into the city beyond. "We won't need the GPS for this one," Nick said. "Just head west until you see land. And let's quit lollygagging—open 'er up a little this time." They needed to hurry; there were still two points to check out—one in the downtown area and one farther north—and there were only a couple of hours of daylight left.

J.T. grinned and twisted the throttle. The boat rocked back, but only a little; Nick's weight in the bow kept it down. Nick had let the boy pilot the boat all day. Why not? If Nick had had any reservations about J.T.'s maturity or ability, they had vanished the night before: When Nick lost his glasses, the boy used the GPS receiver under Nick's direction to guide them both back out of the Lower Nine.

As they neared the end of the houses and saw the Surekote levee in the distance, Nick stopped—something seemed different. He wondered if they were in the right place, but then he looked to the left—there was the old lift bridge across North Claiborne Avenue, exactly where it should be. They were in the right place—but something had changed. He squinted hard but couldn't make it out.

"Look up ahead," he called back to J.T. "Do you see the levee?"

"Sure I see it—can't miss it."

"Can you see the break where we cross over into the Industrial Canal?"

The boy looked. "Nope."

"No? You can't see it?"

"It ain't there."

Nick turned and looked again—the boy was right. Silhouetted against the sun, the levee once again formed an unbroken line across the horizon. The breach had been repaired—there was no longer a way across the Industrial Canal.

Nick spotted a workman standing atop the levee. "Pull up alongside," he told the boy. J.T. steered the boat up smoothly and killed the engine.

"I see you got it fixed," Nick called up. "When did you finish it?"

"Just this morning," the man called back. "Now they can get the pumps going and start draining this place. Great news, huh?"

"Yeah," Nick said. "Great news."

He sat there silently, staring at the spot where the breach used to be. Now his only way across the canal was by car or on foot, across the St. Claude Avenue Bridge—but even if he followed the streets downtown, what then? The city was still flooded; it would be days before the city's massive pumps could drain the entire area and make New Orleans accessible by foot. He would still need to travel by boat, but without a trailer he had no way to haul his own boat across the bridge and into the city. He would have to find another one there, and that would take time—and he didn't have time to waste. *Idiot*, he thought. *Why didn't I look over there when I had the chance?*

Nick squinted at the setting sun. Whatever he was going to do, it would have to wait until tomorrow. *Might as well head back to the DPMU*, he thought. *Might as well get the car back to Beth and get some sleep.*

Won't that just make her day.

Detwiler sat alone in his gray-green boat, motoring slowly around the charred ruins of the burned-out rooftop. He took out his satellite phone and punched in a number.

"Turlock."

"Frank, it's Detwiler. I'm at the house."

"And?"

"There's only one body."

"No sign of Polchak?"

"None. His body could still be underwater somewhere—he might've made it out of the fire and then drowned."

"You think so."

"The guy's got more lives than a cat," Detwiler groaned. "I don't see how he could have—"

Detwiler stopped. He heard a faint beeping sound coming from somewhere nearby—but he couldn't tell where. He looked at the phone; that wasn't it.

"Hang on a second," he said to Turlock.

He slid off the bench and began to search the bottom of the boat—the equipment bag, the cooler, the rolled-up pair of rubber waders.

Nothing.

But he still heard the sound, coming from somewhere farther forward in the boat; somewhere toward the bow; somewhere on the right—

He opened the bait well and found a fist-sized GPS transmitter inside. A red LED was flashing on the top, warning of LOW BATTERY.

"That son of a—" He cocked his arm to throw the transmitter long and hard, but stopped; he picked up the phone instead.

"Frank," he said, "I've got an idea."

39

Nick stopped the silver Lexus fifty yards from the main gate of the DPMU. He reached into the backseat and made sure the blanket was completely covering the boy's reclining form.

J.T.'s head rose up sleepily under the blanket. "Are we there yet?"

"Almost," Nick said. "Go back to sleep. I'll let you know."

He pulled around the corner and up to the gate. A man stepped out of the guardhouse as he approached and held up one hand, signaling for Nick to stop. In the brilliant headlights, Nick could see that the man wore the uniform of the St. Gabriel Police Department.

"'Evening," Nick said as the guard approached his window.

"Nice car."

"I only drive the best." He handed the guard his DMORT credentials. "Nice little town you've got here."

"We like it."

"They tell me that at the St. Gabriel General Store I can get a po' boy, chips, and a drink for under two bucks. Is that true?"

"A man who drives a car like this can afford more than two bucks."

"Yeah." Nick nodded. "You'd think so, wouldn't you?"

The guard studied the credentials, then looked at Nick's face. "Are you Dr. Nicholas Polchak?"

"That's right."

"I'm going to have to ask you to come with me, sir."

"What's the problem?"

"Sir, I want you to pull your car straight ahead and park it right there where I can see you—is that understood?"

"Mind telling me what this is about?"

"Just do as I ask, please."

Nick pulled slowly ahead. As the car rolled forward he glanced in the rearview mirror and saw the guard speaking into his shoulder radio.

Without turning, he reached behind him and shook the sleeping boy. "Hey—wake up. J.T.—c'mon, wake up."

The boy began to straighten.

"No!" Nick warned. "Stay down—keep the blanket over you and don't move. Listen to me."

"What's goin' on?"

He stopped the car at the prescribed spot and turned off the engine. "I have to go somewhere."

"Where? Why can't I—"

"Just *listen*—I've only got a few seconds." He checked the mirror again; the guard was approaching from behind. "Stay under the blanket—whatever you do, don't show yourself. In a few seconds you're going to hear me get out and close the door. When I do, you wait a few minutes—then go and find Beth." He reached over the backseat and dropped the keys on the floor. "Hear that? That's the keys; take the keys to Beth and tell her what happened. Stay with her; whatever she tells you to do, you do it—understand?"

"I want to stay with you, Nick."

"Well, you can't—not right now. Find Beth and tell her what happened—and don't let anybody see you. Think you can do that?"

"Sure."

"Stay with her, J.T.—that way I'll know how to find you."

Nick could hear the guard's feet crunching on the macadam. He opened the door and stepped out. "What's going on?" he asked lightly. "Did I set off a metal detector or something? Darn those fingernail clippers."

"Do you have any personal items in your car, sir?"

"Just my equipment bag in the trunk."

"Get it, please, and follow me."

Nick made no further attempt at levity; he did as he was instructed. The guard led him into the DPMU and directly to Denny's office, then opened the door and stepped aside, motioning for Nick to enter.

"Thanks for the ride in the patrol car," Nick said. "I know where the principal's office is—you could have just pointed." He stepped into the room and found Denny seated at his desk. Denny didn't bother to rise or even look up.

"Hey, Denny, what's the deal with all the—"

"Sit down."

Nick heard the door click shut behind him. He turned and looked; the officer was standing with his hands folded at his waist, blocking the exit.

Nick swung the equipment bag from his shoulder and dropped it on the floor. He pulled a chair up across from Denny's desk and sat down. "Well, here we are again," he said. "Talk about your déjà vu."

Denny looked up. "You're going home, Nick."

"What?"

"You pushed the wrong buttons this time; you jerked the wrong chains. I tried to warn you."

"What are you talking about?"

"You know exactly what I'm talking about. I told you not to recover bodies—you did it anyway. The DEA said you were endangering an important investigation—you ignored them. You recovered two bodies and stored them illegally on an abandoned floor of Charity Hospital."

"I only did that because—"

"I don't want to hear it. You've been conducting your own private investigation again, haven't you? Just like you always do."

"Denny, let me explain."

"I'm not looking for explanations. I don't care why you did it. I'm here to tell you that you're going home. Sorry—it's nothing personal."

"You're right about that," Nick said. "This wasn't even your decision, was it?"

"It might as well have been."

"Who initiated this? Tell me, Denny—you at least owe me that much."

"I don't owe you anything. I've been covering your backside for years now: your rule-breaking and your disregard for authority and your compulsive work habits—not to mention your wacky pet-conspiracy theories."

"Which usually turn out to be true."

"I'm tired of taking the heat for you, Nick. Every time you screw up, I get called into somebody's office. Some pretty powerful people want you to go home this time, and I don't have time to argue with them. Go home, Nick—go back to NC State and teach freshmen about bugs. Screw up there—let them deal with you."

Nick glanced over his shoulder at the St. Gabriel police officer. "Am I under armed guard?"

"The officer is here to escort you directly from the building."

"Do you think we could ask Barney Fife to step out in the hallway for a minute?"

"Why?"

"I'd like to speak to you personally."

"You have nothing to say to me personally."

"Denny—*please.*"

Denny hesitated and nodded to the officer, who then stepped out and closed the door.

"Thank you," Nick said.

"Make it quick."

"I've got a wacky pet-conspiracy theory for you."

Denny closed his eyes and hung his head.

"Just hear me out, okay? I've been looking for bodies in the Lower Ninth Ward. The DEA asked me to—they told you so. The only rule I broke was to bring a couple back—and that was only to collect forensic evidence before it was destroyed. I couldn't bring them here—you told me not to. So I hauled a couple to Charity Hospital and looked them over there. Why not? The whole floor was underwater—what harm did it do? The bodies I took to Charity—I found them in the Lower Nine. One of them was inhabited by caddis flies just like the one I found before; the materials that made up the caddis-fly cases showed that the bodies originally came from out in the bayous. So how did they get back to the Lower Nine after they were already dead? They sure didn't swim back."

"Nick, where are you going with this?"

"So I went out to the bayous and took a look, and guess what I found? An abandoned meth lab, that's what—and while I was there somebody took a shot at me. Somebody didn't want me there, Denny—somebody is using this flood to cover up some unpleasant business. Somebody pulled those bodies out of the bayou and dumped them in the Lower Nine along with the folks who died in the hurricane; they figured that after a week or so they'd all look the same. And they would have been right—except that I found them first."

"Nick—"

"And last night I was checking out another body—a man who died in his own attic. His body was *pink*, Denny—you know what that means: He died of carbon monoxide poisoning, like a guy who offs himself in his garage—only this guy wasn't in the garage, he was in the attic. There were no wood-burning stoves around, no furnaces or heaters—nothing that would have produced carbon monoxide. Somebody gassed the guy, Denny; somebody murdered him in his own attic—and judging from the body, it was *after* the hurricane. You see what I'm getting at? Somebody is *still* using the flood as a way to cover up killings."

"And who's behind this vast conspiracy of yours?"

Nick paused. "I think it might be the DEA."

"Nick. C'mon."

"Or somebody in the DEA—somebody acting independently, without authority. Is that so crazy?"

"Of course it is. Do you have any physical evidence to support these claims?"

"How could I? People keep taking it away from me—but I've seen it."

"And on that basis you want to accuse the DEA of murder."

Nick shook his head. "Somebody doesn't want me collecting this evidence."

"*Nobody* wants you collecting this evidence—that's what I've been telling you from the beginning. Why can't you get that through your head? The DEA *is* involved in this, Nick—they told you so themselves. You're screwing up one of their investigations—that's why they want you to go home. That's right, it's the DEA that wants you out of here—add that to your conspiracy theory. Just get out of here and stop making things harder for the rest of us."

Nick just sat there and looked at him. There were a dozen more things he could have added: the fact that Jerry had disappeared; the fact that he was being followed; the fact that someone had tried to kill him in a flaming attic. But what was the point? Denny hadn't seen the evidence; he had no reason to believe. It would all just sound like more wild and groundless accusations, just paranoid rantings from a sleep-deprived man.

"Okay," Nick said. "I'll go."

"I wasn't asking you, Nick—I was telling you."

"Is it okay if I take care of a few things on the way out?"

"No, it isn't." Denny walked to the door and opened it, motioning for the guard to reenter. There was a second officer with him this time; he was carrying Nick's duffel bag packed with all of his belongings.

Nick frowned. "Is this really necessary? I feel like a shoplifter."

"I'm just following orders," Denny said. "You should try it sometime."

"Thanks for the advice."

"This officer has been instructed to drive you directly to the Baton Rouge Airport, where he'll drop you off. After that it's up to you. Go wherever you want—just don't come back here."

"I hope you know you're being used," Nick said.

"It's happened before. You should know—you're usually the one doing it."

"I'm right this time, Denny. I know you can't see it yet, but I'm right."

Nick walked to the door and looked at the officer carrying his bag. "I hope you folded things neatly," he said. "I'm a stickler about creases."

40

"Excuse me—where is the gift shop?"

The Delta Airlines ticket agent pointed across the hall. "Right there, ma'am."

"Thank you."

Beth hurried across the wide hallway, straightening her hair as she went, the heels of her shoes rapping like gavels on the glossy terrazzo floor. She entered the gift shop and glanced both ways; there was Nick Polchak, standing at a kiosk and squinting at an inflatable fleece-lined neck support.

"Nick—there you are. I came as soon as I could."

"It's amazing," he said. "I've been standing here looking at all this crap, and I'm actually starting to think I need one of these."

"J.T. said someone came and took you away. I had no idea where you were until you called."

"Do people actually use these things? Do they take them out on the airplane and blow them up in front of everybody else? What would other passengers think—it looks like you brought your own flotation device."

"Nick, what happened? What's going on?"

"It could have practical applications, I suppose. If the flight attendant wants to know if you've had too much to drink, she could just test the air in your neck support."

"Nick!"

He turned and looked at her. "This time *you* look terrible."

She glared at him. "That's because I keep getting calls from desperate men in the middle of the night."

"Lucky you."

"Nick, be serious. What happened tonight? What are you doing at the airport?"

"They sent me home, Beth."

"What?"

"The DEA pulled some strings and had my credentials pulled. They're sending me home."

"Oh, Nick, I'm so sorry."

"It makes perfect sense, if you think about it. They don't have to kill me—they just want me out of the way. All they need is time—just a few more days for the water to finish the job. There won't be any evidence left."

"But what about Jerry? Someone will eventually find him."

"Sure, in a week or so—probably at the Superdome, tucked away in a dark corner somewhere. What will that prove? Jerry worked for FEMA—half the people in the Superdome would have killed him if they had the chance."

She stepped closer. "Nick, listen to me: You tried—that's all anybody can do. No one could have worked harder. What you did for J.T.—what you did for the people of the Lower Ninth Ward—Jerry would have been proud of you. *I'm* proud of you."

He looked at her. "Will you miss me?"

"Of course I'll miss you. I know we don't always see eye-to-eye, but I look forward to seeing you at these deployments; they'd be boring without you. The truth is—I still care about you."

"You do?"

She kissed him on the cheek. "What time is your flight?"

He looked at his ticket. "Noon."

"Tomorrow?"

"No, a week from Thursday."

Her mouth dropped open. "What?"

"You didn't think I was really going home, did you? I don't have to leave town—I just can't go back to DMORT again. New Orleans is full of civilian volunteers; there's no reason I can't be one of them."

"Then why did you buy a ticket?"

"The government's paying for it—besides, I get frequent-flier miles."

She glared at him. "Why did you let me go on like that?"

"It's healthy to express your emotions. You can't keep things like that bottled up inside—you might explode."

"I still might," she growled.

"Did you leave a lipstick mark? That's so embarrassing."

"If you're not leaving, then why did you call me?"

"I need transportation."

"I'm not a shuttle service," she said. "Call a cab—get your own ride."

"I don't need a ride, I need transportation. I want you to rent me a car."

"Why me?"

"Because I don't want it in my name. If they're watching my credit card, I don't want them to know I'm still here. They dropped me at the airport and I bought a ticket; as far as they know, I'm gone."

He took her by the arm and led her out into the ticket lobby, past the security entrance and baggage claim and toward the rental car counters at the opposite end of the terminal. "Where's J.T.? Is he all right?"

"I left him sleeping in my bed," she said.

"Keep a close eye on him, Beth. He's just a kid, but you never know."

They stopped at the first rental car location they came to. "I need a car," Beth said. "What's the cheapest thing you've got?"

Nick frowned. "You drive a Lexus and you're sticking me with a Kia? I thought you cared about me."

"I said that under false pretenses," she said. "That's called 'entrapment.'"

Nick turned to the agent. "Have you got anything with GPS?"

"Only on our luxury cars, sir."

"She'll take it."

"Wait a minute—" Beth complained.

"It's a business expense—you can deduct it."

Ten minutes later, Nick was dropping his duffel bag into the spacious trunk of a midnight-blue Lincoln Town Car. "Now, this is me," he said.

"No, this is *me*. Don't fall asleep at the wheel—it's on my credit card."

"Relax, I bought their insurance. I'll try to call you when I get settled in someplace. I'll have to find a pay phone somewhere; I sure wish they'd get the cell phones working again."

"Nick, where will you go?"

"I know just the place," he said. "It's cheap, it's out of the way—and the folks there don't like federal agents."

It was after midnight by the time Beth got back to St. Gabriel. She slipped off her shoes and tiptoed into the dormitory, hoping not to wake either the boy or the female DMORT personnel sleeping nearby.

When she got to her bed, she found it empty.

She checked the floor on either side. She got down on her knees and looked under the bed. She tiptoed to the bed nearest hers and shook the woman awake.

"Wha—"

"Andrea, it's me. Did you notice anybody come in or out of here tonight? Did you see a young boy leave, about ten years old?"

"I didn't see anyone. What's wrong?"

"Never mind—go back to sleep."

She checked the bathroom—it was empty. She went to the DPMU and checked the cafeteria—maybe the boy was hungry, maybe he had gone off in search of an MRE—but there was no one there. J.T. had disappeared without a trace, and there was no one she could ask about him—no one else had seen him enter, and he wasn't supposed to be there.

She stepped outside and looked around. The grounds around the DPMU were dark and still. She hurried across the parking lot to Nick's trailer; she quietly pulled the door open and stuck her head inside. She saw the abandoned spaces that Nick and Jerry had once occupied—but no sign of J.T.

She felt panic rising inside her like a tide; she could feel her heart pounding in her throat. She took long, slow breaths, trying to push it all down. She needed to *think*.

Where would the boy have gone? Maybe he had gone looking for Nick. He knew he wasn't supposed to, but he'd done it before—he had walked five miles alone in the darkness across the city of New Orleans. It was only ten miles to Baton Rouge—but the boy didn't know that Nick was in Baton Rouge—he wouldn't have known where to go. Would he have gone back to the city—back to the Lower Nine? Nothing she considered seemed to make sense.

Suddenly a thought occurred to her: *The entire DPMU is surrounded by cyclone fence topped with razor wire—the only way in or out is through the main gate.*

She hurried to the guard gate and found the officer on duty. "Did you see a boy go out of here earlier tonight—in the last two or three hours? He would have been about ten years old—about so tall."

"Civilians aren't allowed on the grounds, ma'am."

"No, of course not." She stopped and thought. "What about cars? Have any cars passed by here other than mine?"

"We changed shifts at midnight," he said. "I've only been on duty for half an hour, and I haven't seen anybody."

"Do you keep any kind of gate log?"

He took a clipboard from the fence and handed it to her.

"I don't recognize any of these names," she said.

"They're all guests. People who work here, people with valid ID, we just wave 'em through. That's what they told us to do."

She checked the column marked "Time In/Out"—the final entry was at 4:45 p.m. "I don't see any guests listed for tonight."

"Looks that way. Is there a problem?"

"Do you know this area very well? The area around New Orleans, I mean?"

"Yes, ma'am—lived here all my life."

"Can you give me some directions then?"

"No problem. Where you headed tonight?"

She handed back the clipboard. "The bayou."

41

Nick could hear people moving around him, but he couldn't see a thing—everything was dark. He could make out three separate voices, but their words were muffled, as if he were hearing them through a door. The voices sounded busy, efficient, professional; he wondered who they were. He seemed to be lying on his back, looking up; he tried to lift his arm, but it wouldn't move—he was paralyzed.

Now he heard a slow, zipping sound, and a slit of dazzling white light began to open in front of his face, moving down toward his torso. He saw latex-gloved fingers work their way into the slit and spread it wide; he closed his eyes tight against the blinding light. When he opened them again the image cleared: He was at the DPMU, lying on a metal gurney, staring up into the forensic examination lights.

A figure leaned in over him, masked and gowned, studying Nick's face but not looking into his eyes. Now a second figure joined him.

"Cause of death?" the first man asked.

"He pushed the wrong button," his colleague responded. "They found him floating in the Lower Nine."

"Well, let's get to it. Dr. Woodbridge, would you like to open?"

The two men stepped aside and a third figure leaned in—it was Beth, dressed in an impeccable business suit.

"There are traces of blood on his left mandible," one of the men said.

"That's lipstick," she replied.

Now she held up a scalpel in her right hand; with her left hand she felt for the joint between his right collarbone and shoulder. She placed the tip of the scalpel there and pressed—it felt as cold as ice.

Nick tried to scream but couldn't.

She drew the scalpel down and to the right, to the center of his chest, then from the sternum down to the lower abdomen. She made the same cut from his left collarbone, completing the classic *Y* incision that began every autopsy. She peeled the tissues back, exposing his rib cage, then leaned in closer and looked.

"Just as I thought," she said. "He had no heart."

She took him by the shoulders and began to shake. "Wake up," she shouted. "Nick—wake up!"

The image in front of him began to change now. He was no longer staring up at examination lights, but at the rustic wooden roof of a bayou cabin. Beth's face began to change too—it began to soften and blur. Nick felt life flowing back into his body—he felt the power of movement returning to his limbs. He grabbed Beth by both wrists and jerked upright, sending her sprawling back onto the floor.

He pulled up his shirt and felt the skin of his chest.

"What's wrong?" Beth asked.

"Just checking something."

"Nick, I thought you were dead!"

"I'm fine, no thanks to you."

"I couldn't wake you up!"

"You keep nagging me to 'get some sleep,' then the minute I try you wake me up—I wish you'd make up your mind." He felt around on the cabin floor for his glasses and slipped them on. He looked at Beth and blinked. "What are you doing here, anyway?"

"Nick—J.T. is gone."

"What?"

"I left him sleeping in my bed, but when I got back he was gone."

"Are you sure?"

"Of course I'm sure—I looked everywhere. I had no way to call you, so I had to come after you. It took me hours to find this cabin again—I couldn't remember the way. I had to stop for directions half a dozen times." She looked around the cabin, especially in the dark corners. "Why did you come here? Why would *anyone* come here?"

"Exactly," Nick said.

"Where are Boo and Tonton?"

"Checking their traps. I don't know when they'll be back." Nick had only been asleep for an hour or two, just long enough to become completely disoriented. He lifted his glasses and rubbed at the bridge of his nose, trying to clear the cobwebs from his mind.

"Do you think J.T. might've tried to follow you?"

"It's possible—he's done it before. Did anybody see him leave?"

"No—but nobody saw him come in either. He wasn't supposed to be there, remember?"

Nick thought for a minute. "There are only two ways out of the DPMU—over the fence or through the gate."

"But the fence is topped with barbed wire—do you think he would have tried to climb over?"

"Or under. He knew he wasn't supposed to be there—he would have wanted to avoid the cop at the gate."

"Do you think that's what he did?"

Nick paused. "No, I don't. The kid was exhausted—I had to shake him to wake him up. You said you left him asleep in your bed—why would he wake up on his own? Someone must have woken him up; someone must have taken him. We have to assume that he left the same way he came—in a car."

"But who would take him away?"

"Did you check at the gate? Did the guard see anyone leave with a boy?"

"They changed guards at midnight—J.T. could have left before then. If someone took him, he might have been in the trunk—then no one would have seen him."

"Does the gate keep any records? Any list of cars going in or out?"

"Only guests—but they said there were no guests this evening. As long as you've got valid credentials, you can pass right through."

Nick considered this. "Then someone with valid credentials must have taken J.T. away—someone with access to the DPMU."

"Denny?"

"Not Denny—Denny didn't know the boy was there. Nobody knew the boy was there. Nobody could have, unless they were—"

Nick jumped to his feet and twisted the dial on the propane lamp, throwing the cabin into total darkness.

"Nick—what's wrong?"

"We have to get out of here. We have to get away from this cabin."

"Why?"

"Someone must have been watching, Beth—they knew the boy was at the DPMU, and they knew to look for him in your bed. They may have seen you leave too—they may have followed you here."

"Who?"

"Turlock or Detwiler, that's my guess. They're DEA, they have access to the DPMU—they could come and go without anybody looking twice. They're the ones who had me sent home—Denny said so. Suppose they were watching the DPMU just to make sure I left: They might have seen J.T. get out of my car, and they could have followed him to your bed. When you left, they saw their chance to wrap up a loose end—they waited until everybody was asleep and then one of them grabbed the boy. Then you came back and found the boy missing; when the other one saw you leave again, maybe he saw a way to wrap up two loose ends at once."

"Nick, are you sure about this?"

"No. It's only a theory—but we have to assume that it might be correct. We can't take a chance on staying here. This is exactly the way they'd like to find us: together, alone, in an isolated location. Where did you leave your car?"

"Up the road a little, behind yours. I remembered the uncle's rifle—I didn't want to drive up unannounced."

"We'll leave the cars there. If somebody did follow you, he'll be watching the cars and the cabin. He won't approach the cabin until he knows who's inside."

"Leave the cars? Then how do we get away?"

"The same way we got here the first time—by boat."

"Nick. Please tell me you're joking."

"Remember the rental boat we left behind at the abandoned shack? Boo towed it back for us—it's tied up at the dock. If we can get to it without being seen, we can head out into the bayou. They can't follow us there—there's no other boat."

"There has to be some other way."

"Can you think of one? Come on, we have to go right now—once he notices that the lights are off, he might think we're asleep and come after us."

Nick went to the window that faced the bayou and inspected it. It was a single sheet of glass mounted in a frame—there was no way to open it. He thought about breaking it, but the sound would give away their intentions for sure.

"We'll have to use the front door," Nick said. "It's the only way out. Stay close to the shadows and move slowly—and wrap this around you." He tossed her the nutria quilt.

She shuddered. "Do I have to?"

"You'll look like Snow White out there," Nick said. "You'll stand out like a glow stick if you don't cover up."

She wrapped the thick fur around her shoulders. It made her skin crawl, as if it were lined with tiny insects.

"I'll go first," Nick said. "If anything goes wrong, you get back in the cabin and barricade the door. Maybe the Cajuns will get back before it's too late."

"Why don't we just barricade the door now?"

"I said *maybe* they'll get back. I don't like the odds."

Nick slowly opened the door and peered across the open area at the brush that lined the opposite side. He saw nothing—but then again, he didn't expect to. It would be easy to hide in the thick sedge and swamp grass at night. He knew he had to step outside—it was the only way he would ever know if his theory was right or wrong.

A thought occurred to him: *If I am right, I may never know.*

He eased through the doorway and pressed his back against the cabin wall. He heard no sound from the surrounding brush. He kept close to the shadows, sidling slowly down the wall toward the end of the cabin. At the corner he turned his head and waited for Beth; a moment later she stepped out and followed, easing up beside him.

Nick pressed his lips against her ear and whispered, "Stay close to the brush. Keep low. We've got to cross an open area to get to the dock, but let's stay out of sight as long as we can."

She nodded.

They bent down and crept along the brush, doing their best to avoid the serrated blades of grass that would catch on their skin and clothing like the teeth of a saw. A minute later they arrived at the edge of the clearing and stared across at the dock; there was the tiny wooden skiff tied up alongside, pointed out to the bayou as if it were ready and waiting for them.

There was no more concealing brush between them and their goal—they had no choice but to cross an exposed area now, alone and backlit by the glistening bayou behind them. Stealth was no longer possible; speed was their only ally.

Nick turned to Beth. "When I say 'Go,' we run for it. You go first this time—straight out to the end of the dock and into the bow of the boat. I'll be right behind you. We won't use the engine—we'll shove off with the oars so we don't make any sound."

He checked the clearing again. "Ready?"

"Ready."

"Go."

He gently pushed her and she started off; Nick followed a few steps behind. It seemed to take forever to cross the open stretch. They moved as quickly and as quietly as they could, but every crunching step seemed amplified by the empty darkness.

Beth reached the dock first and started out on it at a run. There was no way to hide her footsteps now—they sounded like hammer blows on the brittle wooden slats. Nick was right behind her—but the instant his full weight was added to hers, the rickety pier let out a creaking groan and sagged precariously to the right.

"Nick!" Beth shouted, dropping to her hands and knees on the weather-beaten boards.

Nick immediately stopped and backed away, and the dock straightened slightly. "Get up!" he shouted to her. "Keep going—we've got to do it one at a time!"

Suddenly, the entire area was illuminated by a pair of blinding headlights. Somewhere behind him Nick heard a car door slam shut.

He didn't turn to look.

Beth reached the boat now, tottering the remaining distance like a gymnast on a balance beam. She half-stumbled into the boat, crawling over the center bench and into the bow.

Now Nick started forward again. He weighed considerably more than Beth did, and the old dock registered its complaint with sharp groans and brittle cracking sounds. The pier seemed to wobble with every footstep, shifting left and right beneath him.

He heard heavy footsteps in the distance behind him. Someone was breathing hard, running fast—running toward him. He listened to the sound and tried to estimate the distance.

He didn't have time to pick his footsteps as Beth had done; all he could do was run and hope the old dock would support him long enough to reach the boat. But he couldn't really run—not like he could on open ground—he could only wobble along like a drunken man, and it was maddeningly slow. He saw Beth crouched low in the bow, holding an oar at the ready, staring back at him with panic in her eyes.

The footsteps were closing fast. He imagined that at any moment a hand would reach out and tap him on the shoulder.

When he was six feet from the boat, he jumped. He landed with a crash in the stern, almost overturning the boat. Beth let out a shriek.

"I dropped the oar!" she shouted.

For the first time, Nick turned and looked back—there was Detwiler, running at full speed with his handgun drawn, just a few yards away from the end of the pier. "Forget the oars," he said. "We're out of time." He jerked the cord on the old outboard motor; it sputtered and stopped.

Detwiler stopped at the end of the dock, panting like a dog. He steadied himself and took hurried aim; he squeezed off two quick shots.

They were close enough that Nick could hear the bullets hiss by. "Get down!" he shouted to Beth. He pumped the primer button again and again, drawing gasoline up and into the cylinders, then jerked the starter cord once more; this time the old engine coughed and belched out a puff of blue smoke. Nick twisted the throttle lightly, nursing the ignition along—

It started.

Detwiler was halfway out on the dock now, within easy firing distance. Only the swaying of the dock kept him from taking careful aim, but in a few more seconds it wouldn't matter; in a few more seconds he would be on top of them, and even a blind man couldn't miss at that range.

Nick twisted the throttle hard and gunned the engine; the boat eased forward at a horrifying pace. He kept the tiller fixed, steering the boat straight ahead into the bayou, trying to put as much distance between them and the pier as he could.

He turned and looked back again. Detwiler was aiming directly at Nick's head—only a last-second shift of the dock kept him from finding his mark.

He wouldn't miss again.

Nick felt something brush his left ankle; he looked down and saw a coil of cotton rope playing out over the edge of the boat and disappearing into the bayou. He looked back at the dock and saw the other end of the rope still tied to one of the posts that supported the pier.

Detwiler was at the end of the dock now. He widened his stance carefully and balanced himself; he took careful aim this time, resting the butt of his handgun in his cupped left hand. He slowly closed one eye, and his right index finger curled around the trigger . . .

Suddenly the rope went taut, snapping off the old post like a matchstick. The entire dock collapsed under Detwiler's feet, forming a kind of wooden ramp that sent him sliding headlong into the black bayou water. He landed with an awkward splash—but after thrashing about for only a few seconds, he quickly scrambled to his feet and raised the gun again.

Though he now stood perfectly still, the water around him began to froth and churn. Detwiler suddenly threw his head back and screamed; his body jerked violently to the left, then to the right. Greenish-black snouts lunged at him from the water, snapping and tearing at his flesh, crawling over one another in their frenzy until the water around him boiled with foam and blood.

42

Nick tried the driver's-side door. It was unlocked, just as he'd expected. Detwiler was in a big hurry—he wouldn't have taken the time to lock it behind him. He felt around on the ceiling near the windshield and found an instrument console lined with rectangular buttons; he punched the one closest to him and a blinding halogen map light clicked on, illuminating the front seat and floor.

"What are you looking for?" Beth asked.

"A phone."

"I've got a phone, Nick—cell phones don't work out here."

"A satellite phone. I'm betting Detwiler had one."

There was paper everywhere: empty fast-food sacks and sandwich wrappers, coffee cups with slotted plastic lids, and the last three editions of the *Times-Picayune*.

"And you thought I was a slob," Nick said.

There was a pair of olive-drab Steiner military binoculars hanging from the rearview mirror, and on the front seat there was a Nikon digital SLR with a hefty telephoto lens. Nick popped open a plastic cover on the back of the camera and pushed a tiny button with his thumbnail; he ejected the memory card and dropped it into his pocket.

"This should prove that he was following me," Nick said. "At least it establishes a connection; it's not much, but it's a start."

He noticed a flask-shaped power adapter with a glowing red LED projecting from the dashboard cigarette lighter. A coiled black power cord protruded from the end and disappeared under a pile of maps and magazines in the passenger-side floor well. Nick lifted the power cord and tugged; it was attached to a sleek black iridium satellite phone.

"Bingo."

"Thank God," Beth said. "Now we can call the police."

"What for?"

"Nick, there's a dead man back there in the water."

"He's not going anywhere. Besides, the police have their hands full in the city."

"Then what do you want the phone for?"

"We have to talk to Turlock—right away."

He pushed the Redial button and held the phone to his left ear so Beth could listen too.

"Turlock," a voice on the other end said.

"You people sure work long hours," Nick said. "Tell me, is this DEA policy or more of a personal work ethic?"

There was no response.

"Hello, Mr. Turlock? Mr. Frank Turlock of the New Orleans Drug Enforcement Administration? Talk to me, Frank. It's a satellite phone—the calls are expensive."

"Where did you get this number, Dr. Polchak?"

"I don't have your number, Frank, I have your phone—your colleague, Mr. Detwiler, was kind enough to loan it to me."

A pause. "Is Mr. Detwiler there? May I speak with him, please?"

"That could be a little difficult," Nick said. "The fact is, he didn't actually *loan* it to me—he sort of *willed* it to me, if you get my drift."

No reply.

"But, then, this is hazardous work, as I'm sure you know. Take me, for instance: I've only been in New Orleans for a week, and somebody's tried to kill me three times already—four times if you count tonight. Can you believe it? No wonder our insurance rates are so high."

"Are you telling me that you've killed Agent Detwiler?"

"I don't do that kind of work, Frank—that's more up your alley. No, Agent Detwiler managed to get himself killed."

"How did that happen?"

"He decided to play 'Crocodile Hunter'—only they were alligators, because we're in Louisiana. Alligators aren't as big as crocodiles, did you know that? They still get pretty big, though—maybe half a ton. They're not as mean as crocodiles, either, but that doesn't mean you can go swimming with them—I don't think Mr. Detwiler knew that. Big mistake, I'm afraid."

"What do you want, Polchak?"

"I want the boy. I assume you've got him."

"You want the boy. And that's all?"

"No, I want you to rot in a federal prison for several years—but one thing at a time. You took the boy, Frank, and you didn't take him to hold him hostage. I want him back—don't hurt him."

Turlock didn't reply, and Nick felt a twinge of dread in the pit of his stomach. What he said was true: Turlock didn't take the boy to hold him hostage—he took him to eliminate a dangerous loose end, and he may have already done just that. Nick held his breath and asked the big question: "Is the boy still alive?"

"He might be."

"That's not good enough, Frank—I need to know."

Again, no reply.

"I can tell you're considering your options," Nick said, "so let me help you out. The only reason I haven't already gone to the authorities with what I know is that I don't have all the evidence I need yet, and I don't want to just blow the whistle on you—I want to put you away. But you know what? I don't need more evidence—I can cause you all kinds of trouble right now. Forget the authorities—I'll go to CNN. Why not? If the boy is dead, I've got nothing to lose. The entire government response to Hurricane Katrina has been one big screwup—you think the media won't want to hear about a plot by the DEA to settle some old debts outside the law?"

"Lots of crazy stories are being circulated right now," Turlock said. "Yours would be just one more."

"Maybe—but I can shine a lot of spotlights your way, at least for a while. Can you really afford that, Frank? There would be so many questions, so much *attention*—just the kind of thing the DEA likes to avoid.

But you know what, Frank? I think the DEA would have a few questions of its own—because I've worked with the DEA before, and this isn't like them. This is just a guess, but I don't think you and Detwiler have been acting in an official capacity. I think the two of you screwed up somehow, and you've been trying to cover it up ever since. How'm I doing, Frank?"

"There'd be questions for you, too, Polchak—questions about your work habits, questions about your employment history with DMORT—about your psychological profile. They'd take one look at your résumé and call you a loon."

"I am a loon, Frank—you can ask my psychiatrist. What do I care if people think I'm crazy? I'm a college professor—I'm supposed to be quaintly eccentric. But what about you? You're a DEA agent; you're supposed to be dignified."

"What is this boy to you?" Turlock asked.

"None of your business. Is he alive or not?"

Turlock paused. "He's alive. He's alive and unharmed."

Nick felt no sense of relief. Of course Turlock would say that J.T. was alive—what else could he say? Turlock knew that Nick wasn't bluffing: If the boy was dead, Nick would go to the media—and he would cause trouble.

"Good," Nick said. "Then let me talk to him."

"He isn't here."

"Sorry, Frank. I need to know."

"I wouldn't keep the kid with me, now would I? That would be a little hard to explain at the office. I can put you in touch with him, but it'll take a little time."

Nick clenched his teeth; Turlock was stalling. "How much time?"

"Let's say—a day. Call me at this number tomorrow at midnight; I'll let you talk to him then."

"That's too long. I'm going to the media."

"No, you're not—you can't take that chance. Think it over, Polchak—if you do go to the media, then *I* have nothing to lose. I'll kill the kid for sure—you know I will."

Nick did know. Going to the media would sign J.T.'s death warrant.

The boy's disappearance might raise questions, but the boy himself could give answers—answers that Turlock couldn't afford to have heard. Turlock was telling the truth: The minute Nick went to the media, the boy was dead.

"How do I know he isn't dead already?" Nick asked.

"I told you, he's still alive."

"And I'm supposed to trust you."

"Only for a day—then you can talk to him yourself."

Nick slammed his fist against the dashboard. He knew what Turlock was doing; he knew what would happen next. Nick would make the call tomorrow night at midnight, and Turlock would ask for another day—and Nick would have no choice but to agree again. And with each passing day the bodies would decompose a little more, until no physical evidence remained. At that point, Turlock would be willing to take his chances; Nick could go to the media—but by that time it might not do any good. Worst of all, J.T. could be dead already. Nick had no way to know.

"C'mon, it's a decent offer," Turlock said. "One day of the boy's life for one day of your time. Whaddya say, Polchak?"

"And after I talk to him tomorrow at midnight—what happens then?"

"I don't know yet. It's a little complicated. Why don't we both sleep on it and see what we come up with tomorrow?"

Tomorrow. That's all Turlock needed—time—but Nick needed a whole lot more than that. He needed to come up with something better than the threat of going to the media—a threat that would lose power with every passing day.

One thing he knew for certain: Turlock would never let J.T. go. Nick's only chance was to get to Turlock before the boy was dead.

"Agreed," Nick said. "One day—and that's all. I'll call tomorrow night at exactly midnight. I'll expect to talk to the boy; we can work out some kind of arrangement then."

"Deal."

"Turlock," Nick said.

"Yeah?"

"I want the boy back—I want him alive and unharmed."

"We should be able to work that out," Turlock said. "Let's sleep on it. Let's give it a day. Let's let things—simmer."

Nick heard a click.

He switched off the phone and sat there staring at it. "You were right," he said to Beth.

"About what?"

"I'm not thinking clearly anymore. I'm making bad decisions. Turlock knew I was bluffing. I threatened to go to the media—I practically told him that I didn't have any real evidence. He knows if I did, I'd go to the authorities now."

"There's a dead body back there—that's evidence."

"Sure, that's evidence—and when the NOPD finds its missing officers, and when they finally have time to send somebody out here, they'll find what's left of it—in the gullets of a dozen alligators. They'll look for a hunk of flesh that isn't fully digested, and they'll take a DNA sample and send it to a lab for a couple of weeks—and then what? Then we'll be able to prove that Detwiler was here, but not why. Don't you get it? It's not about evidence anymore, it's about *time*. Turlock's got J.T. He knows I'm expecting to talk to him tomorrow at midnight—that means I've got one day to come up with a better bargaining chip to use against Turlock—something that might keep him from hurting the boy."

"Like what?"

Nick thought for a minute. "I tagged Detwiler's boat, remember? I retraced his path all over the Lower Nine, but he crossed the Industrial Canal and stopped two places in the city itself. We've got to check those places out, Beth—Detwiler stopped there for a reason. If we can find out where he stopped and why, we might find something we can use against Turlock."

Beth looked at him. "Nick—I don't know how to say this—"

"I know," he said. "There's a good chance J.T. is dead already."

"I just want to prepare you."

"Don't prepare me—help me. Get your car and let's go."

43

Tuesday, September 6

J.T. awoke groggily and blinked. His bed was soaking wet, and he felt aching pains across his hips and back and shoulders—he felt hard ridges beneath him, like the metal bars in Aunt Wanda's pullout sofa bed.

The room was dark but very hot; he could see sunlight streaming in from somewhere to his right. He tried to sit up, but the minute he did he felt a wave of nausea come over him; he rolled onto his left side and vomited.

I messed the bed, he thought. *Beth's gonna be mad now.*

He looked down at the bed and realized it wasn't a bed at all. He was lying on a floor of some kind—wooden boards with some kind of yellow stuff between them. The wood, that's what hurt his back; he was lying on boards, only they weren't close together—they were spaced apart. He pushed down on the yellow stuff; it was mushy, like a sponge filled with water. He pushed harder and the yellow stuff gave way. He pulled his hand out of the soggy mass; he wondered how deep the water was.

He finally managed to sit up without retching and looked around the room. The ceiling was slanted on both sides—it came all the way down to the floor. It wasn't a room at all—it was an attic. One end of the attic was dark; at the other end he saw lines of daylight shining through.

He struggled to his feet. His head was throbbing and he could still taste bile in the back of his throat. He looked at himself. His clothes were soaking wet and his skin was wrinkled like a prune. His arms and legs itched; he picked off bits of the yellow stuff and shook them off onto the floor.

Where am I? How did I get here?

He tried to think back to the night before. He remembered Nick waking him, telling him to go and find Beth; he remembered sneaking his way past the DMORT personnel and finding her; he remembered her taking him to her bed and tucking him in. He remembered her kissing him on the forehead too; he reached up and touched his forehead, as if the kiss might still be there. That was all he remembered—after that, he fell asleep.

But there was something else—something that happened later—something he couldn't quite recall. It was a *feeling*—it was a *smell.* He remembered something pressing hard against his face, causing him to wake up—then when he did, he smelled something bad—like plastic bags, like model airplane glue. Then he closed his eyes again and there was nothing else.

And now he was here—but where was he?

"Nick!" he shouted. *"Nick!"* But the sound of his voice hurt his head and he stopped.

The attic was hot—so very hot, and there was no breeze at all. His entire body was dripping with sweat. He peeled off his shirt and mopped his forehead and chest, then tossed it away.

He held on to the rafters and worked his way toward the sunlight. When he reached the wall he tried to peek out between the slats, but the slats overlapped like window blinds and he couldn't see a thing. He crouched down a little and looked up, but all he could see was the clear blue sky and the blazing sun high overhead. The sun hurt his eyes—he squeezed them shut and turned away.

"Nick!" he shouted again. "Beth! Anybody!"

He listened. There was no answer.

He felt his stomach growl. He hadn't eaten since yesterday, and he'd vomited up anything that was left. He had no food and no water, and he felt weak and empty—but maybe it didn't matter; he felt too sick to eat anyway. But he couldn't help thinking about those MREs . . .

He crossed to the dark end of the attic and tested the wall. There seemed to be a three-sided section at the top, just like at the other end, only there were no slats to let in the light—just solid boards. He ran his fingers along the edges and felt splintered wood. He squatted down and felt along the floor; he found long thin sections of broken wood—the slats. *Somebody busted them in*, he thought. He stood up and pushed on the boards—they were thick and hard.

He crossed back to the center of the attic and looked around the empty room—dark on one side, light on the other, with no way out. He felt a jolt of fear.

Then he remembered Nick—Nick had been in an attic just like this, and he had gotten out.

He looked around the floor; he saw a place where the boards framed a rectangular opening with a folded wooden ladder in the center. He worked his way over to it and squatted down beside it. He put one foot on the ladder and pushed down, testing it; one end lowered just a little, then sprang back tight. Now he crawled onto the ladder with his full weight, and it began to slowly descend. He rode it down into the water until he was chest-deep—then the ladder stopped and locked in place.

He climbed back up the ladder and sat down on the edge with his legs dangling into the hole. He looked down into the opening.

I'm a good swimmer, he told himself.

The water smelled like garbage. It looked like ink.

I can hold my breath a long time.

Sweat dripped into his eyes and burned them; he scrubbed his face with both hands and twisted his fists in his eye sockets. His tongue felt thick and sticky; he looked at the water and wondered if it was okay to drink just a little.

"Nick! Beth!"

He stood up again. It was even hotter at the peak of the roof now—it was like sticking his head into an oven. He felt weak and light-headed.

"Help! Somebody help!"

He pounded his fists against the roof and felt stabbing pain. He jerked his hands back and looked at them. He saw blood dripping from tiny ragged holes where the roofing nails had punctured his skin. He put his fists to his mouth and sucked at the wounds; he felt tears welling up in his eyes.

He looked down at the opening again.

44

The monotonous drone of the boat's engine was putting Beth to sleep. The gentle, rhythmic rocking of the bow wasn't helping, either, lulling her like an aluminum cradle. Her eyes kept drooping and her head slowly nodding until the boat struck a chunk of debris or unexpectedly crossed the wake of another boat—then she jerked upright again and stretched, blinking at her surroundings.

She turned and looked at Nick in the stern; he kept glancing back and forth between his GPS receiver and the surrounding buildings. He looked no different than he had the night before; she wondered how she must look to him. She was tired—mind-numbing, tongue-tying, bone-dragging tired. Nick should have felt far worse; but if he did, he didn't show it.

It had taken an hour to make the drive back from the remote bayou to the city, and once they got there they still faced the task of finding another boat. Nick had briefly considered dismantling the old johnboat and hauling it across the bridge in their two cars, with the aluminum hull strapped to the roof of one and the Evinrude and gas tank in the trunk of the other. But the process would have taken hours, and they weren't sure the two of them could have lifted the motor by themselves. They decided instead to head directly into the city, counting on the growing number of search-and-rescue teams to make it possible to beg, borrow, or steal a boat there. They eventually managed to do so, but it took hours more; by the time they located a boat and put out into the flooded downtown, the sun was already high overhead—and Beth was already exhausted.

They set out from the central business district just north of the Convention Center and headed into the heart of the city. They passed the Superdome several blocks away to the left, then crossed under Interstate 10. They were in mid-city New Orleans now, still headed west-by-northwest—exactly where, Beth didn't know. Nick didn't know either; the GPS unit would allow them to retrace Detwiler's path and to stop where Detwiler stopped—but what they found once they got there was anyone's guess.

After Interstate 10 the neighborhood began to change—the steel-and-glass business buildings gave way to more-industrial surroundings. The water looked deep here; a street sign barely protruding said "Tulane Avenue." The road was wide—maybe six lanes across—and they cruised down the exact center, making Beth feel vulnerable and exposed. She had been followed once before—she wondered if it could happen again.

At the intersection of Tulane and Broad Street, Nick slowed the boat to a crawl. On their left was a long gray three-story structure with a multicolumned front. The center six columns rested on a wide stone stairway that disappeared into the water just a few steps down.

Beth looked at Nick. "Is that the place?"

"It has to be," Nick said.

"I don't see a sign."

"Maybe it's underwater." He motored slowly up to the stairway; when he did, the massive front door swung open and a man dressed in the uniform of a sheriff's deputy stepped out.

"The building's closed," the deputy said. "You can't stay here, folks—sorry."

Nick held up his DMORT credentials. "We're not looking for a place to stay—we're looking for information. What is this place?"

"Orleans Parish Criminal District Court."

"Was this some kind of evacuation center?"

"For a couple of days. When the city first flooded, a lot of court employees were trapped here—judges, staff, their families—then folks from the surrounding area started coming too. We had about a hundred and fifty at the peak, but we cleared the last of 'em out last Friday and sealed the building."

"You're still here."

"I'm a sheriff's deputy. A few of us stayed behind to secure the building."

"Looks like you got hit pretty hard here," Beth said.

"Yeah, the water's about eight feet deep."

"Did it do much damage?"

"Flooded the basement completely—right up to the ceiling."

"What's in the basement?" Nick asked. "Anything important?"

"Judges' parking lot, jury rooms, the coroner's office—it's all underwater. The big problem is the evidence rooms."

Nick blinked. "The what?"

"We've got seven evidence and records rooms down there, all of 'em flooded. It's a real mess—stuff dating back seventy years."

"What do you keep in the evidence rooms?"

"Everything—case files, court records, evidence submitted during trials—we store it all down there. They'll have to wait until the water goes down just to see what's left—then they'll have mud, and slime, and mold. They say they'll have to bring in salvage experts just to see what they can save."

"That's got to slow things down around here."

"Are you kidding? It's a disaster. We had three thousand cases pending before the storm, and every one of them just ground to a halt—some of them won't ever make it to court now."

"Why not?" Beth asked.

"How can you have a trial? Defendants, witnesses, they all fled the city—there aren't even enough people left to fill a jury pool. Then there's the evidence—you lose a critical piece of evidence and the trial's over."

"Yeah," Nick said. "That's exactly right."

"It's a problem for the higher courts too. The Fifth Circuit Court of Appeals—that's down by Lafayette Square—they count on us for evidence and records too. When a man files an appeal, the appeals court sends over for his trial record; if we don't have a record for them to review, they order a retrial. But how can there be a retrial without the original evidence? There can't be—if the evidence is lost, the conviction gets overturned."

"And bad guys end up back on the streets," Nick said. "That's got to be frustrating for a lot of people—a lot of hard work down the drain."

"You have no idea," the deputy said.

Nick looked at Beth. "Actually, I think we do."

"That was very educational," Nick called over the engine's roar. "I just love field trips, don't you?"

"Is that why Detwiler stopped at the courthouse—to try to find out what evidence had been lost?"

"Looks that way to me," Nick said. "Try to see it from their perspective: The courthouse is underwater—evidence has been destroyed—a lot of indictments might never make it to trial, and a lot of hard-won convictions might get overturned. That means a lot of bad people back on the streets and a lot of work to do all over again. That's got to be tough, watching years of work about to go down the drain—literally. If I were in their shoes, I might have been tempted to cut a few corners too."

"Is that what you think they did?"

"I'd bet on it. I think Turlock and Detwiler saw the legal system about to break down and decided to settle a few debts on the side. If we could ID the bodies I recovered from the Lower Nine, I'll bet we'd find that every one of them was involved in the drug trade in some way. No wonder they didn't want them identified."

"Would there be some way to connect them all to Turlock and Detwiler?"

"Maybe, through prior arrest records. Some of the victims might have been under investigation by the DEA—that would establish a definite connection. The clincher would be establishing time of death—proving that each of the men died after the hurricane. That would definitely indicate foul play—that's what would set off all the bells and whistles with the authorities."

"Sounds great," Beth said. "Can you do all that?"

"No, I can't. The problem is, I don't *have* the bodies—and by the time they're recovered again, there won't be enough evidence left to establish time of death. If the DNA degrades enough, we might not even be able to identify them."

"Then how does it help us to know all this?"

"Knowledge is power," Nick said. "All we need right now is a better bargaining chip with Turlock—maybe I can construct a better bluff than I did last night. Besides, we've got one more stop to make. Let's hope this next field trip is as educational as the last one."

Nick tried the back door—it was open. That didn't surprise him; why lock the door of a castle when it's surrounded by a moat? The entire neighborhood of Lakeview was underwater, inundated by a breach in the Seventeenth Street Canal half a mile to the west. This house was one of the fortunate few: Situated on a slight elevation, the water came up to the front door and then stopped; the house appeared to be sitting on the water like a barge.

Nick could have sailed right up to the front door. After all, the entire neighborhood was abandoned—who would see? But he thought it best to exercise caution. He didn't know why Detwiler had stopped here, and he had no idea what they might find inside.

He pushed open the door and stepped in; Beth was right behind him. He instinctively reached for the light switch and flipped it several times, but he knew that nothing would happen. The house was already in deep shadow from the late afternoon sun. Nick switched on his flashlight and held it at shoulder level like a knife.

He stopped and listened; he heard no sound from anywhere in the house.

"Hello!" Beth called out. "Anybody home?"

There was no response.

"We're with FEMA," Nick offered, thinking it best not to mention a mortuary team just yet. "Sorry to bother you—we're in the neighborhood, just checking things out. No reason to be alarmed. Anybody here?" They worked their way deeper into the house as they spoke.

"I think we're alone," Beth said.

"Looks that way." They were in a small kitchen now. Nick pointed the flashlight around the room; it was a scene frozen in time, a three-dimensional photograph of someone else's life.

"It's creepy," Beth said. "Like visiting Hiroshima after the bomb went off." She reached for the refrigerator door.

"I wouldn't," Nick said. "The power's been off for a week—the place stinks bad enough as it is."

She noticed it too. It wasn't just the mold and mildew; it was the smell of filth that filled the air—a combination of dust, sweat, and lingering body odor.

Nick pointed the flashlight at the kitchen sink; it was stacked high with dirty dishes, utensils, and glasses. "Somebody needs to tidy up—somebody who's been here since the storm."

"How do you know?"

"The water shut off when the power did—that means the dishes were either there before the storm or somebody's been adding to them since. That's a pretty big stack to let pile up, even for a guy like me. I think somebody's been staying here—somebody who works for the government."

"Why do you say that?"

Nick pointed to the kitchen table—it was covered with empty brown-and-silver Mylar bags. "MREs—they're eating the same food we are. MREs are usually government-issue—whoever it is must be connected with some local agency."

"Probably Detwiler," Beth said. "He stopped here—it's probably his house."

"I don't think so—but it should be easy enough to find out. Look around for a magazine, a diploma, something with a name on it."

They found nothing in the kitchen. In the entryway beside the front door there was a dusty foyer table with a small lamp and a withered houseplant. Leaning against the lamp was a stack of stamped letters waiting for a postman who would never return. Beth flipped through the letters and checked the return address.

"You were right," she called to Nick. "It's not Detwiler's house."

Nick poked his head around the corner. "Who lives here?"

"Never heard of him," she said. "Somebody named 'LaTourneau.'"

45

"Try to remember," Beth said. "What else do you know about him?"

"Almost nothing," Nick said. "Jerry and I met LaTourneau the first morning after the storm—he was the only other guy working the Lower Nine. He said he was with the NOPD—I gave him a hard time about all the officers who didn't show up for work."

"Why did you do that?"

"Just to stay in practice, okay? Get off my back—it's LaTourneau we need to focus on here."

"You say he was in the Lower Nine every day?"

"He was the first one there in the morning and the last one back at night—a one-man rescue team."

"He worked alone?"

"Yeah—except for the day he worked with me."

"He *what*?"

"It was the day after Jerry disappeared. I needed protection, and LaTourneau was a cop—he carried a sidearm. We worked together all afternoon."

"Maybe he wanted to keep an eye on you."

"No, I asked *him*—I practically had to beg. He didn't want to work with me—he wanted to keep working alone."

"Maybe that's what he wanted you to think."

"No way. I can tell when somebody's playing me, Beth—he genuinely didn't want me around. So what's the connection between LaTourneau and Detwiler? Detwiler wanted to kill me—he would have done it if he had the chance. LaTourneau had the chance all afternoon, and he had a gun—but he didn't do it. Why not? It doesn't make sense."

"What else can you remember about him? You were together all afternoon—he must have told you something."

"He didn't talk much."

"Did you ask questions? Did you volunteer anything about yourself?"

"I don't need a lecture on interpersonal communication, okay?"

"Men. If he were a woman, we wouldn't have this problem."

"If he were a woman, he would have talked me to death. Can we get back to the subject? What's the connection between LaTourneau and Detwiler?"

"I have no idea."

"We're not going to figure it out standing here," Nick said. "Let's look around the house and see what else we can find."

They went down the hallway to a small bedroom, only recognizable as the master because of the adjoining bath. There were two closets, one on either side of the bed; the closet on the left was empty.

"He's separated or divorced," Nick said.

"How do you know?"

"That closet is empty—but look at all the hangers. There used to be clothes in there."

"Maybe his wife left before the storm and took her things with her."

"In an emergency you only take basics—you don't clean out the closet."

Beth went into the bathroom and checked the medicine cabinet. "She left a few things here too. You're right, he's probably separated or divorced—and I don't think he's handling it well."

"Why not?"

"Look at the bed—he doesn't even bother to make it up anymore. He doesn't do dishes, he doesn't dust, he doesn't clean—he's lost interest in the house. This isn't *home* for him anymore—it's just a place where he eats and sleeps. Maybe that's why he works such long hours."

"Let's try across the hall—maybe he's got kids."

The bedroom across the hall was equal in size but very different in appearance. The bed was neatly made—the dust ruffle was crisply pleated and every throw pillow was carefully arranged. Each item on the dresser and vanity was neatly ordered too; nothing was on the floor; nothing was out of place.

Nick pointed to a purple-and-gold pennant hanging over the bed. "LSU—she's either a student or a fan."

Beth crossed to the vanity and looked at the photographs sticking out from the mirror's frame. "Student," she said. "Sorority photo—she's a Pi Phi. No graduation photo, though—she's probably still in school." She ran her index finger across the glass top; it left a track in the thick dust like the wake of a boat. She slid open the closet door and looked inside; it was packed completely full. She checked the top dresser drawer; it was full too.

"I've got a bad feeling about this," Beth said. "The girl used to live here, but not anymore—nothing's been touched for months. It looks like she left suddenly, and she left everything behind—all her photos, all her mementos. If her parents kicked her out or if she ran away, she would have at least taken some of her clothing—but everything seems to be here. And nothing's been moved or rearranged—it's like someone's trying to preserve the place as it was."

"I was thinking the same thing," Nick said. "This isn't a bedroom, it's a museum. I think the girl's dead—that's my guess."

"That would explain a lot—the father's long hours, his disinterest in the house—it might even explain the breakup of his marriage."

"Let's keep looking," Nick said.

At the end of the hallway was the smallest of the three bedrooms, little more than a large closet. It was furnished as an all-purpose room—a combination office, storeroom, and gymnasium. In one corner there was a sagging particleboard bookshelf packed with NOPD training manuals and unmarked three-ring binders; in the center there was a rickety bench press with one red vinyl pad split open and urethane foam poking out; in the opposite corner there was a small desk piled high with unopened letters and unread magazines.

Beth went to the desk and shuffled through the papers. She opened the center desk drawer; there was a newspaper clipping on top from the *Baton Rouge Advocate*. She read the headline: LSU Student Dies in Apparent Overdose.

"Nick—look at this."

Nick took the article and read:

> Sherri LaTourneau, 20, a third-year pre-med student at LSU, was found dead in her apartment Thursday, the apparent victim of an accidental drug overdose. According to official sources, LaTourneau's roommate confessed to LaTourneau's occasional use of methamphetamines around the time of final exams. According to sheriff's deputies, the emaciated condition of the body indicated regular and excessive use of the drug. In response, LSU officials have issued a public statement, warning students that "the pressure to succeed does not justify dangerous and illicit practices . . ."

Nick looked at Beth. "You said that you once thought I took meth. What made you think that?"

"I told you: your compulsive work habits, your excessive hours, your inability to sleep—they're classic symptoms. Why?"

"I saw the same things in LaTourneau. He never seems to stop; he doesn't take breaks; and I remember something else now—he told me he can't sleep. I remember thinking, *This guy's just like me*. I figured he keeps going the same way I do, but maybe not. Maybe he's got a different method—'better living through chemistry.'"

"You think LaTourneau is a user?"

"I don't know—that doesn't seem possible. If a man's daughter died of a drug overdose, wouldn't that man stay away from drugs? Wouldn't he find them abhorrent—repugnant—just because of what they did to his daughter?"

"Sometimes just the opposite," Beth said. "Sometimes when a man's daughter dies of a drug overdose, he wants to understand why. He wants to know what she was thinking, what she was feeling, he wants to understand the power of the drug—so he becomes a user himself. Children of alcoholics become alcoholics; friends of suicide victims commit suicide. It's a common psychological phenomenon—it's entirely possible. Did you notice anything else unusual about his appearance or behavior?"

"Like what?"

"Extreme nervousness; dilated pupils; dizziness or confusion; dry or itchy skin—"

"Itchy skin—that reminds me of something else he said. When I told him I work with maggots, he told me he hated maggots. He said they get under his skin—that he could feel them crawling around. I had no idea what he was talking about."

"I think I do," Beth said. "I've seen it in some of my cocaine patients. They call it 'cocaine bugs'—meth users call it 'speed bumps.' It's a form of delusional parasitosis known as *formication*—the delusion that insects or snakes are crawling all over your skin. It's a psychosis that can result from stimulant abuse."

Nick looked around the room. "If you were taking amphetamines, where would you hide your pills?"

"If I lived alone? In the medicine cabinet; why would I bother to hide them?"

"I'll check his bathroom—you check the one across from the girl's room."

Nick hadn't even reached the master bath before he heard Beth's voice: "Nick—come here. Look at this."

He entered the small bathroom and found Beth standing beside the medicine cabinet, ashen-faced. The medicine cabinet was empty except for one orange pill container on a center shelf. Beth was holding the wastebasket. She tilted it toward him so he could see inside; the bottom was lined with empty pill containers that looked exactly the same.

She reached up without a word and closed the medicine cabinet door. Taped to the mirror was a photograph of Nick sitting in the john-boat. Underneath the photo, written in lipstick on the mirror, were the words: "Kill him, Daddy. He's the worst one."

Nick stared at the photo. "Now, that's what *I* call creepy."

"They've been using him," Beth said. "They've been feeding LaTourneau names and locations of people to kill—and using his dead daughter's voice to do it. They're supplying him with meth too. That's your photo, Nick—they're telling him to kill you."

"I get it now," Nick said. "They let LaTourneau do the killings for them, then when they're through with him they just turn him over—just another good cop gone bad."

"Can you imagine anything more despicable? The man is undoubtedly grief-stricken over the death of his daughter—then suddenly his daughter speaks to him from beyond the grave and reveals to him where to find all the drug suppliers? LaTourneau would be more than happy to kill them—he'd think he was doing it for her."

"Who wouldn't?"

"Most people would experience the emotions, but they wouldn't act on them—they would grieve, they would get angry, but the better part of them would win out in the end. Not LaTourneau; Turlock and Detwiler pushed him over the edge—they were feeding his psychosis and using it for their own benefit."

"But LaTourneau doesn't seem psychotic. He saves people's lives all day long—what kind of a killer does that? All day long he—"

Nick stopped.

"What is it?"

"'All day long.' LaTourneau kept telling me not to work at night—to go home—to wait until morning. He said, 'Everything changes at night.' What do you suppose that means?"

Beth took a deep breath. "It means you're lucky to be alive."

"What?"

"He might have been telling you that he didn't want to kill you—to go home before his bad self came out."

"What are you talking about?"

"Methamphetamine abuse produces paranoia—it's one of the most common symptoms. If you take the drug too long or too often, paranoia turns into schizophrenia—a state where your personality splits into different identities, sometimes antagonistic identities. LaTourneau is a good cop, a public servant, a man who saves lives—but he wants to do something very bad too: He wants to kill all the people who killed his little girl. So how does he reconcile these two contradictory parts of himself? He can't—so he mentally splits himself into two different people. The good LaTourneau would never murder anyone; it's the bad LaTourneau who does that."

"But only at night?"

"Sometimes the different identities are linked to environmental cues: A good boy at work becomes a bad boy at home. In his case, a good boy during the day becomes a bad boy at night. Think about it: During the day, LaTourneau is a relentless doer of good. But at night—"

"*—everything changes.* You think that's what he was telling me? 'I protected you during the day, but I'll kill you at night—go home before I switch personalities'?"

"It's definitely possible. He's showing signs of acute psychosis in other ways."

Her expression suddenly changed. "Nick, I just thought of something: We need to get out of here—it's almost dark. If I'm right about this, we don't want to be here when LaTourneau comes home at night—especially when you've got your face plastered across his mirror." She reached for the photo of Nick.

"Wait," Nick said. "Leave it there."

"What? Why?"

"Detwiler stopped here two days ago. If he put the picture up then, LaTourneau has probably already seen it. It won't do any good to take it down now."

"But maybe he hasn't seen it yet."

"We have to assume that he has—and if he's seen it once, I want him to see it again." He picked up a towel from the floor. "Do you have a lipstick on you?"

46

"This is insane," Beth whispered.

"This is a *hunch*," Nick replied. "That's different." He attached the cable from the satellite telephone to the laptop computer. "Let's just hope both batteries hold out. We only need an hour, but the way my luck's been going lately, I wouldn't count on it."

It was almost eleven o'clock now. Nick and Beth sat in the boat in an isolated spot near the center of the Lower Nine. At this hour the neighborhood was completely abandoned; there were no sounds at all and the water was completely still.

"Why would Turlock come all the way out here?" Beth asked.

"Because a body is hard to get rid of—even the body of a boy. That's what this whole thing has been about. Turlock and Detwiler wanted to kill a few people—so why didn't they just shoot them? Because then they'd have bodies with bullet holes, and then people would start asking awkward questions. So they killed them out here—they made them look like natural deaths, and they used the water to cover up any forensic evidence. Now Turlock has a boy to get rid of—a boy who lives in the Lower Nine. Why wouldn't he get rid of him the same way?"

"It seems like a long shot to me," Beth said.

"That's all I've got left," Nick said. "Turlock said the boy wasn't with him—so where is he? I'm betting Turlock stashed him somewhere here in the Lower Nine. It makes sense: It's remote, it's quiet, and it's J.T.'s home—the natural place for the body to turn up later."

"But Turlock would have to get around the same way we do—by boat."

"That's what I'm counting on. I know the DEA has a boat on the Lower Nine—the one Detwiler was using to follow me. If Turlock needs a boat, he's likely to use the same one. That's the good part: I've got that boat tagged."

Nick took the satellite phone and dialed an access number, then opened the GPS program and waited for the map of colored dots to appear.

"Have you decided what you're going to say to Turlock yet?"

"I'm going to tell him everything we've figured out—about the courthouse, about his little vendetta, about the way he's been using LaTourneau. I'm going to tell him that he only has one option—to turn over the boy and cut his losses—not to make things any worse for himself than they are now."

"Do you think that will work?"

Nick paused. "No. He knows there's no way to cut his losses. He's in too deep—he's guilty of multiple murders already. He's counting on the fact that I won't be able to prove anything. He'll never release the boy—he'd be a fool to, and he knows it. He's just buying time."

"Nick," she said gently. "Then why are we doing all this?"

"Because I'm buying time too," Nick said. "If Turlock hasn't killed J.T. already, then I don't think he will—at least not for a day or two. He knows that if he does I might do something desperate, and he doesn't want to risk that. My threat to go to the media bought J.T. one more day of life, that's all. That's what I'm hoping, at least—we should know in about an hour."

"But if Turlock won't let him go anyway, what's the point?"

"I don't need him to let the boy go—I want him to lead me to him."

Nick held his breath as he watched the monitor, waiting for the downloaded data to appear. He let out a sigh of relief when the image shifted, revealing an additional dot.

"Bingo," he said. "Maybe my luck is changing after all."

"What is it?"

"J.T. is alive."

"How do you know?"

"The DEA boat is moving—look at the dot. Turlock is the only one with any reason to be out here at this time of night—and he has no reason to be out here unless he's heading for J.T."

Beth looked at the screen. She saw the flower-petal pattern of multiple dots where the boat had been docked for the last two days—then one additional dot marking a location somewhere in the Lower Nine. The text display beside the dot read 11:00 CST.

"But that doesn't tell us where he's going," she said.

"No—but it tells us which direction he's headed. All we'll do for now is head in the same general direction—that should put us just a short distance away. The GPS unit will broadcast his next position at midnight—by that time he should be with J.T. and waiting for my call. When the computer picks up that signal, we'll know exactly where he is—and when Turlock leaves we can get J.T. out of there."

"I hope you're right about all this," Beth said.

"So do I." Nick set the laptop on the bench in front of him. He started the engine and quietly motored deeper into the Lower Nine.

Turlock pulled his boat up alongside the abandoned house. He shut off his engine and listened for a moment, then turned and searched the surrounding area for prying eyes. He was alone, as he knew he would be. He'd picked this spot for good reason.

He rapped his knuckles on the attic wall. "Hey, kid."

There was no answer.

"Hey, kid, I'm a friend of your buddy Nick. He sent me here to get you—he wants to talk to you."

Still nothing.

Turlock took a hammer and pried off one of the boards that he had nailed across the attic vent. He pointed a flashlight into the opening and searched the attic's dark interior; he spotted the boy's body lying faceup halfway across the room.

He shrugged.

He replaced the board and hammered it on tight again. He looked at his watch: just a few minutes before midnight. He checked the satellite phone to make sure it was powered up and receiving a signal; he laid it on the bench in front of him. He took out his .40-caliber Glock and checked the clip, then slid it back into his shoulder holster.

He pulled the boat into the shadow of a nearby tree and waited for Nick to arrive.

47

Nick pulled his oar from the water and listened.

Nothing.

The black rooftops drifted past like great piles of coal. He snapped his fingers and Beth turned and looked at him; he held up his oar, signaling for her to stop rowing too. He let the boat slowly drift on the glassy water. It was strange: He had spent so much time in this neighborhood that he recognized his current location—he had passed this way half a dozen times in the last week. Turlock knew what he was doing; this section of the Lower Nine had been emptied of survivors days ago—no one was likely to search here again.

This was as far as he dared to go. Nick had no idea how far they had traveled or how near to their final destination they might be, but he couldn't take a chance on overtaking Turlock—that would be the worst thing he could do. His goal was to discover J.T.'s hiding place and then spirit him away—but it would work only if Turlock believed the boy was still in his possession. If Turlock realized that J.T.'s location had been discovered, he would remove the boy himself—or he would kill him on the spot.

Nick lifted the computer onto his lap and checked the screen again; according to the computer's clock, there was less than a minute until midnight. Nick had decided that he would wait for the final GPS coordinate, then disconnect the satellite phone from the laptop and make the call. He wondered if Turlock would actually let him talk to J.T. Probably—he didn't want Nick doing anything stupid. Then after the call Turlock would try to buy more time; he would request another day, and Nick would "reluctantly" agree—because the moment Turlock left, Nick would find J.T. and take him away, and after that there would be nothing to stop him from turning Turlock in, physical evidence or not.

Midnight.

A final dot appeared on the computer screen. Nick estimated the distance from his own location—it wasn't far away.

"Got it," he whispered to Beth.

He disconnected the phone from the laptop and dialed another number.

"Turlock."

"Let me talk to the boy," Nick said.

"He's right here. He's fine."

"Lucky for you. Let me talk to him."

A pause. "The kid's asleep. Let's not wake him, okay? Kids need their sleep."

Turlock was stonewalling. "He won't mind. He keeps late hours."

Turlock didn't answer.

Nick frowned. "The deal was: I wait one day, you let me talk to him."

"No. The deal was: You wait one day, I let the kid live one day. The day's up, Polchak—let's talk about tomorrow."

"No deal. You said one day."

"He's a good kid—real smart—I can see why you like him. We've brought the boy this far; seems like a shame to end it now—but I will, if that's what you want."

"I need to know the boy's alive," Nick said.

"Sounds reasonable. How about this: You call me tomorrow night at midnight—same time, same number—and I'll let you talk to him then."

"That's what you told me last night."

"Like I said, the boy's asleep. I can't help that. He's fine, Polchak, he's right here—I just looked in on him a minute ago."

Nick paused to give Turlock the impression he was considering. "One day," he said, "but that's it. No more excuses, Turlock—tomorrow night I either talk to the boy or I talk to CNN. It's up to you."

Nick disconnected.

"What happened?" Beth said. "I thought you were going to tell him what we found out—about LaTourneau and the courthouse."

"Something's wrong," Nick said. "He wouldn't let me talk to J.T."

"Why not?"

"There are two possibilities: He might just have been playing hardball—letting me know that he's the one in charge." Nick stopped there, and Beth didn't ask him to continue; they both knew what the second possibility was.

"What do we do now?"

"What we planned to do—we wait. Once we're sure Turlock is gone, we'll go to his location and look for J.T."

They sat together in silence.

Nick knew that something was definitely wrong—something he did not bother to explain to Beth. It made no sense: If Turlock never intended to let Nick talk to the boy, why did he come out here in the first place? He didn't need to make the trip to the Lower Nine just to say no—he could have done that from anywhere. Was it possible that Turlock was telling the truth? Did he intend to let Nick talk to the boy, but changed his mind when he found the boy sleeping? The idea was absurd; Turlock wasn't a babysitter—what did he care about waking the boy up?

There was only one other possibility . . .

Nick adjusted his glasses and looked at the computer screen again.

Oh, no.

The overlapping dots—the series of coordinates representing the time that Turlock's boat had been docked—there was something wrong with them. The text displays beside each dot overlapped too, making them difficult to distinguish—but now that he looked more closely, Nick could see it: There was a twenty-six-hour gap between two of the overlapping dots. There could only be one explanation: The GPS unit had been switched off and then on again.

Nick started up the engine and twisted the throttle.

Beth twisted around and looked at him in astonishment. "What are you doing?"

"It's a trap," Nick said.

"Nick—he could hear us!"

"It doesn't matter—he already knows we're here."

Nick jerked the tiller and turned around on a dime, gunning the engine and accelerating away.

"Where are we going?"

Nick didn't reply. He was moving fast, searching up ahead for familiar landmarks, dodging back and forth between the shadowy houses and black mounded treetops looming from the water. He swerved too close to an old river oak and the branches raked across the bottom of the hull like the fingernails of a giant. He misjudged a turn and the boat's right side caught the edge of a rooftop; the boat almost overturned, throwing Beth off her bench and against the port-side rail.

"Nick! What are you doing?"

A minute later they squeezed between two rooftops and emerged into a wide-open area; in the center of the area was a bizarre jigsaw puzzle of wooden coffins, roped together around the edges like a massive log raft. Nick brought the boat up alongside the coffins and killed the engine. He reached over the side of the boat and pushed down hard on the closest coffin, testing its buoyancy. He looked at Beth.

"Get out," he said.

"What?"

"Get out—I'm leaving you here."

"What are you talking about? What's going on?"

"The GPS unit—the one I dropped in Detwiler's boat—he must have found it. Somebody turned it off—there was a gap in the time record."

"So?"

"Anybody could have turned it off, but only one person would have a reason to turn it on again: Turlock. He must have figured out what I was doing. He switched the unit on again because he wanted me to follow him."

"Then let's get out of here!"

"No. I'm going back."

"Are you out of your mind? If he wanted you to follow him, he'll be waiting for you. This was never about J.T.—it was just a way to get you out here so he could kill you himself."

"I came out here on a hunch," Nick said. "Turlock had the same hunch—he knew I might try to follow him, but he couldn't know that for sure. I still think there's a chance J.T. is out here."

"Then why wouldn't Turlock let you talk to him? J.T. is dead, Nick—that has to be the reason. You can't risk your life on the outside chance that he might still be alive."

"Why not? I'm willing to take that chance."

"Nick, you're tired—you're not thinking clearly."

"It seems clear enough to me. If there's a chance that J.T. is back there, I have to go back and look. If Turlock has left already, I'll be okay. If Turlock is waiting for me, he'll be planning to kill me—but I don't think he'll do it."

"Why not?"

"Because of you, Beth. He's forgetting about you; he's forgetting that you know everything I know—about LaTourneau, about the courthouse, about Detwiler and the bayou. If anything happens to me, *you'll* go straight to the authorities—he's forgetting that, but I'll remind him."

"Nick, that's a terrible risk."

"I'll take that risk."

"Then I'm going with you."

"No. One of us has to make it back to the authorities—that's why I'm dropping you here. If things work out all right, I'll come back for you; if not—here, take the satellite phone. FEMA knows about this place—just tell them you're at the coffins."

"But if you don't come back—"

"Then you'll go to the authorities, and we'll still get Turlock."

"But you'll be dead."

Nick shrugged. "Denny wanted a team player; looks like he finally gets his wish. Now—get out."

48

Nick worked his way back between the rooftops, checking his GPS receiver as he went. It wasn't far now—just a few more meters away. Straight ahead of him was a single-story house with an asphalt-shingle roof, no different from six thousand others in the Lower Nine—except for the fact that this might be the last house he would ever see.

Nick spotted the attic vent and motored toward it. The attic was the only portion of the house above water; if J.T. was there, he would be inside. He started to call out as he approached but decided not to—his voice would carry easily over the still water, and if Turlock had recently left, there was no sense in calling him back.

As Nick approached the attic vent, another boat slid quietly out from behind the house. It was Turlock—and he was holding a gun.

"Cut your engine," Turlock said. "Do it now."

"This used to be such a nice neighborhood," Nick said. "Now they're letting everyone in."

"You don't seem surprised to see me. I'm a little disappointed."

"It's sort of like hemorrhoids," Nick said. "You know they'll be back, you just don't know when."

"I know what you mean. I've had the same experience with you."

"Glad to oblige."

"You cost me a partner."

"That wasn't my fault, Frank—you'll have to talk to the alligators about that. You know, I've been reading up on alligators lately. Here's an interesting fact: Alligators can't chew. They just rip off huge chunks of flesh and hold it in their jaws until it decomposes enough to swallow whole. That means your partner should be around for a few days—long enough to get a DNA sample and prove that he was there."

"Now, who would want to do that?"

"Dr. Woodbridge might. She doesn't like people shooting at her—she's picky about things like that." Nick glanced down at Turlock's hand. "We both are."

"You didn't mention that Dr. Woodbridge was with you that night."

"Didn't I? Oh, yes, we've been spending a lot of time together lately. Take yesterday, for example—we made a very interesting side trip to the Orleans Parish Criminal District Court."

Turlock paused. "You don't say."

"It was very educational. A sheriff's deputy there told us all about it—how the basement flooded, how all kinds of court records and case evidence have been destroyed."

"Seems I heard something about that."

"I'll bet you did. That's just the sort of news that would get your attention, now, wouldn't it? I imagine the DEA spends a good bit of time at that courthouse. Orleans Parish—that covers the entire city of New Orleans, doesn't it? I'll bet you boys make quite a few arrests around there—some of them right here in the Lower Nine."

"A few," Turlock said.

"Just think about all those cases that might not make it to trial now—all the past convictions that might be overturned on appeal. All that work—all that time—it's enough to break your heart."

"You have no idea," Turlock said.

"Oh, I don't know, Frank—lots of people feel that way from time to time. Take me, for instance: I've been trying to catch a couple of murderers for a week now, and I'm getting nowhere—I keep losing all the physical evidence."

"Sorry to hear that."

"I'm not the only one who's frustrated. There's a cop who's been working in the Lower Nine—he keeps rescuing people all day long, but they still seem to keep dying at night. Poor guy, he just can't seem to get ahead. Maybe you've heard of him—a guy named LaTourneau."

Turlock didn't answer.

J.T. stood with his ear pressed against the attic vent. He heard every word that Nick had said—and every word spoken by the man he called Frank.

When J.T. first heard Turlock call out to him he almost shouted back, but something warned him not to—something in the man's voice. "I'm a friend of Nick," the man said—but it wasn't Jerry's voice, and Nick never mentioned other friends. Maybe this was the man who put him here—the one who made him sick to his stomach and left him here to rot. Nick would never do that. Nick would never leave him in a place like this, a place so hot that you felt dizzy and weak and you sweated until your skin got cold and clammy and your tongue got glued to the roof of your mouth.

That's why J.T. didn't shout back—that's why he lay down on the floor and pretended to be dead. He heard the man pry off the board—he could hear the squeaking of the nails. And when the man hammered the board back on again, that's when he knew: This was no friend.

When he heard Turlock's voice a second time, it was at the opposite end of the house—the one with the slats. He was talking to someone else this time, but who? J.T. pressed his ear against the slats and listened—and that's when he heard Nick's voice.

He started to shout again—to let Nick know that he was there, just a few yards away, trapped inside the attic, hot and tired and hungry—but again he decided not to. He decided to listen; that's when he knew that Nick was in trouble.

That's when he knew that he had to help.

The attic was as black as a cavern. J.T. quickly felt his way across the floor joists, testing with his foot for the opening that led down into the house. When he found it, he eased onto the ladder and stepped down into the water until it was almost up to his neck. He looked back at the faint moonlight glowing through the slats at the attic's end. That was the wall—that was how far he had to swim.

That ain't nothin', he told himself. *I'm a real good swimmer—I can hold my breath for a long, long time.*

He felt something brush by his leg. He thought about the house—about the way it might be shaped, about windows and doors and where they might be.

I been in lots of houses like this. This one's no different.

He felt a sudden rush of fear. He imagined himself trapped, frantic, with no way to go forward and no way back.

Nick did it, he told himself. *If Nick can do it, so can I.*

He summoned all his courage, took his deepest breath, and dived in.

He headed directly toward the end of the house. That's where Nick was—that's where he needed to go. He swam hard at first, hoping to cover the distance in the shortest possible time—but then he remembered how hard he had to breathe whenever he ran as fast as he could, so he eased up a little and paced himself instead. He swam along the ceiling like a cockroach; the ocean of darkness around him seemed overwhelming, and it was reassuring to feel something real and solid against his back.

Bump! A wall—he felt his first wave of panic.

He felt along the wall with both hands. His memory of other houses told him to go left, and the decision was a good one—in a few seconds he found the top of a doorway and swam through.

But in the process of twisting through the doorway and righting himself again, he became disoriented. He wasn't sure which direction to head now—but he was sure of one thing: He was running out of air, and fast.

He started to swim harder again, but in just a few inches his head bumped something else—something hard. He frantically ran his hands over it: a hinge—a door of some kind. He pulled the door open and tried to reach through, but his hand hit something else—a stack of dishes—cups and saucers. He jerked his hand out and felt the dishes slide out and fall, drifting silently back and forth in the water like leaves settling to the ground. It was a cabinet—he was in a kitchen—but facing which way? Where was he supposed to go now?

He felt his lungs heave, desperate for air.

He turned to the left and swam desperately, but once again in just a few feet his head bumped into something hard—something made of metal this time.

His head was aching, throbbing from lack of oxygen. He felt as if his chest was about to explode. He wanted to cry; maybe he was already crying, but there was no way to feel the tears in water as warm as spit. He floated motionless, trying to think what to do—what Nick would do—but no ideas came to his mind. There was no way forward and no way back, and he could only summon one thought.

Where is my father?

49

"You probably know LaTourneau," Nick said. "He's a methamphetamine addict, and the DEA keeps tabs on people like that. We stopped off at his house yesterday and took a look around. Guess what we found? Somebody's been supplying him with speed, then using him like a hopped-up errand boy to do their dirty work. Now, who would do a thing like that? If you ask me, that's the sort of person who needs investigating; that's the kind of guy you want to keep tabs on."

"LaTourneau started using on his own," Turlock said. "We had nothing to do with that. We got a call from NOPD Internal Affairs—they said they had a drug-abuse situation with one of their officers. They sent him to rehab and gave him a long leave of absence—asked us to find the supplier."

"So you took over his rehab."

"LaTourneau was over the edge when we found him. He was going down anyway—we did the poor guy a favor."

"You call that a favor?"

"We tracked down LaTourneau's supplier. Turns out he was buying from the same guys who supplied his own daughter—the two who set up the meth lab out in the bayou. We made the mistake of telling LaTourneau; the next day he took a boat out there and shot both of them dead."

"You 'made the mistake' of telling him. Now was it really a mistake, Frank? Or were you hoping that he would take care of a little problem for you? I hear that clandestine meth labs are becoming quite a problem for the DEA; so you just let it slip to LaTourneau that you knew where to find one—one that he'd be especially motivated to do something about."

"It was his daughter, Polchak—he lost his head, that's all. We just looked the other way."

"But not for long—because LaTourneau wasn't quite as tidy as you'd hoped he'd be; he just threw the bodies in the water, and you knew that somebody might eventually discover them. So when Katrina came along you saw a way to take care of that little problem; you dredged up the two bodies from the bayou and dumped them in the Lower Nine, didn't you?"

"That's about it."

"But when the hurricane hit—when the courthouse flooded—you got a little more ambitious, didn't you? It wasn't just about covering your tracks anymore, and that's when you realized that LaTourneau could be a very useful guy. Why should you get your hands dirty? You could just give LaTourneau your grocery list and let him do the shopping for you."

"The people he killed were all in the drug trade, Polchak—they were just like the ones who murdered his daughter. Men lose their kids to drugs all the time; most of them never get to do anything about it. We gave LaTourneau that chance—that was the favor."

"Sorry if I don't appreciate the favor," Nick said. "Don't forget, I lost a partner in all this. But now that I think about it, that happened in the daytime—so that wasn't LaTourneau's work, was it?"

"I tried to warn you. You wouldn't let it go."

"Yes, I have that tendency—my psychiatrist keeps warning me about it. Have you met my psychiatrist? Dr. Woodbridge—I mentioned her before. Psychiatrists have a funny way of getting inside your head; before you know it, they know everything that you know."

"What a nightmare that must be."

"Can you imagine? Dead partners, bodies with strange anomalies, clandestine meth labs in remote bayous, attics that blow up the minute you step inside—she knows every detail. And believe me, Frank—if anything happens to me, she'll tell."

"I'll take my chances with her."

"I've made that mistake. I don't recommend it."

"I went to a lot of trouble to get you out here. Do you really think I'm going to let you go?"

"No, I don't," Nick said. "I'm only interested in the boy—he's the only reason I'm here."

"Sorry," Turlock said. "You're a little late."

J.T. began to twist frantically in the water. He shoved hard against the metal surface in front of him—maybe it would move, maybe it would let him by. He felt the metal flex a little and it shifted in the water. Whatever it was, it was big, like a box, with flat sides—and it was floating against the ceiling.

Then he remembered what Nick had told him: *Refrigerators float because they're filled with air.*

He swam underneath the refrigerator and felt along the surface. He found a handle—the door was facing down. He pulled on the handle but nothing happened. He had no leverage—he had nothing to pull against. He jerked on the handle again and again. His lungs were on fire, and the knowledge that there was air just a few inches away made it even worse.

What would Nick do? He tried to think.

He rotated upside down and planted his feet against the ceiling—then he grasped the handle with both hands and pushed upward with all the strength he had left. The door slowly opened and swung down into the water. The refrigerator rocked from side to side, bobbing like a cork, knocking against the ceiling, releasing huge bubbles of air that rolled out from underneath and gurgled up the sides.

J.T. pulled himself around the edge and shoved his head in between two shelves—but he couldn't find the air. Half the space was filled with plastic containers and rotting food that had fallen down against the door. He dug his way through it like a mole, clawing his way up until his head finally hit the back of the refrigerator—then his lungs exploded and he took his first frantic breath. The air was hot and foul, filled with the stench of mold and slime that had been accumulating for a week. But it didn't matter—it was air.

He floated in the darkness, panting like a dog, listening to his rasping breath echoing off the walls just inches from his face.

50

"Where is the boy?" Nick asked.

"He's dead," Turlock said. "Too bad about that."

"You said he was here. You told me he was sleeping."

"I wasn't sure you'd come. I didn't want you running off half-cocked."

Nick nodded toward the attic. "Is he in there?"

"Yeah, he's in there."

"J.T.!" Nick shouted.

There was no reply.

"J.T.! It's Nick! Can you hear me? It's all right—I came to take you away!"

Still nothing.

"You shouldn't lie to the boy," Turlock said.

Nick glared at Turlock; he could barely contain his rage. "Did you put him in there? Did you seal up that attic and leave him in there to bake all day? Shame on you, Frank—he was just a kid."

"Like I said—it's too bad."

"That's it? That's all you've got to say?"

Turlock didn't reply.

"Take a look around, Frank—the whole city's underwater. Lots of good people are suffering right now, and yes—some people are taking advantage. They're roaming the streets, looting the stores, even taking potshots at rescue helicopters—and they're all getting away with it right now, because there's no law. But you don't kill the good ones to get to the bad ones—that sort of defeats the point. I thought you'd be bright enough to figure that out. Apparently not."

"I don't expect you to understand," Turlock said.

"I understand more than you think. See, I'm basically in the same line of work you are—I catch bad guys. And when I see one of them getting away, it really bothers me—it's hard to let it go. I can understand how you feel—I can even understand why you did what you did—but you didn't just want to stop the drug dealers, did you? You wanted to stop the drug dealers *and get away with it*—and that's different. The minute you killed Jerry, everything changed. This wasn't about you saving the world anymore—this was about you saving your own skin."

Turlock shook his head. "You know, I've spent twenty-five years with the DEA, most of it on the streets in run-down neighborhoods like this one—tracking down dealers, breaking up supply rings, kicking down doors, busting a few heads. It's a dirty business, Polchak. I've lost friends and I've lost partners—more than one—but I like to think it's been worth it, because I've managed to take a lot of bad people off the streets. Now a hurricane comes along and threatens to put them all back again? Sorry—Detwiler and me, we couldn't just sit back and let that happen. So we killed a few people—we 'took the law into our own hands'—but what are you supposed to do when there's no law left? You can think whatever you want, Polchak—first watch your own daughter die of a drug overdose, then come and talk to me about 'due process.'"

"How noble," Nick said. "Tell me something, Frank: Where is LaTourneau getting his drugs now?"

"How should I know?"

"You have to know; it's a critical element in all this, isn't it? LaTourneau isn't following your orders—he thinks he's listening to the spirit of his dear departed daughter. To keep that little scam going you have to feed his psychosis—and that requires a steady flow of drugs. I was at his house, remember? I saw the pill bottle in the medicine cabinet and all the empties in the trash. Tell me, does the DEA keep a handy supply of methamphetamine for situations like this? Or have you found another source?"

Turlock didn't answer.

"You told me something in Denny's office—that day we first met. You said that after the hurricane, people in the drug trade would see opportunities to get ahead. You said a dealer might see the chance to become a distributor, or a distributor might try to become a major supplier. Is that what happened here, Frank? Did you and Detwiler see this whole disaster as a chance to move up in the world? Or do you really expect me to buy your 'noble vigilante' angle?"

"Think what you want," Turlock said. "I've got no apologies to make. There wasn't a man we killed who didn't deserve to die ten times over."

"J.T. didn't."

Turlock shrugged. "He got caught in the cross fire—just like you."

Now Nick heard the sound of another boat's engine; it was approaching from behind. He turned and looked, but in the darkness saw nothing. He looked back at Turlock again—Turlock showed no sign of surprise or concern.

"I get it," Nick said. "I've got to hand it to you, Frank, you're very thorough." He turned around and looked again; now he could see the bulbous black hull of the inflatable Zodiac boat cruising silently toward him.

"Evening, partner," Nick called out to LaTourneau as he approached.

LaTourneau said nothing; he brought his boat up parallel to Nick's and stopped his engine. The boats sat lined up in the water like three fingers on a hand—with Nick caught dead in the middle.

"Missed you today," Nick said, hoping to remind LaTourneau of their earlier kinship. "How was the fishing in the Lower Nine? Catch any big ones?"

But the LaTourneau who looked back at him was a different man—his eyes showed no recognition of Nick's identity. They showed almost nothing at all; they were glassy and hollow, and they kept staring at Nick as if trying to determine what kind of creature he was.

Nick looked at Turlock. "Very clever. Why shoot me yourself when you can have your errand boy do it? It'll be his gun—his bullet—and the ballistics tests will prove it. I'll just be one more victim of the speed-freak cop."

LaTourneau pulled a piece of paper from his pocket and slowly unfolded it. When he angled it down to view it in the faint moonlight, Nick could see what it was; it was his photograph—the one from the medicine cabinet mirror. LaTourneau looked carefully at the photograph, then up at Nick.

"Tell me something," Nick said to Turlock. "When you're finished with him, are you planning to kill him or just turn him over to the authorities?"

"I'll have to kill him," Turlock said. "His brain's so fried that he probably wouldn't remember me anyway—we've only met at night, and at night he's on another wavelength. But I plan to kill him—that'll wrap up a lot of loose ends, and it won't look bad for me either. I can see the headline now: 'DEA Agent Solves Bizarre String of Murders'—including yours, Polchak. Sort of ironic, if you think about it."

"Keep talking, Frank. He can hear every word you're saying."

"Like I told you, at night he's on another wavelength. LaTourneau can't hear me; he can't hear you either. Go ahead, try to talk him out of it if you want to—it won't do any good. At night he can only hear one voice."

Nick looked at LaTourneau. *That's what I'm counting on,* he thought.

LaTourneau squinted at the photograph, then at Nick again. His eyes were wide and they were blinking like camera shutters; his fingers were trembling like tuning forks. He stood up slowly in his boat and unholstered his gun. He held the photograph in his left hand and the gun in his right; he slowly raised the gun and aimed it at Nick.

He looked down at the photograph one last time. He read the words again, written in lipstick across the front: "This man is your friend, Daddy—Turlock is the bad one."

Turlock smiled at Nick. "Sorry, Polchak. Nothing personal."

"You're wrong," Nick said. "This is personal."

LaTourneau fired twice over Nick's left shoulder. Both shots caught the astonished Turlock square in the chest, knocking him backward over the edge of the boat and into the oil-black water.

51

Nick stared at the water behind Turlock's empty boat, half-expecting to see a wounded man struggle back to the surface—but the water quickly grew quiet and still, healing over its ugly wound, adding one more piece of garbage to its toxic brew.

Nick slowly turned and looked back at LaTourneau, still standing in his boat with his gun hand extended. The weapon was shaking visibly; Nick was amazed that the man could aim and even group his shots in his present condition. LaTourneau was staring at the water too—staring with a look of astonished confusion, as though he had just been a witness to Turlock's death instead of the cause.

LaTourneau ignored Nick—he seemed to look through him as though he didn't even exist, and Nick hoped things would remain that way. *He's on another wavelength*, Turlock had said, and he was right. LaTourneau was tuned in to a different galaxy right now, capable of receiving only one signal—the voice of his dead daughter.

Nick's gamble had paid off: LaTourneau interpreted Beth's lipstick-scrawled message just as he had all the others—as a message from beyond. Detwiler had spoken to LaTourneau in his daughter's own voice; Nick realized that he had to do the same, because no other voice could ever contradict hers. He erased Detwiler's message from the medicine cabinet mirror and had Beth write another in its place—a message that had just ended Turlock's life.

Now Nick sat perfectly still, waiting, watching LaTourneau's face, hoping that he might consider his daughter's wishes finally fulfilled and quietly sail away—but it wasn't happening, and Nick thought he knew why: Detwiler's original message had been on the mirror for two days—a message instructing him to kill Nick. LaTourneau must have seen it before it was erased—and he still remembered.

LaTourneau looked down at the photograph again—then he looked at Nick.

Nick could see the confusion in his eyes—he was struggling to reconcile the two contradictory messages. What did his daughter want him to do? She said that Nick was bad—then she said that Turlock was the bad one. Did she change her mind? Maybe both men were bad—maybe she was only telling him to kill Turlock *first*.

LaTourneau looked at the photograph—then at Nick.

Nick saw the change coming over his face.

"LaTourneau, listen to me. You've been manipulated—Turlock and Detwiler were behind all of this—they've been using you to kill the people they wanted dead. They're the ones who left the messages for you—the ones on your bathroom mirror."

But it was no use. Just as Turlock had said, LaTourneau was on another wavelength—Nick's voice didn't even register.

At that moment Nick heard a splash and a choking sound behind LaTourneau's boat.

"Nick!"

Nick blinked in astonishment. "J.T.! Is that you?"

"I'm here, Nick! I got out!"

Nick looked at LaTourneau—his face showed no recognition of the boy's voice or presence behind him. Nick wanted to stand up, and he wanted to look over LaTourneau's boat and see the boy's face, but he didn't dare move; any sudden motion might cause LaTourneau to fire, and that would undoubtedly prove fatal—Nick was only half as far away as Turlock had been.

"Where are you, Nick? I'll swim over—"

"No! Stay where you are! LaTourneau's got a gun."

There was a pause. "But he's on our side."

"Listen to me, and do exactly what I tell you. I want you to swim to the house and climb up on the rooftop. I want you to stay there until somebody comes to get you. Do you understand me? LaTourneau won't hurt you—he won't even know you're there."

"I want to come with you, Nick."

Nick looked at LaTourneau; the man's left arm dropped to his side and the photograph slipped from his hand—then he slowly aimed the gun at the center of Nick's chest.

"Get up on that rooftop!" Nick shouted. "Do it right now!"

"I been on a rooftop," J.T. grumbled. "I ain't goin' back."

There was another splash, and Nick saw a pair of hands shoot up over the edge of LaTourneau's boat and jerk down hard. The boat pitched violently to port—LaTourneau stumbled backward and fired one shot into the air above Nick's head. When his legs hit the side of the inflatable boat his knees buckled, sending him rolling back over the edge and into the water behind him.

A moment later, J.T.'s head popped up in front of Nick's boat. "Hi, Nick!" he said with a grin.

Nick frantically started his engine, nursing the throttle until he heard a steady rumbling roar.

"Grab on!" he shouted to J.T.

The boy complied, hooking both arms over the side of the boat.

Nick hit the gas. As the boat began to accelerate forward, he reached across and grabbed J.T. by the back of the pants, dragging him up over the edge and flipping him onto his back in the bottom of the boat. Nick looked back over his shoulder—

He saw LaTourneau climbing back into his boat.

"He's still coming!" J.T. shouted, staring into the darkness behind the boat.

"Get down!" Nick yelled back. "He'll spot us for sure if you keep standing on that bench—get up in the bow and keep an eye out for Beth."

"Where is she?"

"I left her somewhere."

"You don't remember where?"

"I left her on the coffins. They should be around here somewhere—keep an eye out for them."

Nick glanced back over his shoulder. He knew that LaTourneau would follow, and he knew that he would have no trouble picking up his trail. LaTourneau didn't need GPS—on the glass-smooth water, the wake left by Nick's boat would look like the tail of a comet. And to make matters worse, the Zodiac boat had a much more powerful engine—LaTourneau would overtake them in a matter of minutes.

"There!" J.T. pointed to an area beyond a row of rooftops. Nick saw nothing—but he knew enough to trust J.T.

They approached the coffins at full speed. Beth had apparently heard their engine and was standing near the edge, waiting for them. She looked relieved to see Nick again—and utterly astonished to see J.T.

"What did you—how in the world did you ever—"

"There's no time—get in," Nick said. "J.T., do you remember how to drive this thing?"

"Sure. Why?"

"I want you to take Beth away from here. Head in that direction—that's west. Keep going until you hit the levee, then leave the boat and keep going on foot."

"What about you, Nick?"

"I'm staying here."

Beth took a step away from the boat. "Oh no you don't."

"Beth, listen to me."

"You left me once tonight—you're not leaving me again."

"LaTourneau is right behind us—he'll be here in a few seconds. He killed Turlock, Beth—he saw the note we left for him and it worked. But now he thinks his daughter wants him to kill me too. He doesn't care about you two—it's only me he's after, and as long as you're with me, you'll be in danger. That's why you're going on without me."

"And what happens when he finds you?" Beth said.

"I'll figure that out when the time comes."

"And we're just supposed to sail off and leave you here?"

"I knew you'd catch on—now get out of here."

"No," she said. "I'm a team player, too, Nick. I'm staying—I'll try to talk to him."

"You can't talk to him, Beth, he's almost catatonic. He can't hear you—he won't even know you're there—he can only hear his daughter's voice, and he thinks she's already spoken."

Beth paused. "Pull the boat around behind the coffins."

"What?"

"Do as I say—if you both duck down in the boat, he won't be able to see you."

"What are you going to do?"

"I'm going to talk to him."

"Beth, you're not listening."

"I have an idea, Nick. Let me try it—I'm in no danger if he only wants you."

Nick shook his head in frustration. "Nobody follows orders around here."

He took the boat around behind the coffins and stopped the engine. He grabbed ahold of the rope that bound the caskets together and pulled the boat in tight; the gunnels stuck up just above the lids. Beth was right—when Nick and J.T. ducked down low, the rectangular johnboat looked like just another coffin.

If LaTourneau spotted them, that's exactly what it would be.

Nick peeked up over the edge of the boat and looked at Beth. She was working her way from coffin to coffin toward the very center of the raft. Each coffin dipped down slightly when she stepped on it, sinking and rising like a piano's keys.

She looked over at Nick. "Do you have a blanket or something?"

"No blankets," he said. "All I've got is a tarp."

"Toss it to me. Then get your head down—do you want him to see you?"

Nick did as he was told.

In the distance, he could hear an approaching engine.

52

Beth stood in the center of the casket raft like a figurine on a dashboard. The canvas tarp was wrapped around her like a shroud, covering her entire body and forming a hood over her head that completely obscured her face. From beneath the hood she watched the black Zodiac boat slip out from the darkness between two rooftops. It was a shadow moving among shadows, like a bat flying toward her in a cave. The image triggered something nameless and primitive in her mind, and it made her shiver.

He was less than thirty yards away now, almost even with the coffins, and he showed no signs of slowing down. Beth prayed that he might continue on by—but when LaTourneau saw that the trail he was following had suddenly ended, he cut his engine, and the night became as silent as a tomb.

LaTourneau turned and looked in her direction.

When he did, Beth slowly raised both arms to the side. She wanted to make sure she was seen—to be the focus of his full attention instead of a certain object behind her. It worked—she saw his eyes turn to her and stare.

She said nothing at first; she just held her pose to allow the visual impression to sink in—to create a nameless and primitive sensation of her own. She counted slowly to ten, then whispered a single word.

"Daddy."

The whispered word carried through the air like an electric current. LaTourneau blinked and shook his head.

"Daddy."

"Sweetheart," he whispered back. "I've missed you so much."

"I've missed you, too, Daddy."

He took a step toward her. "Please, sweetheart, let me come to you—"

Beth let out a piercing shriek. "Stay back! You can't come to me. You can't touch me. It isn't . . . allowed."

LaTourneau stumbled back and stood there, blinking in confusion. Beth watched him: He was displaying athetosis—his hands and arms were constantly writhing over one another like snakes, and he picked at his skin with his fingernails. His entire body trembled—he looked as if he might convulse at any time. He looked feverish; he was drenched in sweat—she wondered what his body temperature must be. She knew that meth could produce hypothermia, stoking the body's metabolism and driving its temperature as high as 108 degrees. He was burning up right in front of her eyes.

"I'm sad, Daddy," she said.

"Why are you sad, sweetheart?"

"I don't like to see you this way. I miss you—the old you. Not this one—not the one who hurts people. That makes me sad."

"They took you away from me. They come out at night—"

"Tell me what you did today. Tell me about the morning. Tell me all the good things you did. Did you save anyone today? Make me happy, Daddy—tell me."

"I can't—remember."

LaTourneau was in an advanced stage of amphetamine psychosis. He wasn't at all like her cocaine patients, but Beth knew that meth doesn't work like cocaine: Cocaine is quickly metabolized and eliminated from the body, while meth remains in the nervous system longer, permanently altering the brain. She could see that LaTourneau's schizophrenia was profound—that he had driven a permanent wedge between his two personalities. He was incapable of even remembering the actions of his other self—events that had occurred only a few hours ago. She wondered if there was any possible way to reintegrate his two personalities. It would take years of therapy—and the poor man didn't have years to live.

"I want you to rest now, Daddy. You've done everything I asked. Your work is done—you're finished now. It will make me happy to see you rest."

"I don't need to rest, sweetheart—I can keep going."

"You have to rest. You have to sleep. It will make me happy."

"I tried," he said. "I can't."

Beth knew he was right. LaTourneau was no longer capable of rest; he was like a truck screaming downhill without brakes, and there was no runaway truck ramp to slow him down. It was only a matter of time before he crashed in flames—and maybe killed someone else when he did it.

"I want you to stop taking the pills," she said. "I want you to promise me."

He seemed confused at this. "But—it's how we talk to each other."

"No, Daddy, that's what killed me. I don't want it to kill you too."

"*They* killed you. Just tell me who they are—tell me where to find them."

"I won't send you any more messages. There won't be any more names or addresses on the mirror. I want it to stop, Daddy. I won't be happy until it does—do you understand?"

He blinked. "You won't talk to me anymore?"

"You can talk to me anytime you want. I'll always be near you."

He took a step forward again. "I can't live without you."

"No—stay back!"

But there was no stopping him this time. LaTourneau swung his legs over the starboard side of the boat and slid off into the water, never taking his eyes off Beth. He began to swim toward her, but his motions were erratic and awkward and his progress was slow.

"Go back to the boat, Daddy! Turn around and go back!"

But he slowly kept coming, flailing like a man beating eaten by sharks, coughing and choking, barely keeping his head above water.

Beth was horrified; his metabolism was already accelerated by the drugs—how much of this could he take before his heart ripped apart like a rupturing tire?

She heard the roar of an engine behind her—Nick and J.T. sped out from behind the coffins and made a wide arc toward LaTourneau's boat; when they reached it, Nick jumped across into the Zodiac boat and J.T. crawled back to take Nick's place.

LaTourneau was halfway to the coffins now.

"LaTourneau!" Nick shouted. "Stay where you are!"

But he didn't seem to hear Nick's voice. He just kept coming, locked onto Beth's shrouded form, desperately seeking to be reunited with his daughter. Beth realized that nothing would stop him or turn him back—unless his daughter was no longer there.

She shook off the tarp and let it drop around her feet.

"My name is Beth Woodbridge," she said. "I'm a psychiatrist, Mr. LaTourneau—I can help you."

LaTourneau thrashed in the water, shaking his head, trying to clear his clouded mind. "Sweetheart—where are you?"

"I want you to keep coming, Mr. LaTourneau—try to make it to the coffins. You can do it—just keep listening to my voice."

But LaTourneau no longer heard her voice. He just kept staring at her—through her—searching for something that had been there just a moment ago.

His flailing began to slow.

"No!" Beth shouted. "Keep going!"

"I can't . . . live . . . without you . . ."

His body stopped moving, and his head disappeared below the water.

Beth sank to her knees and began to weep.

53

Wednesday, September 14

Nick and Beth watched J.T. through the glass door. The boy was sitting in the cafeteria at Baton Rouge General Hospital, leisurely picking his way through his third dessert.

"He looks pretty good," Nick said.

"Kids are resilient," Beth replied. "All he really needed was some fluids and a good night's rest—that's more than I can say for you."

"How long was I out?"

"Three days, more or less. I'll bet that's the longest you've ever slept."

"Oh, I don't know—we've had some long conversations."

"How are you feeling?"

"I'd like to get out of here."

"That's a good sign."

"When can I go?"

"Your doctor wants you here one more day; the nurses all want you to leave immediately."

"I don't get along well with nurses," Nick said.

"They don't take it personally—I told them you don't get along well with anybody."

He looked at her. "I'll probably be sorry for asking this, but—how are you feeling?"

"Do you really want to know?"

"Just give me the highlights; I'll let you know if anything sounds interesting."

"I'm better," she said. "It was a little rough at first—I didn't expect my conversation with LaTourneau to turn out that way."

"That wasn't your fault, Beth."

"I thought I could reach him."

"You can't reach everybody. Haven't I taught you that?"

She smiled. "Never."

"What about the boy—how's he feeling?"

"Don't worry, Nick, they took real good care of J.T.—I made sure of it myself."

Nick shook his head in admiration. "Can you believe that kid? He got out of that attic all by himself. He held his breath and swam out—and he stopped to breathe out of a refrigerator along the way! A *refrigerator*—I never would have thought of that."

"What did you expect? He's a chip off the old block."

Nick looked through the glass. "Not anymore."

Seated beside J.T. was an African-American man about Nick's age. He was a pleasant-looking man, dressed in a coat and tie, leaning on the cafeteria table and smiling at the boy as he watched him eat.

"I didn't know he had an uncle," Nick said.

"Neither did he. That's the great thing about the Family Assistance Center: Sometimes we manage to reconnect family members who lost track of each other a long time ago. Mr. Walker lives here in Baton Rouge; he lost contact with his brother years ago. When he heard about the flooding in the Lower Ninth Ward he remembered J.T. He contacted us just yesterday."

"What do you know about him?"

"I know he's legally entitled to take custody."

"Beth."

"He owns a welding supply company. He's been married for fifteen years and he's got two children of his own—one of them a boy. He goes to church. He's got a good marriage, a stable family, and he's a nice man. Is that enough?"

Nick stared at the boy. "No."

Beth patted him on the back. "You knew you couldn't keep him just because he followed you home."

"I know. I just thought—"

"Go talk to him. And here, don't forget this—I wrapped it for you." She handed him a box wrapped in silver-and-gold paper with a fluffy white bow pasted on top.

Nick took the box and began to tug at the bow.

Beth slapped his hand. "Hey! It took me fifteen minutes to make that."

"It's too girly."

"Just give it to him—he won't care."

When Nick stepped through the cafeteria door, J.T. looked up and grinned. "Hey, Nick!"

The uncle rose and extended his hand. "Dr. Polchak. I'm Lucien Walker—J.T.'s uncle."

The two men shook hands.

"I want to thank you for looking out for my boy."

"We looked out for each other," Nick said.

"I was just about to get a cup of coffee. Can I get you anything?"

"No, thank you."

"I'll be a few minutes. You take your time." He turned and left.

Nick sat down beside J.T. "So what's the verdict? Is hospital food better than MREs?"

"Nothin's that good," J.T. said.

"So—you feeling okay?"

"Sure. No problem."

"I brought you something." He slid the box across the table. "Beth made the bow."

"What is it?"

"There's only one way to find out."

J.T. tore the paper away and opened the box; inside was a pair of Steiner military binoculars. The boy beamed.

"Those are top-notch," Nick said. "I got them from a guy who used to use them for surveillance—he didn't need them anymore."

"Thanks, Nick!"

"I like your uncle. He seems like a nice guy."

J.T. shrugged.

"Baton Rouge is a great town. I think you'll like it here."

"Are we goin' out today?"

"What?"

"On the boat—are we goin' out?"

Nick paused. "No. We did what we needed to do. They've got plenty of people to take over for us now. I have to go home soon."

"Where?"

"North Carolina."

"Where's that?"

The other side of the world, he thought. *Nine hundred miles and five states away.* "It's not far," he said. "Just around the corner."

"When will you be back?"

Nick didn't reply.

J.T. put the binoculars back in the box.

"I just had an idea," Nick said. "Have you ever seen a Formosan subterranean termite?"

"Nope."

"I thought you knew everything. They call them Super Termites. They eat everything in sight—they can eat through bricks if they want to."

"Cool."

"Guess where the largest infestation in the world just happens to be? In the French Quarter, right in the heart of New Orleans. If I get back this way, would you like to drive over and take a look under some buildings?"

J.T. threw his arms around Nick's waist. Nick pulled him in tight.

"Bye, Nick."

"Good-bye—son."

Nick stood up and gave J.T.'s head one last rub.

The uncle returned now. "Are you boys finished here? Then let me walk you out, Dr. Polchak."

At the door Nick turned to Mr. Walker and said, "May I ask a favor? This might sound really stupid, since you're his actual blood relative and all."

"Don't worry," Mr. Walker said. "I'll take good care of him."

"Like he was your own son," Nick said. "He deserves it."

Nick opened the door and stepped out.

Beth was waiting for him. "There. That wasn't so bad, was it?"

"I guess not."

"It ripped your guts out, didn't it?"

Nick shook his head. "You know, for someone who's supposed to encourage mental health, you sure seem to enjoy pain."

"It's a good sign, Nick. I know it hurts, but it's a good sign."

Nick turned and looked back at J.T. "I still don't get it."

"What?"

"He hasn't had a father since he was four years old. Why was he suddenly looking for one now?"

"Because his world was coming apart at the seams. A father is a powerful thing, Nick. A father is more than a man, he's a symbol of something larger—a reminder that the universe is a safe place to live—that someone out there loves you, and that things will turn out all right in the end. J.T. had no real family before—he had all of the insecurities that come with that—and then suddenly his whole world was washed away in a flood. No wonder he was looking for a father—a lot of people are right now. Maybe we all need one."

"But you can't just pick out a father."

"Not a biological father, maybe, but a father figure."

"But why me?"

Beth smiled. "Because you're tall; because you're smart; because you try to do the right thing; and because you never, ever quit. You make a pretty good father if you ask me. What more could a boy want?"

"Thanks."

"By the way, I talked to Denny again last night."

"And?"

"He's cooling off—but he still wants you to go home. He says your two-week deployment is almost up anyway."

"Tell him it isn't fair—I spent half of it unconscious."

"I already did. He says you spent the other half working round the clock, so it evens out. Where will you go, Nick—back to NC State?"

"I'd like to stop off in Fort Wayne first. Jerry's got family there. I know they've already been notified, but I want them to hear it from me."

Beth squeezed his arm.

"I guess I won't see you until our next deployment," Nick said.

"Don't kid yourself. According to DMORT regulations, I'm allowed to check up on you periodically after your deployment—just to check for any post-incident mental health issues."

"Is that really necessary?"

"In your case? I'll call you tomorrow."

Nick leaned in close to her and whispered, "Have you ever considered, Dr. Woodbridge, that between the two of us, I might be the sane one?"

"Stop it—you're scaring me. Seriously, Nick, I'd like to check in from time to time. Think you can handle that?"

"I just handled a psychotic cop and two deranged DEA agents."

"Is that a *yes* or a *no*?"

"Suppose I call you?" he said. "That way we can talk as friends."

"Can we do that?" she asked.

"I can. How about you?"

She smiled. "I'll give it a try."

"About Denny," Nick said. "How mad is he? Is this whole DEA thing going to mess up my next deployment?"

"That will depend on my summary evaluation," she said. "DMORT will be counting on me to assess your mental and emotional fitness for future duty."

"Terrific," he said. "Another entry in my file of personality disorders. What are you going to write this time?"

"I'm going to write: 'Nick Polchak—almost human.'"

Nick frowned. "Well, you don't have to get insulting."

AUTHOR'S NOTE

Because *First the Dead* takes place in New Orleans in the days immediately following Hurricane Katrina, I made my fictional characters subject to the same limitations everyone shared during that time: a lack of reliable information, erroneous and exaggerated news reports, and unfounded rumors about conditions and events in the city. It was reported early on, for example, that dozens of evacuees in the Superdome had been murdered and that bodies were beginning to pile up. Forensic teams later searched the facility, prepared to recover as many as two hundred victims. They found only ten bodies in total, four of which had been carried in from the streets outside. Of the remaining six, four died of natural causes, one of a drug overdose, and one from apparent suicide. Though the conditions in the Superdome were certainly deplorable, the early reports of widespread murder were erroneous—a part of the flood of urban legend that surrounds an event when reliable communication breaks down.

In the same way, it was reported that between one-third and one-half of all New Orleans Police Department officers had deserted their posts following the storm. This, in fact, was another urban legend; only 15 percent of the NOPD's officers failed to report for duty, many because they themselves were victims of the storm. I allowed Nick Polchak to believe this urban legend—that half of the NOPD had deserted—because that's the report that was circulating in those early days. Nick would have had no way to know that the number had been grossly exaggerated, and so he would have accepted it—just as many of us did.

Though my story required that I repeat this urban legend, I would like the reader to understand that it did not turn out to be true. The NOPD's officers are dedicated and committed individuals, many of whom repeatedly risked their lives in the rescue efforts following Katrina, and I believe they deserve our respect and admiration.

YOU CAN HELP THE PEOPLE OF NEW ORLEANS

The following is a list of some of the fine organizations either providing direct relief assistance to victims of Hurricane Katrina or collecting funds on behalf of other relief efforts. They would greatly appreciate your contributions; please visit their individual Web sites if you wish to do so.

American Red Cross
www.redcross.org

Direct Relief International
www.directrelief.org

Habitat for Humanity International
www.habitat.org

World Vision
www.worldvision.org

All of these organizations meet the *Standards for Charity Accountability* set by the BBB Wise Giving Alliance. For more information, visit their Web site at: www.give.org

A TIMELINE OF HURRICANE KATRINA

Friday, August 26, 2005—Landfall minus three

Hurricane Katrina crosses Florida and moves into the Gulf of Mexico, gathering energy from the warm seas. At 10 p.m. CDT the National Hurricane Center predicts that Katrina will strike the town of Buras-Triumph, Louisiana, about sixty-five miles southeast of New Orleans. This early prediction proves to be uncannily accurate.

Saturday, August 27—Landfall minus two

By 5 a.m. Katrina is a Category 3 storm. By 9 a.m. officials in the parishes closest to the Gulf issue a mandatory evacuation order. In the parishes surrounding New Orleans—Jefferson, Orleans, and St. Bernard—the evacuation order is only voluntary.

Sunday, August 28—Landfall minus one

By 7 a.m. Hurricane Katrina is a Category 5 storm with sustained winds of 175 mph and gusts up to 215. At 10 a.m. the National Weather Service issues a bulletin predicting "devastating" damage. At noon the Superdome is opened for those who cannot flee the city.

Monday, August 29—Landfall

At 6:10 a.m. Katrina makes landfall, but flooding in residential areas begins an hour and a half earlier due to an eighteen-foot storm surge pushed ahead of the storm. The levees along both sides of the Industrial Canal are quickly overtopped; by 7:45 the levees along the eastern side fail completely, allowing a twenty-foot wall of water to rush into the neighborhood and wash houses off their foundations. By 8 a.m. water is seen rising on both sides of the Industrial Canal; one hour later there is six to eight feet of water in the Lower Ninth Ward. By 10:30 a.m. both the London Avenue Canal and Seventeenth Street Canal levees fail, flooding downtown New Orleans.

Tuesday, August 30—Landfall plus one

Sandbagging of the Seventeenth Street Canal levee fails. Governor Blanco estimates that 50 to 100,000 people remain trapped in the flooded city. Officials call for anyone with a boat to assist in the rescue efforts.

Wednesday, August 31—Landfall plus two

Hurricane Katrina is downgraded to a tropical depression. Eighty percent of the city is now underwater; floodwaters in the city and in Lake Pontchartrain finally equalize at three feet above normal sea level, leaving the average home in six to nine feet of water. The NOPD is ordered to abandon search and rescue efforts in order to control widespread looting in the city; a curfew is put into effect.

Thursday, September 1—Landfall plus three

National Guardsmen, accompanied by supply trucks and buses, finally begin to arrive in number at the Superdome, transporting evacuees to the Astrodome and Reliant Center in Houston.

Sunday, September 4—Landfall plus six

Evacuation of the Superdome is completed.

Monday, September 6—Landfall plus eight

The Seventeenth Street Canal levee breach is finally repaired and officials begin to pump water out of the flooded city. Sixty-seven pumps will be able to remove more than five million gallons per minute, but officials estimate that the pumping could still take a month.

Wednesday, March 1, 2006—Landfall plus six months

DMORT finally closes down its operations in Louisiana. During its six months of tireless efforts, about a thousand DMORT volunteer team members processed approximately 1100 victims of Hurricane Katrina as well as 612 disinterred caskets from flooded cemeteries, some of which were discovered thirty miles from their original place of burial.

ACKNOWLEDGMENTS

I would like to thank the following individuals and agencies for their assistance in my research for this book: the National Oceanic and Atmospheric Administration Central Library Photo Collection; Diane Galatas, Public Relations Director for the Orleans Parish Office of Communication Services; Robert Ricks of the National Weather Service in Slidell, Louisiana; Michael Smith, Deputy Circuit Librarian of the 5th Circuit Court of Appeals; Marcia Kavanaugh, Public Information Officer, Orleans Parish Criminal District Court; and all the others who took the time to respond to my e-mails, letters, and calls.

I would like to say a special thanks to my research assistant, Tommy Downs, for patiently tracking down the countless facts and statistics that formed the basis of this story. And thanks to all the others who contributed to the creation of this book: my literary agent and friend, Lee Hough of Alive Communications; story editor Ed Stackler for his insight into plot, pacing, and point of view; copy editor Deborah Wiseman for her unerring red pen; my publisher, Allen Arnold, and my editor, Amanda Bostic, of Thomas Nelson for their helpful suggestions on the story; and the rest of the Nelson staff for their kindness, dedication, and patience with demanding writers.

ABOUT THE AUTHOR

TIM DOWNS has received high acclaim for his novels, including a Christy award for *PlagueMaker*. He is also the author of *Chop Shop* and *Shoo Fly Pie*. Tim lives in North Carolina with his wife and three children.

ALSO BY TIM DOWNS

PlagueMaker

Head Game

Shoo Fly Pie

Chop Shop